Editor's Note

Jonathan Wilson, Editor

C000146830

As we don't mention nearly as often as we used to, *The Blizzard* was born in Sunderland in March 2010, at the table in the back corner of the Chart Room in Fitzy's, in the days before they spruced it up and it was still comfortingly grubby. So there was a sense both of pride and appropriateness when we held our first event outside London in the National Glass Centre in Sunderland. And there were, of course, in the spirit of pilgrimage, a couple of pints of White Amaryllis in Fitzy's afterwards.

I'm not entirely sure how these events came about. We had our launch event, when Issue One was released on the website, in the Princess Victoria pub in Shepherd's Bush. The aim of that was clear: we got along as many journalists as possible — and it was the night before the Champions League final at Wembley, so the cream of the world's football media was in London - plied them with booze and asked them to say nice things about us. That was partly about rewarding the writers who'd taken the gamble and written for us with no guarantee of getting anything in return, but mainly about generating publicity.

Then Rough Trade, who've stocked *The Blizzard* from the start, asked if we'd like to put on an event in their Brick Lane store. It was sort of a launch event for Issue Two but this time we got along readers and did a question and answer session with Tim Vickery and Iain Macintosh. That seemed to be well-received, so when Foyles on Charing

Cross Road offered us space to put on a similar event we happily accepted for the launch of Issue Three. This time I was joined by Philippe Auclair and Gabriele Marcotti. By this stage it wasn't really feeling like a launch. I'm not sure what it did feel like but it seemed like fun.

For Issue Four, we went to Wembley. I moved sideways to join Philippe and Gab on the panel as the much more capable Dave Farrar took over the presenter's chair. That was an incredible night, and not just because Wembley laid on free pies. There were more than 200 people there and a real sense of occasion, of *The Blizzard* as... as what? As a journal, of course. But also as a community, perhaps even as a movement, readers and writers together fighting for a type of journalism that doesn't exist elsewhere. The video of that night's discussion can be viewed on our website.

London, with its vast population, almost guarantees an audience: a tiny minority there is a lot of people. We were determined, though, not to become Londoncentric. So after the success of Sunderland, when Philippe and I were joined by Iain again, with Marcus Speller presenting, we're off to Dublin for this issue. Keep checking the website for details of where we might turn up next.

We never envisaged doing these events but they seem already a central pillar of what *The Blizzard* is.

September 2012

Contents

The Blizzard, Issue Six

Introduction

03. Editor's Note

❖ Portugal

07. **Ben Shave, The Curse of the Golden Whistle**

     How corruption and inefficiency have squandered the legacy of Euro 2004

22. **Luis Catarino, The Flight of the Eagles**

     In the early sixties Benfica rose to topple Real Madrid, only to be cursed by Béla Guttmann

31. **Andy Brassell, The Pretenders**

     Only two sides outside *Os Tres Grandes* have won the Portuguese title. For both a repeat seems unlikely.

39. **Vitor Sobral, The Dragons' Cap**

     Porto's rise in the late seventies was inspired by the innovative coaching of José Maria Pedroto

❖ Interview

45. **Karel Häring, Antonin Panenka**

     The Czechoslovakia great discusses how his famous dinked penalty came about and the impact it's had

❖ Euro 2012

53. **Jonathan Wilson, The Essential Backdrop**

     Euro 2012 raised major questions about the nature of fandom and what comprises a tournament

66. **Barney Ronay, The First Twitter Tournament**

     In Euro 2012, newspapers were very rarely first with the news as social media came into its own

❖ Theory

73. **Philippe Auclair, Directing the Pianists**

     Brendan Rodgers discusses the importance of possession football and what he's learned from José Mourinho

79. **Antonis Oikonomodis, Ivan the Reasonable**

     Ivan Jovanović explains his philosophy and how he hopes to build on Apoel's success last season

84. **Tim Vickery, The Rise of the Technocrats**

     How attitudes to the dictatorship shape Brazil's change of approach in the seventies

92. **Federico Farcomeni, The Second Coming**

Zdeněk Zeman talks about attacking, romance and his challenge after returning to Roma this season

⇨ **Photo Essay**

100. **Aníbal Greco, River's Return**

Images of River Plate's battle to win promotion from the purgatory of Nacional B

⇨ **The Lost**

115. **David Bartram, The Paper Tiger**

How politics and society have stood in the way of a Chinese boom

126. **Iain Macintosh, The Coach on the Couch**

Is being addicted to Football Manager a medical condition?

133. **James Young, The Far Corner**

How football in the north-east of Brazil struggles to keep up with the giants of the south

⇨ **Polemics**

144. **Gabriele Marcotti, Care for the Community**

Could a radical rejig of television schedules help create a greater bond between clubs and their fans?

151. **Tom Dart, Location, Location, Location**

Which is more important? How it looks or where a stadium is?

⇨ **Fiction**

157. **David Ashton, The Limping God**

His football career ended by injury, John Brodie's life is going nowhere until he is sucked into the world of crime

⇨ **Greatest Games**

167. **Dermot Corrigan, Spain 1 Ireland 0**

World Cup qualifying play-off, Parc des Princes, Paris, 10 November 1965

⇨ **Eight Balls**

179. **Sheridan Bird, Classic Footballs**

A selection of the best footballs through the ages

Information

188. **Contributors**

190. **Subcriptions**

191. **About The Blizzard**

192. **T-Shirts**

FSC
www.fsc.org
MIX
Paper from
responsible sources
FSC® C008152

6

Portugal

"There has been an extended
collective abdication of
responsibility on the part of those in
charge of football in Portugal."

The Curse of the Golden Whistle

How corruption and inefficiency have squandered the legacy of Euro 2004.

By Ben Shave

Aveiro. Sunday, 20 August 2011. 6.10pm. Players from Beira-Mar and Sporting waited in the tunnel of the Estádio Municipal, bobbing up and down in the tense moments before kick-off. Ten minutes later, they were still there. The match, due to begin at 6.15pm, had been thrown into jeopardy by a frantic, uncoordinated search for a refereeing team, after the appointed official, João Ferreira, had refused to take charge following yet another week of controversy and vitriol.

Sporting had begun the 2011-12 season at home to Olhanense the previous weekend, with their new coach Domingos Paciência fielding four new signings and including four more among the substitutes. *Os Leões* were still in the middle of a summer overhaul, with the president Godinho Lopes busy making good on his promises of investment on the pitch and a bullish reassertion of the club's identity and tradition off it. Lopes had been elected the previous March after a campaign notable for accusations of vote rigging and money laundering, characterised throughout by a distinct lack of unanimity among the candidates as to what exactly was best for a once-proud institution fallen on hard times.

Lopes, who surrounded himself with the great and the good of Sporting's past (Manuel Fernandes, second only to Fernando Peyroteo on the club's all-time goalscorers' list, was a particularly vocal supporter), defeated Bruno de Carvalho by a margin of less than 1%, a result that was confirmed amid rancorous scenes outside the Estádio José Alvalade. Throughout the campaign De Carvalho, a youthful, dynamic figure who promised Marco van Basten as coach and €50 million worth of investment 'guaranteed' by Leonid Tyagachev (then the president of the Russian Olympic Committee), Alexander Nazarov (the former governor of the Chukotka region of north-eastern Russia) and Yuri Pachechin (a construction magnate), was regarded as the clear favourite. A poll conducted by *A Bola* on the Monday before the election predicted that his margin of victory would be 24.1%, and when early exit polls on Saturday March 26 showed him to be ahead, most Sportinguistas went to bed with the sound of a sweeping broom echoing through their consciousness.

However, they had reckoned without Sporting's voting system. Although all *sócios* are eligible to vote, those with smaller membership numbers (who have been paying their dues the longest) are entitled to more votes than those with larger numbers: 1-19 were given 25 votes, while 76,642-83,034 had just one. At around 6am on Sunday March 27, the shrewdness of Lopes's strategy in targeting the older generation with his regular references to past glories was revealed. De Carvalho's followers were furious and police had to intervene to prevent supporters of the same club from attacking one another at the Campo Grande bus station.

De Carvalho immediately challenged the outcome, saying that "the aim is to clarify everything that happened and to spell out the rules that had to be complied with, and some of which were not. We are preparing to impugn the elections. We will go ahead with a court injunction."

Despite the brouhaha, Lopes managed to defy the expectations of many by steering the club through a largely positive pre-season that saw the arrival of Domingos — one of Portugal's foremost young coaches — and a host of signings. Some were necessary (Alberto Rodríguez, Stijn Schaars); others big names to attract fans who had deserted the Alvalade in their droves over almost a decade of instability and underachievement (Diego Capel, Jeffrén Suárez, Ricky van Wolfswinkel). A 3-0 loss to Valencia in August's

presentation game barely made a dent in the collective euphoria, with Lopes declaring the 48,952 attendance (the second highest since the Alvalade opened in 2003) a sign that club and support were once again united.

The 33,248 who witnessed the disjointed display against Olhanense could have been forgiven for recalling such pronouncements with a rueful air. Sporting performed in the manner of a team adapting to life under a new coach, as was natural with a host of new arrivals on the pitch. It was hardly a major cause for concern and had Hélder Postiga and Yannick Djaló not been so profligate in their finishing, Sporting would have won comfortably. Domingos admitted as much following the final whistle but also insisted that the referee Carlos Xistra "had a very bad night. The officiating must be commented upon because it is part of a game of football." Later in the week, Lopes reprised Domingos's refrain with gusto, condemning "the lack of impartiality shown in Sporting games" and delivering a document to the president of the Liga Portuguesa de Futebol Profissional (LPFP)'s Arbitration Commission, Vítor Pereira outlining Sporting's various grievances against Xistra[1].

The use of inflammatory rhetoric by presidents, coaches and players has become a lamentably common ploy in

---

[1] *Although he would take Sporting on a 10-match winning run during the autumn, Domingos departed — less than 24 hours after Lopes dismissed rumours that he would be removed as "ridiculous" — in February 2012, with his side 16 points behind the leaders Benfica and out of the running for a desperately-needed Champions League spot. Sources at the club attempted to foster a media rumour that he had entertained overtures from Porto, for whom he starred as a player during the mid-1990s. His replacement, the Under-19 coach and club idol Ricardo Sá Pinto, oversaw a slight upturn in form that culminated in a semi-final loss to Athletic Bilbao in the Europa League.*

football, not least because in the age of 24-hour news it provides an ideal means of deflecting attention away from shortcomings on the pitch. It is tempting to hypothesise that the practice has become so widespread simply because policing the multitude of hints, insinuations and thinly-veiled conspiracy theories in a coherent, structured fashion would create an unrealistic workload for whichever body was unfortunate enough to be lumbered with the task. There has been an extended collective abdication of responsibility on the part of those in charge of football in Portugal and so the attacks on referees go on unchecked with nobody apparently too concerned for the long-term consequences.

This time, though, the referees hit back. João Ferreira communicated his refusal to oversee Beira-Mar's game against Sporting through a statement issued by the Associação Portuguesa de Árbitros de Futebol (APAF) and his fellow officials swiftly declared their solidarity. As kick-off drew closer, media analysts and administrators alike pored over the available legislation in search of a workable solution. Speaking to TVI, the former referee Pedro Henriques confirmed that it was in theory possible for a player from one of the two teams to take the whistle but also stressed that the ultimate responsibility lay with the appointed LPFP delegate to oversee the process. For his part, Vítor Pereira assured the press that a contingency plan was in place although the circus that led up to kick-off suggested the finer details had never been worked out.

In their minute-by-minute report, *Maisfutebol* reminded a rapt audience that a similar event had taken place in

October 1998. On that occasion, Paulo Costa had refused to oversee Sporting's meeting with Farense and the Category B referee Andrelino Pena had been called into action.

Eventually, after a warm-up that delayed kick-off by a further 10 minutes, Fernando Martins, a worker in the health industry and referee in the Aveiro district league who had been at the game as a spectator, emerged from the tunnel to a chorus of whistles and got the match underway. Following a dull 0-0 draw, *Público* reported that the decision to select Martins and his assistants Fábio Silva, Nuno Simões and Nuno Soares had been reached at a meeting convened an hour before kick-off between the LPFP delegate and the clubs. For his part, Martins, who had a mercifully controversy-free 90 minutes, described the outcome as "a dream come true".

Conspicuous by their absence from the *polémica* were Portuguese football's governing body, the Federação Portuguesa de Futebol (FPF). Carlos Esteves, president of the Arbitration Council, spoke to Rádio TSF 24 hours before the match and confirmed that although there had been conversations between the LPFP and the FPF regarding the situation, he and his fellow Council members had received "half a dozen calls from second category referees" stating that if requested to oversee the game, they too would refuse. Esteves therefore concluded, "It is the responsibility of the Liga."

This brief interview highlighted the crux of an issue that has defined Portuguese football for decades: a disconnect between the national governing body and the two professionalised leagues overseen by the LPFP. The origins of this disconnect can be traced back to the birth of the game in Portugal.

The exact date and nature of football's introduction to Portugal remains open to debate but, writing in 2011, Hugo Relvas credits the likes of Ginásio Clube Português, Club Lisbonense and Carcavelos Club with key roles in the game's formative years. It's generally accepted that *os três grandes* (Benfica and Sporting of Lisbon and Futebol Clube do Porto) appeared between 1904 and 1906 (although Porto's official website states their year of foundation as 1893) with Boavista thought to have been established in 1903. Associations for Lisbon, Portalegre and Porto were established in 1910, 1911 and 1912 respectively, with the intention of coordinating regional tournaments.

1914 saw the creation of the União Portuguesa de Futebol (UPF), but the outbreak of World War One put any aspirations for a national competition on hold until 1921-22 when the inaugural Campeonato de Portugal (played as a knock-out tournament) was won by Porto, who defeated Sporting in the final. In 1926, the UPF was reconstituted by government decree into its present incarnation as the FPF, although the nation's extended political turmoil meant that the new entity was only legally established in 1938, the same year that the first recognised national championship (also won by Porto) was held.

Under António Salazar's corporatist, nationalist and repressive Estado Novo regime, which lasted from 1932 to 1974, public institutions existed as instruments through which the social order could be maintained. Relvas describes how "the regime used football as a way to promote the patriotism of the Portuguese people, believing that if people were talking and 'living' football they would not be concerned about oppressive measures."

The Estado Novo intervened in football when it suited, preventing, for instance, Eusébio's move to Italy: indeed, only Jorge Humberto made the journey from Portugal to Italy during the Salazar era, departing Académica for Inter in 1961 and moving on to Vicenza before returning to Coimbra – the place where Salazar studied, taught, and took his first steps into the political arena.

The authoritarian grip of the Estado Novo not only allowed the *grandes* to retain their most gifted players, but it also preserved the increasingly outmoded structure of the FPF for half a century. The Sindicato dos Jogadores Profissionais de Futebol (SJPF) was not established until 1972, by which time Salazar had passed away and the pervasive presence of the Estado Novo was beginning to wither. Eusébio was among the members of the first steering committee, along with his fellow luminaries António Simões, Fernando Peres, and Artur Jorge.

Four years after the *Revolução dos Cravos* [Carnation Revolution] unleashed a maelstrom of economic, social and political change in Portugal, football (specifically that in the north of the country) had its own landmark 12 months.

After 19 years without lifting the national title, Porto, coached by the great José María Pedroto and with the current president Jorge Nuno Pinto da Costa as sporting director, edged Benfica to wrest the championship away from Lisbon, an event which has since come to be viewed as a key moment in the club's modern history. Da Costa, an omnipotent figure at the Dragão for the best part of three decades, has pointedly contrasted Benfica's relative lack of success post-Salazar compared to that which they enjoyed during the Estado Novo years and, while such declarations are in one sense simply barbs aimed at an eternal rival, the re-emergence of Porto as an active power in the Portuguese footballing sphere is not just significant in the history of the club, but in that of the game in Portugal itself.

A power struggle between Da Costa and his predecessor Américo da Sá saw the former (along with Pedroto and a host of stars including Fernando Gomes) depart during *O Verão Quente* [The Hot Summer] of 1980; but the duo returned to consolidate their grip on the club two years later, drawing on the foundation of popular support created by the back-to-back titles won at the end of the 1970s.

1978 also saw the establishment of the LPFP (albeit only as a department of the FPF) under the leadership of João Aranha and subsequently Lito Gomes de Almeida. Relvas describes it as "without significant autonomy and power of decision" until 1988 but the gradual shift towards a footballing disestablishment had begun.

Work undertaken by the SJPF and the APAF (which had been formed in 1986) to move the game towards a more professional, modern approach continued through the decade and extended talks between Aníbal Cavaco Silva's Partido Social Democrata (PSD) and the LPFP resulted in the granting of partial autonomy to the country's two national divisions, from 1990-91. At the same time, the modernising forces that swept across the European game from the late 1980s were also affecting Portugal: those clubs who wished to pursue a more independent, flexible model of governance — one that placed the interests of profit above all else — exerted great pressure on newly appointed LPFP president Valentim Loureiro to secure full autonomy.

In many ways, Loureiro represents the emerging contradictions at the heart of Portuguese football's drive towards modernisation. Born in 1938 and a veteran of the bloody, protracted war that Salazar's Portugal waged between 1961-75 in an attempt to retain control over Angola, Loureiro is infamous for his consumption of offices, titles, and positions. President of Boavista from 1978 to 1997 (the mantle was then passed on to his son João), the early years of his administration at the Estádio Bessa were marked by the establishment of the Supertaça Cândido de Oliveira, the now traditional curtain-raiser to the new season, contested by the most recent winners of the Liga and the Taça de Portugal. An active and influential figure in the northern PSD since the 1970s, Loureiro utilised his numerous contacts from the political and sporting spheres to facilitate the talks regarding LPFP autonomy and wielded a great deal of political capital in the initial attempts to overcome the fudged legislation which only granted partial independence. 1993 was a good year for Loureiro: he was elected president of the Gondomar Câmara Municipal and managed to negotiate the law which laid out a definitive separation of professional and non-professional football in Portugal, with the LPFP in charge of the former and the FPF of the latter. Loureiro's cause was helped by the fact that since the *Caso Saltillo* scandal of 1986, public and more importantly political perception of the FPF had become increasingly negative. The scandal was sparked by the treatment of Benfica's António Veloso after a disputed positive doping test shortly before the squad were due to depart for the Mexico World Cup. Veloso was later cleared of wrongdoing, but not before he was dismissed and Fernando Bandeirinha was called up as a last-minute replacement. The tension was raised further once the *Selecção* arrived in Saltillo (via Frankfurt and Dallas) to find that their accommodation was some way below the standard they had expected, particularly in terms of privacy and training facilities. The build-up to the tournament was marked by a steady flow of sensationalist stories devoured eagerly by the Portuguese public and a war of words between the squad and the FPF, conducted via a series of press releases and interviews. The squad, incensed by the treatment of Veloso, their accommodation, paltry win bonuses and the expectation that they would advertise FPF partner brands without receiving additional financial reward, threatened to strike, although they eventually backed down after widespread condemnation at home and abroad.

Things didn't improve once the tournament began. The group stage proved little short of a disaster, with an improbable 1-0 victory over England

swiftly giving way to losses against Poland (1-0) and Morocco (3-1) which were in turn listless and humiliating. The Selecção didn't qualify for an international tournament for a decade and the *Caso Saltillo* was a major contributor not only to the FPF's fall in stature as an institution but to the chronic financial issues that plagued it throughout the late 1980s and early 1990s. Loureiro's relentless lobbying and the seemingly increasing validity of the argument that the failing economic health of the Portuguese game was being eroded by the archaic FPF resulted in the separation, rubber-stamped by Cavaco Silva's government.

The first national championship to be organised by the autonomous LPFP began in August 1995, one month after the election of Pinto da Costa as president. Despite being behind the establishment of the LPFP as a separate legal entity, Loureiro's burgeoning political career meant that in 1994, he had been replaced by the Benfica president Manuel Damásio, with the arrival of Da Costa a move designed to minimise the risk of the backbiting and mutual enmity which generally emerges whenever officials from Benfica and Porto are required to be in the same room. However, this delicate balance proved impossible to maintain for an extended period of time and Loureiro returned to office in December 1996, much to the disgust of Benfica and Sporting, who chose to remove themselves from the process.

The Eagles were particularly isolationist in the nineties under the presidency of João Vale e Azevedo, which ended with the former lawyer imprisoned on charges of embezzlement and the club indebted to such an extent that the effects are still being felt more than a decade later. After being granted parole, Vale e Azevedo decamped to London where he continues to fend off criminal charges stemming from his short reign in charge of Portugal's most successful club. Between 1994 and 2004 Benfica lifted just two Taças de Portugal and no national championships, while Vale e Azevedo continues to contest an extradition order.

The establishment of the LPFP as an independent actor coincided happily with Portugal's return to prominence on the international stage. The *Geração do Ouro*, spearheaded by the iconic creative axis of Luís Figo and Rui Costa and coached by the up-and-coming Carlos Queiroz, had won consecutive Fifa World Youth Championships in 1989 and 1991, the second of which was secured with a penalty shoot-out victory over Brazil in front of 127,000 at the Estádio da Luz. At a time when the *Caso Saltillo* was still at the forefront of the footballing public's consciousness, this triumph over a more fashionable Lusophone rival provided hope for the future which began to bear fruit with qualification for and an encouraging group-stage performance at the 1996 European Championship.

Although the foundation of the LPFP and the national side's rise were connected only in the sense that the likes of Costa, Figo, Fernando Couto and Vítor Baía starred for LPFP member clubs, the notion of new beginnings on the pitch was undoubtedly reflected behind the scenes. As part of the changes in law

negotiated during the early 1990s, the country's traditional multi-sport clubs (of which football was and almost always is the predominant branch) were for the first time allowed to convert their professional football divisions into separate companies, which in theory retained the associative, *sócio-*driven foundation, but with additional room for flexibility in areas such as professional management and — crucially — generation of revenue. The structure known as *Sociedade Anónima Desportiva* (SAD) has to date been adopted by fewer than half of the LPFP's 32 current members, but has allowed the *grandes* (as well as other traditionally better-supported clubs such as Braga and Marítimo) to operate primarily as businesses rather than member-owned associations.

Despite the willingness of Cavaco Silva's government to rubber-stamp this change in the national game, the FPF and its 22 member associations were not entirely abandoned. Indeed, the FPF retains its status as a body with *utilidade pública* (UP), which is accompanied by recognition and more importantly financial support from the government.

With the LPFP now ahead in terms of marketing and sponsorship (thanks largely to the continued patronage of the online gambling and alcohol industries), the maintenance of grassroots football in Portugal is considered to be a matter of government responsibility. Despite this, UP status was suspended in March 2010 by Laurentino Dias, then Secretary of State for Youth and Sport, in what was presented as the final straw in an argument over voting reform which had dragged on for the better part of three years. The crux of the issue lay in the fact that despite the establishment and progression of the LPFP, the 22 member associations still held a 50% voting bloc in the FPF's General Assembly, with the LPFP accounting for just 20%. The politics of the game did not represent its modern economics.

In addition, the continued existence of two differing sets of judicial structures (one for the FPF and one for the LPFP) created a situation whereby clubs could call upon two sets of rules when discussing disciplinary cases. A notorious consequence of this legal irregularity took place in February 2010, when the LPFP Disciplinary Committee handed down suspensions of four and six months to the Porto players Hulk and Cristian Săpunaru following a fracas in the tunnel of the Estádio da Luz in which the pair were adjudged to have physically assaulted a steward after a 1-0 defeat at the hands of the eventual champions Benfica. Porto chose to appeal the decision to the FPF, which subsequently reduced the sentences to three and four matches respectively. Porto supporters still consider Benfica's 2009-10 title win to be tainted as a result — more fuel for the fire.

The civil case is still dragging through the courts but regardless of the outcome of any eventual trial, it acutely exposes the inherent contradictions and weaknesses of a system that calls upon two sets of rules to police a single sporting competition. The LPFP president Hermínio Loureiro, who had taken over from his namesake Valentim in 2006, resigned in protest and the subsequent muckraking between the two institutions culminated in Dias's decision to pull the plug temporarily five months later.

The stakes were raised in March 2011, when Fifa waded in with the inevitable threat of sanctions. Showing his usual preoccupation with adequate standards of governance, Sepp Blatter said, "We are worried about the situation in Portugal. The Portuguese federation has to approve the statutes." Thankfully, the mutual loathing between the FPF and the LPFP did not extend to a desire for self-destruction and an agreement was reached for the statutes to be adopted a fortnight later. The whole unedifying episode illustrated the fragility of the foundations on which football in Portugal rests — foundations that have appeared especially rickety ever since the elephant known as *Apito Dourado* ['Golden Whistle'] barrelled its way into the room, back in 2004.

Understanding the historical context of Portuguese football's current state is vital, particularly as it offers an insight into those key figures that shaped the way in which it attempts to operate. Probably no single episode has contributed as much to the raising of the tension as *Apito Dourado* and its sister investigation, *Apito Final* ['Final Whistle']. Without them, it is hard to imagine the prevailing environment of paranoia, accusations and —particularly among supporters of the *grandes* — a notable rise in incidents of supporter violence and vandalism being tolerated, and in some cases tacitly encouraged, by those in power. For many, the varying processes that fell under the *Apito Dourado* label merely confirmed long held suspicions as fact.

Under the Estado Novo, Portugal's various police forces enforced the will of the state, particularly in the area of public disorder. Corruption, in its numerous forms, was uncovered and acted upon only when it suited the requirements of those at the very top of the political and economic apparatus. The vast majority of the people responsible for carving out the modern Portuguese footballing landscape have done so with a similar lack of regard for the power of public institutions (albeit with far less damaging consequences for society as a whole), but on the morning of 20 April 2004, the Polícia Judiciária (PJ), arrested 16 of them following an investigation which lasted a year and involved around 150 officers, probing match-fixing, specifically the corruption of referees.

The list of those detained reads like an LPFP-issue contacts book: the president Valentim Loureiro, António Pinto da Sousa (head of the FPF Arbitration Council), José Luís Oliveira (Loureiro's deputy in the Gondomar Câmara Municipal and the president of SC Gondomar)... A widely circulated PJ statement also confirmed that about 60 offices and homes had been searched across the country.

Displaying remarkable vivacity for a man whose offices had just been searched, the FPF president Gilberto Madaíl seized the opportunity to revel in his rival's apparent demise, saying he was not surprised by the arrests, following "insinuations which have been made over years." For his part, the then-prime minister (and a PSD colleague of Loureiro) José Barroso neatly sidestepped all invitations to make a substantive statement, merely saying, "I hope everything will be cleared up." Of course, Barroso could afford to be vague,

with his departure for the European Commission Presidency fast approaching.

His vagueness was unfortunate but with Portugal about to host an international tournament for the first time and able to field a group of players with genuine aspirations of winning the competition, the last thing that anyone wanted taking the headlines was a corruption scandal that threatened to cut to the very core of the national game. The minister for sport José Luís Arnaut also declined to comment on the case ("our rule of law is based on the constitutional principle of total separation between the executive and the judiciary"), choosing instead to forecast "a great time of celebration and affirmation of football in Portugal".

Government attempts to distance itself from the case were compromised by the fact that they had, along with the tournament director António Laranjo, been preparing for the championship since it was awarded to Portugal in 1999 (though it should be noted that Barroso was only elected in 2002) and that public funds had been instrumental in the construction of seven new stadiums and the extensive renovation of three more.

Given the eventual outcome of the case, it does not bear thinking about what might have happened had Angelos Charisteas not managed to nod home ahead of Costinha, ensuring Greece beat Portugal in the final and sealing one of the most unlikely achievements in the history of football. Portugal awoke on 5 July 2004 with a sore head and a scandal that showed little sign of ending. Yet while Loureiro, Pinto da Costa, his associate António Araújo, and a succession of referees passed through the court of Gondomar, charged with a wide variety of corruption-related offences and banned from contacting one another, progress remained slow as 2004 ticked into 2005. *Público's* reports from the time make for depressing reading and reinforce the notion that neither the public nor the sporting judicial systems were equipped to deal with such an extensive case, one based around hundreds of hours of wiretaps. Defendants declared themselves free to go, media outlets provided conflicting reports as to their status and it seems that although documents and charges were filed, they were simply added to an ever-growing pile.

However, December 2006 saw the publication of *Eu, Carolina*, a sensational (in every sense of the word) memoir by Carolina Salgado, former escort and companion of Pinto da Costa. Salgado (who dedicated the book to her former lover) accused the Porto president of being far more immersed in the scandal than his initial charges alleged. Press and public alike eagerly devoured the details of her long-term relationship with the man credited for revitalising the country's pre-eminent club at the time. With all the key ingredients of a scandal (sex, violence, and powerful men being caught in the act) present and correct, sales were astronomical. That led to the deputy attorney general Maria José Morgado being appointed to breathe new life into an investigation that had seemed all but over.

The veracity of Salgado's claims were naturally the subject of much debate but the key outcome of her exposé was the decision taken by prosecutors to re-examine accusations of bribery centred

on two Porto matches (against Beira-Mar and Estrela da Amadora) from the title and Champions League-winning season, 2003-04, as well as a 3-2 Benfica defeat at Nacional. From being a case focused on activities at Gondomar, a small club from the greater Porto region, all eyes were now fixed on the winners of seven of the last ten national titles and two referees: Augusto Duarte and Jacinto Paixão.

On 6 March 2007, it was confirmed by the judge Pedro Miguel Vieira that Herminio Loureiro (who, despite being delisted by the PSD, had been re-elected as president of the Gondomar Câmara Municipal as an independent), Pinto da Sousa and José Luís Oliveira would stand trial on over 70 charges of corruption, their defence having failed in an attempt to have the wiretaps labelled unconstitutional. Artur Marques, representing Oliveira, had the line of the day, telling the press in sanguine fashion, "there is no tragedy, just a decision I disagree with."

With Loureiro no longer wielding as much influence at the LPFP, a theoretically unrelated investigation dubbed *Apito Final* was launched in 2007, using the same evidence compiled by the public courts and led by the chief of the disciplinary committee, Ricardo Costa. However, while Portuguese law dictated that the courts were unable to file charges against institutions, the LPFP handed down punishments to both clubs and individuals, all relating to 2003-04. Porto were found guilty of attempted corruption, fined €150,000, and had six points deducted from their 2007-08 total (though this did not alter the destination of the title), while Da

Costa was suspended for two years and fined €10,000.

The club chose not to challenge the verdict, which led to a Champions League ban from Uefa — although that was reversed after an appeal. Boavista were relegated to the second tier and fined €180,000 for corruption: national champions in 2001, they now compete in the regional II Divisão and came perilously close to extinction in September 2011 [for more details, see Andy Brassell's piece later in this issue].

União de Leiria, who had already been relegated, were docked three points and their president João Bartolomeu was suspended for a year. The club secured a return to the top flight at the first attempt, but were evicted from the Estádio Dr Magalhães Pessoa by the local municipality in the summer of 2011 over unpaid rent. One official declared the club "brought nothing of value" to the area — though that did not prevent União from securing use of an alternative stadium in nearby Marinha Grande in exchange for funding the construction of three artificial pitches for public use. The club created international headlines in May 2012 when a player strike over months of unpaid wages led to coach José Dominguez having just eight men at his disposal for a relegation six-pointer against Feirense. Unsurprisingly, Leiria have chosen not to apply for the second professional tier in 2012-13.

Three referees (Duarte, Paixão and Martins dos Santos) and three linesmen were handed suspensions ranging in length from two to six years.

Despite having overcome the constitutional wrangling that had stymied the civil case, the LPFP's verdicts were placed in jeopardy by the same oddity that saw the bans on Hulk and Săpunaru overturned in 2010. Although Porto chose not to appeal to the federation over their points deduction, Pinto da Costa and Boavista did contest their respective punishments and, on 7 July 2008, the FPF Conselho de Justiça met to consider their cases. However, amid high farce pieced together by the media in subsequent days, the five members present voted to suspend the president Gonçalves Pereira and reject the appeals — but not before Pereira and his deputy had claimed that one of the members, João Abreu, was ineligible to rule on the case, and departed, declaring the meeting closed. Although the verdicts were upheld on 30 July, Pinto da Costa sought recourse with a higher legal authority and, in May 2011, the Tribunal Administrativo do Sul declared the section of the meeting that rejected the appeal to be legally "non-existent".

The FPF has pledged to challenge this decision, while the Boavista president Álvaro Braga Júnior has voiced his expectation that the club will be restored to the top flight, with accompanying financial compensation — despite the fact that the non-existent section of the meeting did not concern them. The case, unsurprisingly, continues, and although reports in February indicated that *Os Panteras* could be on the verge of a legal breakthrough, no one at the Bessa is holding their breath.

While *Apito Final* remains entrenched in a legal quagmire, *Apito Dourado* is, legally speaking, complete. On 18 July 2008, Valentim Loureiro, Pinto da Sousa and José Luís Oliveira received suspended sentences for abuses of power, but all three were acquitted on corruption charges relating to the selection of referees for SC Gondomar matches during the 2003-04 season.

Shortly before celebrating 27 years as Porto president on 23 April 2009, Da Costa was (along with Augusto Duarte and António Araújo) acquitted of all charges of corruption relating to the Beira-Mar game by the Tribunal de Gaia. The court rejected Carolina Salgado's accusation that Duarte and Araújo visited Da Costa two days before the match so that the Porto president could hand Duarte "a thick envelope" containing €2,500. Judge Catarina Almeida described the meeting as "suspect and unwise", but having rejected Salgado's version of events (the court heard during the trial that she had asked for €500,000 not to publish her book), concluded that it alone was not sufficient evidence to remove reasonable doubt. Salgado was sentenced to 300 hours of community work by the same court in October 2010, after being found guilty of defaming Pinto da Costa.

Nine months earlier, six videos had appeared on YouTube, containing wiretap recordings featuring Pinto da Costa, António Araújo, Valentim and João Loureiro, Jacinto Paixão, the Porto director-general Antero Henrique and even Deco in conversation. Little of what was being said would have been unfamiliar to those with inside knowledge of the investigations (not to mention more observant members of the public, such had been the extent of the leaking of information since April 2004), but under Portuguese law the use of wiretaps as evidence is only permitted for specific offences. At the time of writing,

the identity of the person who posted the wiretaps remains unknown.

It has been argued in some quarters that inadequate standards of governance, contradictory regulation and ineffective communication and cooperation between its varying institutions do not, or should not, sit at the top of the list of problems currently afflicting Portuguese football. Issues associated with economic short-termism are arguably having the greater impact on a day-to-day basis. The need to create a legacy for the Euro 2004 stadiums has seen clubs such as União de Leiria, Beira-Mar, Académica and on occasion Portimonense play home matches in desolate, expansive arenas, populated by no more than 3,000 hardy souls surrounded by empty seats. Financing the upkeep of these stadiums has also created tensions between municipalities and their footballing tenants — not only Leiria, but Beira-Mar and Académica have also locked horns with their respective local authorities on occasions. Sending the *Selecção* across the country for friendlies and the introduction of the Taça da Liga has done little to plug the gap.

Issues with salaries are also common — Vitória de Setúbal, Belenenses and Boavista are just three to have paid wages in arrears at some point during the 2011-12 season. This is, of course, indicative of the wider financial crisis afflicting Portugal as a whole — the contraction or minimal growth of sponsorship and television monies, combined with an all-too-numerous 'floating' class of supporter, has forced many clubs to diversify their methods of revenue-seeking, or go the way of Campomaiorense, Salgueiros, Estrela da Amadora and now Leiria.

The proliferation of third-party ownership has been one major consequence of this: following the creation of the Comunidade dos Países de Língua Portuguesa (CPLP) in 1996 and the Bosman Ruling the year before, players from Portugal's former colonies (primarily Brazil but also Angola, Mozambique, Cape Verde, Guinea-Bissau and others) were granted the right to citizenship. The accompanying economic rights precipitated a flood of player imports and the continued absence of regulation in the area of player ownership ensured that Portugal swiftly became the ideal entry point into Europe, not only from the perspective of adaptation, but also for those agents seeking either an instant financial return on their 'investment', or a long-term pay-off, as has happened with the likes of Ramires, Lucho González, Lisandro López, Pepe, and many more.

The problem is exacerbated (and the practices made nigh-on impossible to police) by the fact that only Benfica, Sporting and Porto are required to disclose detailed information with regards to their transfer dealings, as the *grandes* are the only Portuguese SADs to be publicly traded and therefore regulated by the Comissão do Mercado de Valores Mobiliários [Securities Market Commission].

The issue has received increased coverage in the English-speaking media following the sales of Ramires and David Luiz to Chelsea from Benfica, both of which involved a number of third-party investors at various stages. The now-infamous transfer of Bébé from Vitória de Guimarães to Manchester United in August 2010 also attracted global attention. However, what many observers have missed alongside the possible implications for Portugal's traditional elite — despite all being saddled by debts of questionable sustainability Benfica, Sporting and Porto are as close as Portuguese football gets to a sensible investment — is the impact that third-party ownership is having in less publicised areas. Clubs of more reduced financial means are routinely signing away large percentages of transfer fees as they try to compete on and off the pitch and retain a relationship with dwindling numbers of supporters.

There has also been the inevitable slow down in the production of youthful talent — Portugal's Under-20 side may have reached the final of the World Cup in 2011, but of the 21-man squad, only Cédric Soares and Caetano are competing regularly at the top level in their home country. The rest are either handed occasional substitute appearances, on loan to lower-league sides, or scattered across Europe with similarly limited first-team opportunities. The decrease in Portuguese talent (particularly at the *grandes*) has become a sore point for many supporters, but as long as the economic incentive exists for clubs to import players from elsewhere, they will surely do so. Similarly, the departure of the most talented before their 23rd birthdays is now the norm, with Porto's João Moutinho a rare exception.

Amid this climate of uncertainty, 2011 saw elections at the FPF and LPFP. In the latter, Mário Figueiredo defeated Euro 2004 tournament director António Laranjo by 27 votes to 21 — although none of the *grandes* supported his candidacy. A 45-year-old lawyer who practised at the Porto firm that represented Pinto da Costa throughout his legal adventures, Figueiredo has also made a number of bold declarations since taking office in January. His most immediate task is averting further financial catastrophe, following a court ruling that Bwin (a sponsor of many teams and, since 2010, the Taça da Liga) remove all advertising and sponsorship from Portuguese sporting competitions. The Associação Portuguesa de Casinos and national lottery operator Santa Casa filed a suit in 2005, claiming that Bwin (and potentially other gambling sponsors such as BetClic) enjoy an unfair advantage, as they are not subject to comparable levels of government tax or gambling legislation. Eduardo Serra Jorge, representing Bwin, said after the ruling, "It is time for the state to legislate and tax online gambling instead of banning it. Regulating it is in the interest of the consumer, the economy and the state budget." The Sporting Clube da Covilhã president José Mendes struggled to envision a future without sponsorship from the likes of Bwin and BetClic: "The Liga Orangina [second tier] clubs are already bankrupt."

The list of concerns continues to grow but examine every one and a direct link can be traced back to those responsible for the development and sustainment of football in Portugal. A brief period of hope for relations between the LPFP and the FPF dawned in December 2011 when Figueiredo's predecessor, Fernando Gomes, a former marketing and financial executive at Porto, successfully stood for the top job at the FPF, Gilberto Madaíl having stepped aside. But rather than drawing upon shared experiences and collaborating with a view to bringing about some positive change, the duo almost immediately plunged the game into a fresh constitutional crisis over the thorny issue of expanding the Liga.

Historically, Portugal's top professional division has been made up of anything between 12 and 18 teams. The upheavals of the late 1980s created a particularly fluid attitude towards structuring, but in 2007, a sensible compromise of 16 was reached. For a country of 10.5 million inhabitants, the vast majority of whom follow one of three teams, the idea of any more than 16 participants is unrepresentative, financially unworkable and unrealistic.

This remains as true as it ever was, but Figueiredo based his election campaign on a promise to re-introduce an 18-team Liga and to allow B teams to compete in the second tier, an unprecedented move (B teams are not an unfamiliar presence in Portugal, but unlike in Spain they have never been allowed to participate in professional national competitions). The finer details of this pledge were not made public but following a meeting of the LPFP's 32 member clubs in March, the gist of it became all too clear. After his proposed play-off system was not ratified by the self-interested Liga clubs, Figueiredo, in a depressingly inevitable move, attempted to convince the FPF and the general public that in order to fill the 18 places, there need be no relegation at the end of 2011-12.

The competitive implications of this were obvious and in an environment so chronically devoid of financial resources, the temptation in some quarters to make a quick buck from what would essentially be meaningless matches proved too tempting to ignore. To his credit, Gomes swiftly used FPF privileges to veto the proposals, insisting that any expansion would have to be implemented within the framework of fair competition. In one sense the self-interest of the Liga clubs (who hold two votes at LPFP general meetings, with their second-tier counterparts holding one) was to blame for the impasse: had they accepted a round-robin play-off between the teams that finish 13th and 14th in the Liga, along with the 3rd- and 4th-placed sides in the Liga Orangina, with the top two staying up and the bottom two going down, they may well have ended up with an 18-team Liga and the financial windfall from the two extra televised matches they so crave. Yet the fact that a man of Figueiredo's supposed standing and experience failed to foresee this scenario (his assertion that competition would not be affected

by the absence of relegation because "nobody wants to finish last" was as laughable as it was concerning) is yet another reflection of the deep-rooted incompetence, unwitting or otherwise, that has paralysed football in Portugal.

In the event, relegation went ahead and the 2012-13 Liga Orangina will feature B teams from Porto, Benfica, Sporting, Braga, Marítimo and Guimarães. Figueiredo's latest projects are the introduction of foreign officials and a collectivisation of television rights. Say what you will about the man, but he thinks big. However, the contrast between his grand designs and the hand-to-mouth existence of the clubs who provided his mandate is acute.

Following his victory in December, Gomes declared "our goal will be to promote Portuguese football, building on the good things that have been achieved in the last 15 years." Learning some lessons from the last 110 would be a good starting point. Ⓑ

The Flight of the Eagles

In the early sixties Benfica rose to topple Real Madrid, only to be cursed by Béla Guttmann

By Luis Catarino

When is the beginning of anything? It's always possible to search further back and find the causes of the causes of great events but, realistically. the foundation stones of Benfica's European successes were laid in 1954 when Otto Glória arrived in Portugal.

In December that year the Estádio da Luz was inaugurated and that had a huge impact on the club, generating increased revenues and providing a top-class stage for them to perform on. The real key was probably Glória himself and the culture of professionalism he introduced. He was a Brazilian who had led the *carioca* side América on a European tour the previous year and had impressed Benfica's chairman Joaquim Bogalho. His impact was immediate as he took Benfica to the title in his first season, ending four years of domination by Sporting.

Glória paid far more attention to diet and medical examination than had ever been done before, and established the *Lar do Jogador* — literally, the Player's Home. The idea was not just to accommodate young players and those who came from outside Lisbon, developing their sense of responsibility, discipline and loyalty, but also to give the technical staff somewhere to billet and to control the entire squad in the 48 hours before games.

Most players in Portugal were still amateurs, something Glória would not countenance. He demanded full-time professionalism and his refusal to allow his players to hold down second jobs was the main reason that Rogério Pipi, a flamboyant inside-forward who was one of the most iconic players of the time, abandoned Benfica. While his brilliance on the pitch was appreciated by the fans, Rogério was also one of Ford's top salesmen in the country, making far more money from selling cars than from football. Forced to choose between Benfica and his work, Rogério moved to the lower-ranking Lisbon side Oriental.

Perhaps most shocking was Glória's refusal to allow the president and other board members to enter the dressing-room to speak to players. That was unprecedented in the Portuguese game but Bogalho was astute enough to accede to Glória's wishes and leave the coach to get on with it.

Glória won his second league title in 1956-57, but after finishing second behind Porto two years later, missing out on a third title by a single goal, he allowed his contract to expire and joined Belenenses. The new Benfica chairman Maurício Vieira de Brito, a coffee tycoon with a considerable fortune in Angola, turned to the coach who had led Porto to the title — the Hungarian Béla Guttmann. He was an astute and charismatic tactician who had played a huge part in restructuring the club after the departure of the fiery Brazilian Yustrich and had been idolised by the Porto fans. His desertion was seen by them as a terrible betrayal and his joke that the humid air in the north was causing him health problems did nothing to soothe their fury.

At Benfica, Guttmann had no need to engage in such restructuring. Glória's five years at the club had left a solid base and Guttmann was able to build on it, winning the league in his first season, going unbeaten for their first 25 matches, losing eventually at Belenenses with the title already all but secured.

In their contract negotiations, Vieira de Brito hadn't taken Guttmann seriously when he'd asked for a 200,000-escudo bonus if Benfica won the European Cup. "Make it 300,000, my friend," Brito had said, unable to believe that a Portuguese team could topple Real Madrid. It was a miscalculation with long-lasting repercussions.

Benfica were keen to enhance an international reputation that had stagnated since winning the Latin Cup, a precursor to the European Cup featuring the champions of Portugal, Spain, France and Italy. Coached by Ted Smith and inspired by Rogério Pipi, Benfica had beaten Bordeaux in the final in 1950. It

was the first international silverware of any significance won by a Portuguese club and, as well as prompting celebrations across the whole country, it made Benfica an appealing guest for friendly matches. That summer, though, spurning a number of requests to stick to their original plan, they headed to Lobito in Angola.

Just a few days after their Latin Cup success, Benfica lost to a local all-star team, for whom a tall young striker scored twice. Rogério Pipi urged his club to sign him and so the 20-year-old José Águas joined Benfica for the rest of the tour. He would go on to become one of the club's most important players. He also prompted a change of policy. Benfica had always prided itself on employing only Portuguese players[1], but the example of Águas persuaded them to look to Africa, considering players from colonies such as Angola and Mozambique who were classed as Portuguese citizens.

In 1960-61, it soon became apparent that Guttmann hadn't been joking about his bonus. They beat Hearts, then Újpest and AGF, before overcoming Rapid Vienna in the semi-final. Their opponents in the final in the Wankdorfstadion in Bern were Barcelona, who had already eliminated the five-times European champions Real Madrid. With the Hungarian trio of László Kubala, Sandor Kocsis and Zoltan Czibor supplied by the graceful Galician playmaker Luis Suárez, Barça were firm favourites.

[1] *The policy ended in 1979 when the Brazilian forward Jorge Gomes became Benfica's first foreign player.*

"On the eve of the final," the Benfica defender Ângelo said, "the Barcelona players didn't even look at us in the training session. They probably thought they were going to play against a bunch of losers."

Having gone behind, Benfica came back to win 3-2, Águas scoring the first and another of their African players, the Mozambican Mário Coluna, adding the third after an own goal from the Barça keeper Antoni Ramallets. A Kubala shot hit both posts, but Benfica held out. So great was the surge of emotion at the final whistle that Vieira de Brito suffered a minor heart attack. Yet in some ways that final wasn't even the key event for Benfica that year[2]. Of more significance in the long-term was the signing of a player who decades later would have a statue in Estádio da Luz: Eusébio.

Like his father and his elder brother, Eusébio grew up a Benfica fan. As a teenager, his goal was to enter the youth ranks of Desportivo LM, a club from the Mozambican capital Lourenço Marques (now Maputo) that had a link-up with Benfica. His dealings with them, though, didn't go well. "The first time I tried my luck at Desportivo LM they didn't like me and even refused to give me equipment to train," he said. "My pride was hurt but I went back a second time."

He had no greater success, though. For some reason, the Desportivo LM youth coach refused to consider Eusébio. He and a few other hopefuls from the Os Brasileiros club, where he'd been playing, gave up on Desportivo and walked to the Sporting LM club instead. They gave Eusébio a trial in which he and his friends were so successful that the club treated them to a lift home in their Volkswagen van.

Eusébio was still unsure about joining Sporting, though, and not just because it was the club associated with Benfica's major rivals in Lisbon. "In my neighbourhood no one liked Sporting," he explained. "It was a club that belonged to the elite and the police. They didn't like black people."

Nonetheless, Eusébio signed and, whatever the racial opinions of the club's leadership, his quality was obvious. He was promoted from the Under-19 side and, aged just 17, he began to shine among the seniors.

He was spotted by José Carlos Bauer, a Brazilian coach who had played for Guttmann at São Paulo, and was leading his Ferroviária de Araraquara side on a tour to Lourenço Marques. Bauer knew he couldn't afford Eusébio but, soon after, he met Guttmann in a barber's shop in Lisbon and recommended the young forward.

Benfica had signed the goalkeeper Costa Pereira and the midfielder Mário Coluna from Mozambique, but others from Lourenço Marques had slipped from their grasp. The multifunctional Hilário, for example, had been diverted to Sporting, while the forward Matateu chose Belenenses instead.

---

[2] *That season, Benfica retained the Portuguese championship, scoring 92 goals in their 26 matches*

Benfica saw Eusébio as a younger version of Matateu, not only because of his origins but because of his combination of explosiveness and subtle technique. Both were examples of what in Lourenço Marques was known as a Magágaga, someone very powerful with a ferocious shot. This time, Benfica were determined they would get their man.

The Eagles reached terms with Dona Elisa, Eusébio's mother, who signed a contract stipulating that her son could play only for Benfica. Sporting, assuming Eusébio was theirs as he played for their feeder club, were blind to the danger. When they did finally approach Eusébio, they offered him only a trial. He reacted badly to that, at which Sporting tried to raise all kinds of bureacratic obstacles to prevent Eusébio joining their great rivals. Eventually, though, he joined the Eagles for a fee of 400,000 escudos.

Guttmann was so excited by Eusébio in his very first training session that he turned to his assistant Fernando Caiado and shouted, "Gold! Gold!" The centre-back Germano was just as impressed. "I'm fine because I'm a defender. But as for you guys," he said, turning to the forwards, "be ready because one of you will be out of the starting line-up for sure."

It took a year from Benfica's initial offer until Eusébio played for them. He flew to Portugal in December 1960 — using the alias 'Ruth Malosso' to escape attention — but he was only confirmed as a Benfica player five months later, shortly before the European Cup final. He couldn't play in that game, though, because of Uefa's rule that only players who had been registered with their clubs for a minimum of three months could play in European Cup matches.

Even though he was ineligible, Eusébio travelled with the team for the away matches in Aarhus and Vienna to become accustomed to the atmosphere of continental competition. He didn't go to Switzerland for the final, though, watching it on television in the *Lar do Jogador* in Lisbon. The Portuguese football federation had refused to rearrange Benfica's Portuguese Cup last-16 second-leg tie away to Vitória de Setúbal that was scheduled for the following day. Eusébio, making his competitive debut in what was essentially a reserve side, scored but also missed a penalty, saved by Félix Mourinho, the father of José.

It was a fortnight later that Eusébio really came to public attention, against the Brazilian giants Santos in the Tournoi International de Paris at the Parc des Princes. Benfica, though, were tired and Santos led 4-0 by half-time. Guttmann, figuring he had nothing to lose, threw on Eusébio for the inside-forward Santana. He responded with a hat-trick; although Benfica lost 6-3, all the talk afterwards was about Eusébio. "Who is that boy?" Pelé, two years Eusébio's senior, asked Mário Coluna. Eusébio was no longer a player to be left on the bench; Santana, an imaginative Angolan, was the player who made way.

Having collected his 300,000 escudos bonus, Guttmann asked for a salary increase of 65% if he won the European Cup again in 1962. His obsession with money was understandable. He had lost a huge amount of money in the

Wall Street crash, endured the worst of Europe's anti-Semitism in the thirties, was interned during the Second World War and coached in Romania at a time when inflation was so rampant he demanded to be paid not in cash but in fresh food.

It soon became apparent that, with Eusébio in the side, Benfica were easily good enough to retain their title. They beat FK Austria comfortably in the first round, and drew Nürnberg in the quarter-final. Conditions were snowy, but Guttmann told his players "snow is only a problem if it's more than half a metre in height". Benfica lost 3-1. In front of 70,000 fans at what became known as the 'Inferno da Luz', though, it was a different story and Benfica won the second leg 6-0. "In this place," Nürnberg's captain Max Morlock said, "you can only play with cotton wool in your ears."

In the semi, Benfica faced Bill Nicholson's Tottenham Hotspur, who had won the double the previous season and were on their way to a second successive league title. Two goals from José Augusto gave Benfica a 3-1 win in the first leg in Lisbon but they came under intense pressure on a damp pitch at White Hart Lane. A goal from Águas cancelled out Bobby Smith's early opener and, although Danny Blanchflower converted a 54th-minute penalty, Benfica held out for a 4-3 aggregate win.

Real Madrid awaited in the final in Amsterdam. They were more respected than they had been a year earlier, but there was a lingering sense that they'd been fortunate against Barcelona the previous season. After all, there'd been a shot from Kubala that had bounced around the frame of the goal before finishing up in Costa Pereira's arms: a clear case of luck — unless it was Guttmann's sorcery.

There was an otherworldly genius about the Hungarian and before kick-off, in his odd blend of Portuguese and Italian, he found exactly the right words to motivate his side. "During the Paris Olympics of 1924," Guttmann said, recalling his days with the Hungary national team, "I met some celebrities. One of them was the great idol Paavo Nurmi, the Finn who won the 5000m gold medal with a superb time of 14:31. Yet, in the Rome Olympics in 1960, an unknown fellow from New Zealand [Murray Halberg] completed the same distance in one minute less." Evolution, he pointed out, was a natural thing in sport, and records achieved in the twenties meant nothing today. "Football is the same," he went on. "The best players in that period would nowadays be considered lower-ranked ones nowadays." His meaning was clear: Alfrédo Di Stéfano and Ferenc Puskás had been great once, but now they were past it.

Before the game the zoo in Rhenen, in the far south-east corner of the Netherlands, gave Benfica a bear cub as a mascot. Vieira de Brito was enchanted by the gift and, startling everybody around, he took it with him into the VIP area in the stand[3]. One of the ball-boys that night, meanwhile, was a 15-year-old Johan Cruyff.

---

[3] *The bear joined Benfica's squad on the return flight to Portugal and was afterwards kept in the Lisbon zoo.*

Benfica used a variant of 4-2-4 for much of the season, their shape matching the formation Vicente Feola, Guttmann's former assistant at São Paulo, had used with the Brazil national team at the 1958 World Cup. Just as Orlando had been the fourth defender for Brazil, dropping back from midfield to cover for Bellini, so Fernando Cruz did the same for Benfica, filling the space whenever the centre-back Germano was pulled out of position by Puskás[4].

The Benfica full-backs Mário João (right) and Ângelo (left) weren't as attacking-minded as Brazil's, but they were noted for their energy and tenacity. Mário João, though, struggled to contain the rapid Paco Gento, and Real Madrid led 3-2 at half-time, Puskás having scored a hat-trick. Benfica's chances seemed slim, but Guttmann remained bullish. "Don't worry," he said, "we're going to win this thing. They're dead tired."

Of all Guttmann's managerial gifts, probably his greatest was his ability to make his players believe they were the best in the world. Perhaps they were; certainly in the second half they played like it. Guttmann was the leader off the pitch, but on it the chief was Mário Coluna, the 'Sacred Monster', who could get his message across with the merest glance.

He had joined Benfica at the same time as Otto Glória in 1954 and had been the most important figure in the team's transition from W-M to 4-2-4. Having joined the Eagles as a striker, he had struggled to find a place in the team because José Águas was a more natural finisher. Coluna was moved to inside forward, where it became apparent that his good technique, robust physique, leadership qualities, tactical awareness and decision-making could be even more useful if he played deeper, operating as the more offensive of the two central midfielders. He was dominant in the second half against Madrid and scored a brilliant equaliser, volleyed home in a manner reminiscent of his goal against Barcelona a year earlier in Bern.

Guttmann's prediction turned out to be correct. The Real defender Pedro Casado suffered a thigh injury and, with substitutes not yet permitted in Uefa fixtures, he was left to limp on the right wing in a side effectively reduced to 10 men. This was Eusébio's moment. Receiving the ball in midfield, he accelerated by Di Stéfano. He was charged by Pachín inside the box and a penalty was given. The Real Madrid centre-back José Santamaría, angered by what he thought was a dive, raced up to Eusébio and called him a "maricón". Eusébio had no idea what the word meant, so sought enlightenment from Coluna, who had taken on the role of Eusébio's mentor[5]. Calm and firm as ever, Coluna said to his protégé, "Just take the penalty and call him cabrón." He did, and gave Benfica a 4-3 lead.

[4] When Brazil won the 1962 World Cup that covering movement was no longer visible because there was already a flat line of four defenders, with the centre-backs Mauro and Zózimo playing side by side.

[5] He already knew Eusébio's family from Lourenço Marques and Doña Elisa had written to him asking him to take care of her son in Lisbon.

Behind for the first time in the final, Di Stéfano turned to Puskás and said, "We're done." Eusébio all but confirmed the win with a goal from a free-kick move and very nearly completed a spectacular hat-trick two minutes later, bursting from half way and drawing a fine save from José Araquistáin. Characteristically, he then shook the goalkeeper by the hand.

Eusébio had been in awe of Di Stéfano before kick-off, and when the final whistle blew, he raced towards the 35 year old, even as the crowd poured onto the pitch. The Argentinian gave him his shirt and Eusébio promptly stuffed it into his shorts to make sure nobody would steal it from him. Photographs of the celebrations show him punching the air with one hand and clutching a bulge in his shorts with the other.

Benfica finished the season third in the league, but that mattered far less than retaining the European Cup. With fluid, cohesive, quick-passing football, they had proved themselves one of the world's great sides. Apart from the powerhouse Eusébio, the attacking line featured José Augusto, a right-winger with an eye for the goal, who was considered by Gabriel Hanot, the editor of *L'Equipe*, to be "as good as Garrincha". Then there was the thrilling António Simões, a promising teenager included in the senior squad for the first time that season. The fearless 'Mickey Mouse' was a right-footed left-winger with such flair that Guttmann had no option but to move the left-winger Domiciano Cavém into central midfield so Simões could fit in the first team[6]. And they all benefited from having the captain José Águas as a striker who, with aerial ability and a capacity to hold the ball up and distribute intelligently, bound the whole side together.

As Brian Clough said, "You win something once and people can say it's all down to luck. You win it twice and it shuts them up." That could serve as Guttmann's epitaph at Benfica. Enticed by a fabulous contract from Peñarol, the Wizard said goodbye to Portugal, confirming his theory that "the third year is always fatal for a coach." Moreover, he said that without him they would never again win the European Cup.

Portugal in the sixties was going through a period of social and economic turmoil. Thousands of troops were sent by the dictator Salazar to fight in the Colonial War in Angola, which began in 1961. Football had an impact there. "When Benfica played," the novelist António Lobo Antunes wrote, "our troops turned the speakers with the radio commentary towards the woods and this way we were never attacked. War stopped in those moments because even the MPLA[7] liked Benfica. It was weird because it didn't make any sense being at war against people who shared the same club."

[6] *Simões remains, at 18 years and 139 days of age, the youngest player ever to win a final of the European Cup / Champions League.*

[7] *MPLA: People's Movement for the Liberation of Angola.*

Benfica remained strong after Guttmann's departure. Having Eusébio was, of course, a major advantage. He could have gone to Italy, but the government of Salazar was determined to keep him in the country. Speaking to Gabriele Marcotti in 2004, Eusébio referred specifically to interest from Juventus and Internazionale, "And yet I was not allowed to move. Why? Salazar was not my father and he was certainly not my mother. What gave him the right? The truth was that he was my slavemaster, just as he was the slavemaster of the entire country." Along with the fado singer Amália, Eusébio was the most famous Portuguese citizen in global terms and the fact he was born in Africa could be used for propaganda purposes to claim that Portugal's relationship with its colonies was good.

These days, Eusébio walks with a pronounced limp, the result of a career in which he was regularly forced to play with the aid of pain-killing injections. He has had surgery on his left knee on six occasions and, as a result, can only drive cars with an automatic gearbox. He insists that he doesn't regret a thing; that his awards, including the 1965 Ballon d'Or, were worth the pain.

Benfica, meanwhile, struggle on, seemingly unable to shake off Guttmann's curse. Since 1962, they have played in five more European Cup finals and lost them all. Their last appearance in a final came in 1990, aganst AC Milan in Vienna, where Guttmann is buried. Before the game Eusébio visited the Jewish cemetery and prayed by the grave of his former coach. Whether he was praying for the curse to be lifted or not nobody knows, but if he was, it made no difference. Frank Rijkaard scored the only goal as Arrigo Sacchi's side retained their crown.

The World's Best FREE Online Soccer Manager Game

www.soccermanager.com

The Pretenders

Only two sides outside Os Tres Grandes have won the Portuguese title. For both a repeat seems unlikely.

By Andy Brassell

A hand-to-mouth existence is nothing new in Portuguese football. Outside the power of *os três grandes* of Benfica, Porto and Sporting, lies a desert of indifference. In this commercial wasteland pitiful attendances are commonplace, with attendances below 1000 registered in 13 top-flight matches in 2010-11.

The feelgood factor from Euro 2004, a tournament that generated so much national pride, quickly began to fade. This season União Leiria moved out of their own Euro legacy, the €50m, 30,000-capacity Estádio Dr Magalhães Pessoa, unable to afford the rent and overheads having never filled it during eight-and-a-half years of residence. They now play in the modest, 6,000-capacity Estádio Municipal in nearby Marinha Grande. Towards the end of April, 16 of the first-team squad rescinded their contracts after going months unpaid and the team started a subsequent league match against Feirense with just eight players. After finishing bottom of the table, Leiria failed to meet the entry requirements for the Liga de Honra (second division), so prepared for semi-professional life in the regionalised third tier under a new board.

Yet official Portuguese Liga statistics make the club the 11th-best supported in the country. In 2010-11, 11 of the Liga's 16 clubs averaged gates below 5,000, with five of those averaging less than 3,000. Yet the problem isn't restricted to provincial Portugal. The rot has long since spread to the big cities. Perhaps the least surprising development in this direction was in early spring 2011 when the perpetually broke Estrela Amadora, the club from the Lisbon suburbs that produced Manchester United's €8m signing Bebé, finally closed the doors of the Estádio da Reboleira for the last time.

The Estrela president António Oliveira made public his hope that a charitable windfall from their former charge's move to England would have saved them, given that Bebé had been at Guimarães for only six weeks before the United deal. In truth, that would have been an act of benevolence too far. He had joined the northern club from Estrela on a free transfer granted in lieu of unpaid wages. Bebé had frequently been subbed a few hundred Euros by his agent here and there to get by. Neither he, nor Guimarães, owed Estrela a debt.

If this slow death was relatively predictable, the fall into ruin of Belenenses and Boavista has been even more painful to watch. In a country in which there is no denying the hegemony of *os três grandes*, these two clubs stand out as, remarkably, the only clubs outside that clique to have been crowned champions since the Liga was first arranged in its current round-robin format in 1938.

Situated back from the River Tejo, some 8km to the south of Reboleira, the Estádio do Restelo feels almost too prestigiously situated to be home to a football club, above and beyond even the positioning of the Santiago Bernabéu on the power vein of the Paseo de la Castellana in Madrid. The sense that this is the case is further accentuated by Belenenses's current problems.

The 1946 champions have spent the last two seasons struggling near the foot of the Liga de Honra. At the club's annual general meeting in summer 2011, president António Soares warned that "bigger gate receipts alone won't resolve our problems. These problems need new solutions and personally, I don't think we'll manage to get out of this situation without new partners." Haemorrhaging money and playing in front of dwindling crowds, gravity means that the club's privileged geographical position is today more of an anomaly that a genuine advantage.

That hasn't always been the case. Visitors to Belém, the fashionable and picturesque suburb in which the club is based (*Os Belenenses* meaning 'the ones from Belém') don't have to go far to spot the very genesis of the club. Some 70 metres from the entrance to the presidential palace, on the opposite side of the road, is a stone bench engraved with the legend *Aqui nasceu o CF "Os Belenenses" 23-9-1919* — Belenenses was born here on 23 September 1919. Collating the club's illustrious origins and restricted present, a short stroll 50 paces to the west of the bench brings you to the town's club shop, a tiny green kiosk with enough space for the shopkeeper to have just about enough elbow room to open a newspaper in quiet periods.

If the shop emphasises that the club has become a niche concern, the presidential palace gives clues to something that was more than a football club in pre-democracy Portugal, and Belenenses's strength meant something in the thirties, forties and fifties. "At this moment in time Portugal was governed by a dictatorship," said Carlos Manuel Pereira of the Lusa news agency. "The history of Belenenses was closely tied to that of the military. Various generals in turn served as club presidents and they gave the club strength and visibility both nationally and internationally."

Belenenses had played on the Campo do Pão de Fio, a modest green off the Rua de Belém, the suburb's main street, facing the Tejo — and on the edge of which the club's kiosk now symbolically rests. The team was often displaced in its early years, frequently playing on a site in Lumiar, where Lisbon's international airport stands today. In January 1928 it gained a solid base in Belém, setting up at the Campo das Salésias. Estádio do Restelo was built on the existing site to replace it and opened in 1956.

Permanence in Belém had been a big factor in making Belenenses the dominant force in Portuguese football pre-Liga, and the club won three national titles in the 1930s. "Being in a noble part of Lisbon," Pereira said, "tied to voyages of discovery and Portugal's 16th-century expansion, being in the place from where ships left for Brazil and India, gave the image of it being a 'rich' club, and the club made the most of it."

The league title was clinched with a 2-1 win on the season's final day, at Alentejo side SL Elvas, on 26 May 1946 but the balance of power quickly tipped across Lisbon to Sporting, with the golden period of *Os Cincos Violinos* — 'the Five Violins' — the name given to the attacking quintet of Jesus Correia, José Travassos, Vasques, Albano and the Portuguese league's all-time record scorer, Peyroteo. Yet Belenenses were still able to compete at this point.

"Just as Benfica had Eusébio and Mário Coluna from Mozambique," said Pereira, "Belenenses had the brothers Matateu and Vicente, two players who made a big impact on Portuguese football." Matateu was the first Luso-African star of the Portuguese game, while Vicente captained Belenenses to a second Taça de Portugal title in 1960 before starring for Portugal in defence at the 1966 World Cup in England.

On two afternoons per week, you can walk around the trophy room at the Restelo. Two storeys of cups and pennants await behind the barred door. Many of them were awarded for other disciplines — like most clubs in Portugal, Belenenses is a multi-sport club — including swimming, rugby and handball. When I visited, the club historian and museum curator Ana Linheiro proudly pointed to a black and white photograph of herself on the wall, taken around the time of her 1944 and 1945 national swimming titles.

The museum is full of reminders of the extremely well-connected history of the club. One pennant, from Real Madrid, commemorates Belenenses's December 1947 visit to play the Spanish side on the occasion of inaugurating the Estadio Santiago Bernabéu (or the Estadio Real Madrid Club de Fútbol, as it was then). The view from the upper floor, through battered windows out into the stadium and towards the glistening Tejo and Belém's central strip, reminds you where you are. Yet the club itself appears trapped in there, suffocated by its illustrious past.

"Today, it's exactly this location that is preventing the club having financial sustainability," Pereira said. "They can't build a new stadium and they can't build commercial add-ons to lease — and give them a financial return — because of the visual and environmental impact that it would cause, with the Estádio do Restelo being behind the Mosteiro dos Jerónimos [the imposing 1490s monastery which has been a Unesco world heritage site since 1983]."

Belenenses's decline arguably began in the 1960s, when they — along with the rest of the country — were left in Benfica's slipstream, as Eusébio, Coluna and company led Portugal to triumph in Europe. Belenenses were Portugal's first Inter-Cities Fairs Cup entrant, debuting with a 3-3 draw away to Hibernian in September 1961. Unfortunately for the Blues this was pretty much a non-event even at the time, as Bela Guttmann had led Benfica to become the first side other than Real Madrid to win the European

Cup, beating Barcelona in Bern, four months earlier.

There were warning signs of the hardship to come in 1981, when it first became clear there were serious financial problems at the club. The inexperienced coach Artur Jorge bore a significant portion of supporters' wrath for the situation and Belenenses were relegated from the top flight for the first time in their history at the end of the season, in May 1982. In the season following relegation, a 19-year-old José Mourinho played for the club. His father, the goalkeeper Félix, had also played for Belenenses in the late sixties and early seventies, finishing runners-up to Benfica in 1973 and later having a brief spell as assistant head coach.

Belenenses went back up in 1984 and the previous problems were treated as a blip. Or not treated, if you prefer. "Even when Belenenses were earning a lot of money," Pereira said, "they didn't take financial sustainability into account. They won another Taça de Portugal [in 1989] while being coached by [the 1974 Brazil World Cup captain] Marinho Peres, but good sporting results like this and participation in the Uefa Cup hid the club's financial weakness. For this [competition] they had to sign good players but they didn't have the money for it. They borrowed, didn't pay their taxes and today they're suffering for all these mistakes."

Remarkably, Belenenses were in the Uefa Cup as recently as 2007, and welcomed Bayern Munich to the Restelo in October of that year in the first round, eventually losing 3-0 on aggregate. Again, the headline disguised the reality of the club's situation. Belenenses should have been relegated in 2006, but were reprieved when an administrative dispute between the Liga Portuguesa de Futebol Profissional (LPFP) and Gil Vicente saw the northerners sent down in their stead. They later had a similar escape, in 2009, finishing second-bottom but let off when the financially stricken Estrela went in their place. Moreover, just 7,000 had attended the game with Bayern at the 20,500-capacity Restelo.

Today, that would be considered a bumper crowd. In their last season in the top flight — 2009-10 — the 15 Liga games at the Restelo produced an aggregate attendance of 50,658. Last season's average in the second tier was 1,396. "At this moment, there are no investors with the capacity or the will to put in the €10m-plus to make the club viable," Pereira said. "After the death of president Cabral Ferreira [in 2008] there was the chance of the Brazilian company Traffic Sport investing, but the then-president Fernando Sequeira rejected the proposal, and this proved to be a big mistake."

These errors keep stacking up. A recent partnership agreement signed with AC Milan gives the Italian giants access to the club's academy products but — bizarrely — doesn't require them to pay any compensation for any players they decide to take on. Losing out on valuable talent is nothing new for Belenenses. "Bebé was training at Belenenses," Pereira said. "The club didn't want to commit to signing him to a contract, so he went to Guimarães instead and they sold him to United for €8m. A decade before, the same thing happened with Pedro Pauleta." Those who don't slip through the net can expect wages to arrive late.

While the roots of Belenenses' status lie deep in the past, the rise of Boavista to surpass them as Portugal's fourth most-decorated club is a more modern phenomenon. Despite now playing in the suburbs of Porto, Boavista were born on the banks of the river Douro, where the port wine lodges that give the city its fame reside.

The club was formed in 1903 as the Boavista Footballers by workers from the Graham distillery and initially run by a six-man board, made up of three English representatives and three Portuguese. A schism quickly developed and a dispute arose in 1905 with the church-going English wanting games played on Saturday and the Portuguese keen to switch to Sundays. A general assembly vote in April 1909 came down on the side of the Portuguese.

The rights to the Campo do Bessa — the site on which a full stadium, Estádio do Bessa, was later built — were also ceded to the victors and the ground was officially inaugurated under that name in April 1910, with a game against the local side Leixões. In that year, the Boavista Footballers became Boavista Futebol Clube.

This workers' team thus began a respectable history, albeit one hardly laden with trophies. Until 1975's Taça de Portugal win, the highlight had been winning the second-tier title (then, pre-Liga de Honra, the Segunda Divisão) in 1937. The club's first silverware had come with the ten-team Campeonato do Porto in 1914, on 28 June — the same day that Archduke Franz Ferdinand was assassinated in Sarajevo.

Things began to change under the reign of Valentim Loureiro, a former army major who was Boavista president for a marathon term stretching from 1972 to 1995. He also served as LPFP president for 10 years from 1996. Valentim's son João succeeded him at the Bessa in 1997 and presided over a decade of unprecedented success which took in the Liga title in 2001, another Taça de Portugal, a Supertaça de Portugal (played out between Liga and Taça winners) and three Champions League qualifications.

To say Loureiro the elder has had his finger in a few pies is something of an understatement. Latterly a local politician, he was also chairman of the ostensibly impressive but disastrously loss-making Porto Metro. Opened in 2002, the total cost of the light railway in Portugal's second city had risen to almost €3.5bn by 2007, having made a record €120m annual loss in 2006. Nevertheless, the board still paid itself a total of €650m in that year. A new line, the metro's sixth, opened in January 2011. Debts mounted to over €2bn.

"Valentim Loureiro was for Boavista what Geppetto was for Pinocchio," wrote Manuel Dias in his 2001 book *O Futebol no Porto*. "If the old carpenter saw his wooden doll transformed into a boy of flesh and bone, this tenacious leader made from a club of small dimensions and limited ambitions one of sporting power on a national scale... and he didn't even need the help of a fairy godmother."

Nowadays, the oil in the magic lamp has run dry. Boavista would be grateful for Belenenses's league placing at least, languishing as they are in the modern day Segunda Divisão; the regionalised third tier, where their local rivals are Gondomar, the satellite town which Valentim still serves as Mayor. The stadium there holds fewer than 2,500.

The shock with Boavista is that they always seemed so well run, among a field of basket cases. Throughout the nineties the club appeared to be balancing the books with what was almost a cottage industry in moving players on to Benfica, notably Nuno Gomes and João Vieira Pinto. Again, the sheen of success — and, in this case, regeneration — concealed what was going on behind the scenes.

Of course, winning a title in 2001 is light years away from the experience of doing so in the nascent professionalism of 1946. For a club of Boavista's size, it is almost equally a curse as it is a blessing. Success necessitates big bonuses, improved contracts and high overheads for the scale of 'production' required for Champions League matches. A plethora of demands, in short, that the club's infrastructure was ill-equipped to cope with.

What really did for Boavista was the *Apito Dourado* [Golden Whistle] enquiry and the subsequent *Apito Final* [Final Whistle] investigation, both centred around accusations of match-fixing via influencing officials. In the former enquiry, which began in 2004 and concluded in 2008, Valentim was found not guilty of corruption, but guilty of "abuse of power" and given a suspended jail sentence of three years and two months.

Apito Final had dire consequences for Boavista, above and beyond besmirching of individual reputations. In May 2008 the club was relegated for "coercion" of match officials in three Liga games, against Belenenses, Benfica and Académica. João Loureiro was suspended from office for four years. In the same enquiry, the champions and city neighbours Porto were docked six points for attempted (but crucially, not successful) bribery — a penalty which didn't affect their comfortable Liga title win. The Porto president Jorge Nuno Pinto da Costa was banned for two years in the same judgement.

This ruling was upheld by the Federação Portuguesa de Futebol (FPF)'s Conselho da Justiça [Justice Council] two months later, despite neither the president nor vice-president of the council attending the hearing. The irregularity in this panel's conduct saw both Pinto da Costa's ban and Porto's points penalty revoked by a Portuguese administrative court in 2011.

Despite this and the fact that Porto's criminal judges absolved Loureiros, the referee Jacinto Paixão and the referees' chief Pinto Correia in July 2010 of the charges brought in *Apito Dourado* regarding the Boavista v Estrela match in April 2004, Boavista are still waiting for their own recompense. "We continue to believe that the truth will come out," said the club president Álvaro Braga Júnior in a press conference that followed the failed appeal. Boavista have kept believing, but it has done little good. In April 2009, supporters marched the 4km up the Avenida da Boavista to the Câmara do Porto [city hall] to protest, with *Justiça Para O Boavista* as their slogan, which was reprised in a May 2011 march and is regularly seen on a banner which follows Portugal's national team around Europe.

Before the march Braga Júnior told *Jornal de Notícias* that "the city has already lost Salgueiros but, now, can't afford to lose Boavista, which has 105 [*sic*] years of history." Salgueiros went to the wall in May 2005, but a phoenix club, Sport Clube Salgueiros 08, was formed three years later.

Braga Júnior was in no way exaggerating the extent of Boavista's inability to cope with the sanction. After a disastrous 2008-09 season they fell straight through the second tier, but seemed to be granted a reprieve when Vizela were demoted for corruption. In July 2009, the LPFP's executive committee withdrew the offer and demoted Boavista to the Segunda Divisão after they failed to deliver the €150,000 required in financial guarantees, despite the board claiming in a statement they were "just a step away from providing them".

Boavista are still there, battling for promotion in front of crowds in their hundreds at the Bessa. The old stadium retains a strong sense of its English roots, with the stands close to the pitch, but it feels like a long time since matches were played in front of full houses here during Euro 2004.

There was little drip-down from those three heady weeks. A 2010 report by TVI noted that Boavista earned just €1.01m in rights from Euro 2004; a figure that appears even more paltry when compared to the harvest reaped by *os três grandes*: €79m for Benfica, €94m for Sporting and a staggering €133m for Porto.

Without having had much of a tangible benefit from the Euro 2004 bump, the club is still lumbered with its share of costs. Boavista spend €11,000 per month just to light the Bessa. At the current rate, it takes seven home games to make enough money to cover it.

Last year brought the tenth anniversary of Boavista's title triumph, though the party was understandably a muted affair. A low-key lunch was organised in Porto city centre in May 2011, with Martelinho, Rui Bento and the former Portugal goalkeeper Ricardo among the attendees from the championship-winning side. In a further attempt to drum up enthusiasm via nostalgia, the club produced a promotional video for this season.

It was filmed at the Bessa, and included interviews with past greats including Ion Timofte, Nelo and the title-winning midfielder Petit. Its title was *"Eu acredito"* [*I Believe*] with all the protagonists and various fans reciting the phrase to camera to conclude the film, affirming their faith in Boavista's ability to bounce back. If they had the grace to participate, most of the players involved also had the realism to look a bit sheepish while they were saying it.

There is little option but to keep on trying. It seemed as if a breakthrough had been made on February 28, when the Tribunal Administrativo e Fiscal de Lisboa ruled the decision by the CJ's skeleton board null and void. An emotional Braga Júnior greeted the decision and called for the "swift reintegration" of Boavista into the top flight. They're still waiting.

Manuel Maio replaced the weary Braga Júnior as president in June, and he hopes to right the enduring wrongs with fresh energy. "We will only beat our difficulties and be able to have the security we need," he told the club's website, "via the club being returned to its due sporting place which the club's by right – in the first division of Portuguese football."

Boavista, and Belenenses, are swimming against the tide in the current Portuguese climate and have begun to look like relics from a bygone era. Ana Linheiro looks after the Belenenses trophy room on her own, dusting the trophies and neatly collating the daily sports press in arch lever files, as she has done for years. "I used to have someone who helped me to polish the trophies," she says, "but the club had to let her go at the end of last season. The club has no money. What can you do?"

When Estrela Amadora finally folded, it took a week for the administrator Paulo Sá Cardoso to announce to the world that the club was no more. Despite their places in history, both Belenenses and Boavista are local concerns too, so while they will continue to be represented as a dogged minority, the rest of Portugal will turn a blind eye, with even football fans still offended by the public expenditure on white elephant stadiums for Euro 2004 and unlikely to be clamouring for a bailout. As Portugal stares into a gaping economic black hole, it seems that many of its public have decided that some things are simply more important than football.   Ⓑ

The Dragons' Cap

Porto's rise in the late seventies was inspired by the innovative coaching of José Maria Pedroto

By Vitor Sobral

It was 1978. A summer's day in Porto, a city famous for its port wine and from which the nation of Portugal derives its name. José Maria Pedroto leant back into his seat on the bench at the Estadio das Antas with a smile on his face.

Porto were 4-0 up against Sporting Braga in the last game of the season. They were level on points with Benfica at the top of the Portuguese league, but with a vastly superior goal difference. There was nothing that the side from Lisbon could do to stop the championship from heading north. Nineteen years after they last claimed the Portuguese title, Porto were champions again. The northern capital celebrated as if it had just been liberated from occupation.

It was only four years after a revolution had removed the country's repressive, centralised dictatorship. But for the man they called Zé do Boné, the Portuguese name for Andy Capp (Pedroto always wore a floppy cap), the war to dominate Portuguese football was just beginning.

Pedroto was born in the northern Portuguese town of Lamego in 1928, along the famous Douro River on which Porto's port wine barrels are floated. An intelligent right-sided midfielder, Pedroto rose through the ranks at Leixões before moving on to Belenenses and finally achieving success with Porto.

He also captained the Portugal national team, where it's said that his word carried far more weight than that of the coach. His teammates would often gather in his room to discuss the strategy for the upcoming game. But it would be as a coach that Pedroto would truly make his mark on Portuguese football. He earned his badges before the age of 30 and after successful stints in the youth ranks of Porto and the national team, the progressive young coach honed his skills at Académica de Coimbra.

He slowly grew into the role and, after a stint at Leixões, the then 37 year old took little Varzim to an astonishing seventh place in 1966. Inevitably his old team Porto came calling, but the club's lack of ambition, despite its large fan base, frustrated Pedroto. He won his first trophy, the 1968 Taça de Portugal, with the Dragões during his three-year stint. But Benfica still dominated the championship and Zé do Boné left Porto in 1969.

It was at Vitória de Setubal that Pedroto finally found a club that, although relatively small compared to the big three, shared his ambitions. He brought together a talented group of players and moulded them not only into determined competitors in Portugal, but on the continent too. One of them was the tireless, technical midfielder Octavio Machado, who played under Pedroto in Setubal and later on at Porto. "He got the best out of players. He always set the team up to play in a way that suited the players he had," Machado recalled. "He taught us how to keep the ball, where to play the ball, but most of all he taught us how to play each game with the same mentality."

The team came third in the Portuguese league in Pedroto's first season, playing attractive, possession-based football. A predatory striker by the name of Vitor Baptista finished off the moves, while an Angolan winger with a club foot, Jacinto João, dazzled opposing defences with skills akin to those of Garrincha. A statue of João stands outside Setubal's Estadio do Bonfim today.

But it was in Europe that Setubal truly upset the established order. In the 1969-70 Inter-City Fairs Cup, Rapid Bucharest were dispatched with ease in the first round. A continental mismatch against Liverpool was next, but Setubal outplayed the English side to win 1-0 in the first leg, before a 3-2 defeat at Anfield eliminated the Reds on away goals.

Setubal lost to Hertha Berlin in the third round, but the success over Liverpool reverberated. In those days, such a result against any English opponent was unthinkable for a Portuguese side outside of Benfica and Sporting.

It was only the beginning. The next season, Setubal saw off Lausanne and Hajduk Split in the opening two rounds,

before dispatching Anderlecht in the round of 16. They would fall against Leeds United in the quarter-finals, but only because of a Peter Lorimer away goal.

Then in 1971-72 Setubal hammered the Soviet Cup holders, Spartak Moscow, 4-0 at the Estadio do Bonfim before defeat to Romania's UTR Arad in the next round. But the disappointment didn't last long as Pedroto led the Sadinos to second place in the Portuguese league. It remains Vitória's highest finish.

The next season they beat Fiorentina and Internazionale in the Uefa Cup before defeat to Tottenham in the last eight; the club's reputation as the giant killers of Europe was confirmed.

For a time, 1973-74 looked like being the crowning glory for Pedroto and Setubal. After 12 rounds of the championship, Vitoria led the league. But in the middle of the title fight, politics intervened. Tensions were rising in Portugal as the population tired of the country's repressive regime. Setubal's president, Antonio Xavier de Lima, whose business ventures benefited from the conservative government, banned players from speaking without his authority.

That enraged Pedroto, who had always treated his players as a second family. On the verge of his first championship, Pedroto walked out on the club. Rather than be disappointed by the coach's decision, the team rallied around the man they loved. "The players were always in solidarity with Pedroto," Machado said. "We always preferred him to the president."

The special relationship between Pedroto and his players was one of the keys to his success. Comparisons with his compatriot, José Mourinho, are inevitable but there's little evidence to suggest that the special one was a student of Pedroto. Although Mourinho was born in Setubal and his father played for Vitória, Mourinho senior had left to join Belenenses before Zé do Boné arrived at the Bonfim.

Despite Vitória's excellent start in 1973, they never recovered from Pedroto's departure, and the club finished the season in third, four points adrift of Sporting. In Setubal today, locals who remember that campaign have no doubt that Vitória would have been champions had Pedroto stayed.

Aged 45, Pedroto headed north to Porto, but not to the club of his heart. Instead it was to the city's second team, Boavista. The side with the checkerboard shirts hadn't won a trophy of significance or finished higher than fifth in their history. Even Pedroto doubted he could make them challengers. But it took just one season to achieve success. In 1975 Boavista won the Portuguese Cup and finished fourth in the league.

It was no fluke. In the following season, the Cup was retained and Porto's second team outshone their more illustrious neighbours by finishing second behind Benfica.

Success at Boavista came with a change in formation, as Pedroto again adapted his tactics to suit his team. Luis Freitas Lobo, one of Portugal's most respected football analysts, was in his teens at the time, but remembers Pedroto's Boavista as tactical innovators. "They played a 4-4-2 diamond with the full-backs

attacking regularly," Lobo recalled. "They also had a magnificent playmaker in João Alves, who was given freedom to roam. This system was very advanced at the time in football."

Portugal's national team, which had struggled after the decline of the 1966 World Cup generation, soon came calling and he took the job in 1974. Grouped with England and Czechoslovakia in Euro 76 qualifying, few gave the Portuguese a chance.

The first game was against England at Wembley; it was widely held that a narrow defeat would be a good result. Pedroto analysed his opponents with rigour. The English, he realised, were much taller than the Portuguese, so any cross into the box would spell disaster. Pedroto effectively played two left-backs and two right-backs, to close the flanks and force the wingers inside. England barely managed a cross as Portugal held on for a famous scoreless draw.

Back in the league Boavista were stealing the limelight. Porto had to act. After an unsuccessful invitation to switch sides, Pedroto finally crossed the divide when his good friend, Jorge Nuno Pinto da Costa, was appointed as the Dragões director of football. The two formed a formidable partnership as Zé do Boné set his team up to win the battles on the pitch, while Pinto da Costa revelled in the political war off it.

In the late seventies, no one could have imagined the combination would prove to be so successful. "At that time Porto was not the dominant team we know today," said Professor José Neto, who was Pedroto's assistant at Porto the following decade. "In the late 1970s, if Porto finished fourth or fifth it was a good season. Even thinking of challenging for the title was unimaginable."

In Pedroto's first season in charge, Porto won the Taça de Portugal and finally, in 1977-78, the Lisbon dominance was broken with that famous win against Braga at the Estadio das Antas. Pedroto insisted that it was just beginning as he turned Benfica into a common enemy, a galvanising force with which to motivate his troops. Even the colour red was banned from the stadium, as the former Porto defender Augusto Inacio found out when he wore red trousers to training.

A second title was won in 1979 but after a controversial Cup final in 1980, Porto's hierarchy grew tired of the constant attrition and showed both Pedroto and Pinto da Costa the door.

It would be only a temporary respite for Benfica, but in the meantime Zé do Boné went further north to coach an ambitious Vitória de Guimarães. During his time in the city Pedroto lectured at a local university when a student there asked him a simple question, "What is the importance of the game in relation to organising training?"

The coach's inquisitive mind was sparked and that student, a young José Neto, was invited to his office to discuss it further. "I would go to his office and he would ask me about what I think of this and what do I think of that," Neto recalled. "Eventually I had to tell him, 'Excuse me, Sir, but I'm the one that should be asking questions: you're the expert here.'"

To help Pedroto, Neto decided to surprise his mentor with a thorough statistical analysis of the game between Guimarães and Penafiel. When Neto showed the coach his findings at training, Pedroto was immediately intrigued and told his assistant to stop the session so they could all discuss the results. Many believe this was the first time such an analysis had been studied on a Portuguese training ground.

Pedroto boasted that Neto would be the man who would help win the title, and when Pinto da Costa returned to lead Porto as president, Zé do Boné brought the professor with him. In 1982 the war with Benfica resumed as Pedroto and Pinto da Costa revolutionised the Dragões with astute psychology as well as modern training methods and tactics. "One of his mantras was, 'Watch the game and I'll tell you how you train; watch training and I'll tell you how you'll play,'" Neto said.

The domestic title was once again within reach as the coach's methods began to bear fruit in Europe. In 1984, Porto reached the Cup-Winners' Cup final against Juventus. By then, though, Pedroto was seriously ill, bed-ridden with terminal cancer.

The Italians' superior experience helped them win 2-1 but the Porto players, who were distracted by their newfound stardom, still believe that they would have won had Zé do Boné been in the dressing-room that day. Pedroto died six months later but the foundations he laid at Porto endured and the Dragões fulfilled their potential by winning the European Cup in 1987.

At a time when Portuguese football's confidence was at its lowest, Pedroto showed the country that it could be a world powerhouse. His mantra of "he who owns the ball, owns the game" is still adhered to in Portugal today.

Luis Freitas Lobo believes that there have been four coaches that have changed Portuguese football: Cândido Oliveira, José Maria Pedroto, Carlos Queiroz and José Mourinho. But it's Professor Neto who gives his mentor the most fitting tribute. "More than the titles that he won with Porto," he said, "or what he achieved with Vitória de Setubal, more than giving Boavista its character, it's his doctrine that's the greatest legacy for Portuguese football."

44

Interview

"I wanted them to talk about my
actions and my goals in pubs..."

Antonín Panenka

The Czechoslovakia great discusses how his famous dinked penalty came about and the impact it's had

By Karel Häring

When you call Antonín Panenka, you can't hear the ring-tone while you wait for him to answer. Instead there's a brief quiz. A serious voice asks you, "The most famous Czech footballer with a moustache is:

a) Antonín Panáček [the name means 'a doll']
b) Antonín Panenka
c) Antonín Nanic ['worthless']
d) Antonín Panic ['virgin']?"

Before you can answer the same voice says, "Wrong answer. You shouldn't try to use a mobile phone with such low intellect." The joke lasts about 30 seconds but usually you have the chance to hear it in full as Panenka doesn't answer his phone quickly. More accurately, he often doesn't pick up his phone at all. That says a lot about a man still best known for his dinked penalty in the final of the 1976 European Championship, the one re-enacted in Euro 2012 by Andrea Pirlo and Sergio Ramos. There aren't many players who bother with a special ring-tone but, more than that, the difficulty getting hold of the 63-year-old Panenka demonstrates that he doesn't spend his retirement sitting on the sofa living on his memories and waiting for calls. I met him during a doubles tennis tournament. He limps because of problems with his hips and

isn't particularly rapid around the court but he has great feel in his hands and can manipulate opponents as he used to torment goalkeepers with his penalties and free-kicks. Between matches, he spoke about his long career.

● *Your name will always be linked with the famous penalty in the European Championship final in 1976. Do you regard that as a blessing or a curse?*

It's somewhere inbetween. Obviously I'm proud and happy about the penalty but, on the other hand, when you say the name "Panenka" everyone thinks only about the penalty. My football motto was, "Play for joy and the entertainment of the fans and yourself." I wanted them to talk about my actions and my goals in pubs and other places. I tried to achieve that through my career but the penalty overshadowed all the other moments. So I'm proud of the penalty but a bit ambivalent.

● *But you're not allergic to questions about it?*

Definitely not. It'll be the thousandth time I've talked about it but that's part of it. You have to cope with it. Whether I want to or not, my penalty kick is part of football history and my career so I'm still open to talking about my feelings and memories of how it happened. I'm happy that the idea of this way of penalty still hasn't died, that there are others who imitate me. And it makes me happy when I hear a TV commentator saying, "It was a Panenka penalty." It happened 35 years ago but even children know about it. It's maybe already in its third generation.

⊕ *What do you think when you see someone try it?*

I am happy but it's not only about trying. It's not easy. I practised it hard for two years. It's not just about taking a penalty and kicking the ball into the centre of goal because you take a risk in attempting a finish like that. I had it perfectly rehearsed.

⊕ *What's your favourite Panenka?*

Maybe Zinedine Zidane or Thierry Henry. I think the penalty still has incredible success. I used the chip maybe 35 times and failed only once. Before that, I took penalties in a 'normal' way and failed more often. This is still a big weapon.

⊕ *Your penalty became one of major topics of Euro 2012 thanks to Andrea Pirlo and Sergio Ramos. Did you think that could happen?*

I don't think anyone expected it but it obviously made me happy. And it also confirmed what I´ve been saying for years. It's a big weapon. If you do it properly and with the right timing, the success is 100%. I observed all the keepers during the penalties and no one stayed in the centre.

⊕ *I know it wasn´t easy to reach you the day after Andrea Pirlo´s goal. Your*

phone was very often busy. How many interviews did you do?

I don't remember the number but I was on the phone all the morning and afternoon. I refreshed my German after many years as I had calls from almost all the true football countries, including Argentina: from Spain, Germany, Austria, Italy, France. It was mad. I am happy that the journalists described it as 'Panenka's penalty'. When they write that even in England, it must mean something (laughs).

⊕ *Which of both chipped penalties did you like more?*

Pirlo did it better. His penalty was similar to mine, Ramos sent it a bit higher but on the other hand it was more surprising as he is a defender. But one thing is clear, both had to practise it beforehand. It wasn't coincidence.

⊕ *How would you describe the secret of converting a penalty?*

It's always been a fight between shooter and keeper — who can keep his nerve longest? No keeper will stay in the centre — that's what I based my strategy on. The keeper is waiting and when I bring my foot to the ball, he is choosing one side or the other. When I kick the ball lightly, the opponent is already on the move and can't recover. However if I kicked it too strongly, he could make some reflex save. And that's why I used slow lobs. It takes a while but the keeper can't get back.

⊕ *It sounds so easy...*

But it isn't. You have to persuade the keeper that you want to kick it normally. I always tried to do it with my movement or with my eyes. I wanted to get him where I wanted.

⊕ *I can understand that you were successful with your first attempts but didn't keepers come to expect it?*

We played against Dukla Prague a few weeks before the European Championship. Their keeper Ivo Viktor, my international teammate, knew that I used to take penalties that way. But he didn't stay on his feet. It's difficult for a keeper not to dive to one side because if you stay still and concede the goal, others will ask why you didn't try anything.

⊕ *How long did you practise it?*

About two years. After almost every training session I took on our goalkeeper, Zdeněk Hruška. He was very good at penalties, defeated me and it cost me quite a lot of money because we had some bets. I thought what I could do to beat him. That was the first idea. However, the basic thing was that I practised penalties every day. If I did it only once or twice a week, I would never have developed it.

⊕ *What were the reactions of your coaches?*

They left the decision to me. They knew that I would take it that way. The good thing was that they didn't write about it too much in the papers at that time and Sepp Maier didn't attend matches of Bohemka [Bohemians 1905]. So it was easier for me [laughs].

⊕ *When you took the penalty in the final in Belgrade, was it one of your earlier or your later attempts?*

The tenth — maybe even fewer than that.

⊕ *But your teammates didn't trust you too much. The goalkeeper Ivo Viktor wasn't happy...*

That's right. We shared a room during the tournament and he told me before game that it would be an extreme audacity from me, that it was too risky and that if I did it, he wouldn't allow me into the room. But in the end, he let me in...

⊕ **Did you think later about what would have happened to you if you had failed?**

I am a skilled turner so I joked that I would now be a turner with 30 years' experience in ČKD [one of the biggest engineering factories in Prague]. Maybe my career would have been terminated, I don't know. It's true that I heard an opinion at that time that they would punish me because they would take it as a ridiculing of the system. Maybe I would be something like a public enemy and I would have had to work somewhere as a stoker.

⊕ *So you had to be really sure about not missing...*

One thousand per cent [laughs]. But it was also partly because of the euphoria we experienced during the tournament. No one really rated us before the tournament. Even if we'd lost in the final, people would still have hailed us in Czechoslovakia. It was the Germans who were under pressure.

⊕ *Is it true that Sepp Maier didn't talk to you for many years after the final because of the penalty?*

When he heard my name, he didn't

react well. I remember that a lot of western journalists wrote at that time that I ridiculed him. But it wasn't right. I saw it as the easiest way to convert a penalty. The problem was that I had been unknown before while he was one of the best keepers in the world. It wasn't easy for him.

⊕ *But you met last year in Prague, 35 years after Belgrade. Has Maier accepted it?*

Yes, it's fine now. We played golf and had some beers.

⊕ *Have you ever thought about how much you would have profited from such a moment if you'd done it, say, 30 years later when football was much more commercialised?*

Obviously we would have profited from the victory and the penalty much more; the situation in marketing is absolutely different. At that time, we were told after our return to keep our feet on the ground. Nowadays, it would be much more commercialised. We could earn more and our lives would be easier.

⊕ *How much money did you earn for winning the European championship?*

16,000 koruna [about £530], while the Germans would have earned much more. But it's not all about money — the sporting value is much bigger.

⊕ *What are you memories about the final game? You led 2-0 but conceded two goals.*

We knew that in the semi-final, the Germans were also 2-0 down but

managed go through. Determination is typical of their character. We kept the lead almost till the last minute but then we conceded an equaliser from a strange corner. However, for me it was good. Without it, I wouldn't have had my penalty...

⊕ *Why did the team succeed in Belgrade?*

The basic thing was that that team was a perfect mix. All the players were good with the ball but there were various types: fighters, very fast lads like Pivarník, motivators like Ondruš, technical players like Móder or me. And very good strikers — Nehoda along with Masný. It wasn't talked about much before the tournament but we had had a good run of results in the build-up. But being a team from eastern Europe, they didn't take us seriously.

⊕ *During the era of Czechoslovakia, there were sometimes problems between the Czechs and Slovakians in the team. Coaches had to be careful not to have a big majority of one group. However you, Nehoda, Viktor and Vesely were the only four Czech players in the 76 team. Why wasn't it a problem?*

The spirit of the team was great and the atmosphere fantastic. I remember that in some previous teams, there was some distance. I wouldn't call it a problem but for example, when we had dinner, Slovakian players ate at one table, the Czechs at another one. And it was similar during tactical preparation. It was done first for the Slovakians in the team, then for the Czechs. Obviously it's not ideal. But in our team, it didn't matter, we were united and the credit goes to [our captain] Tonda Ondruš, who was the man who made us united. We had a lot of fun with him. And don't forget that we also had very good coaches — Václav Ježek and Jozef Vengloš.

⟳ After winning the final, most of the players went to collect their medals in German shirts. Did you have a problem with Communist officials then?

It was funny that all players had swapped their shirts except me and people called me the only patriot. But the reason was a bit different. I took the last penalty and my teammates had already swapped it so I didn't have time to do it. But after the ceremony, I also did it [laughs].

⟳ What was the life of footballers during the Communist era like?

Normal. We didn't care about politics. We were so-called professionals but in fact the only advantage was that we didn't go to work. Of course, we were more famous so we didn't have to stand in a queue for oranges or bananas. We earned more money than most of the people but the difference wasn't so big as today. It's incomparable.

⟳ How much did you earn at that time?

I was 30, had two children and got 2300 koruna [about £80] a month. I could earn another bonus of between 1200 and 1600 koruna from football but only if we won matches. So overall, I earned about 4000 while most of people had between 2000 and 2500.

⟳ One of the biggest advantages of being a footballer was the opportunity to travel abroad while 'normal' people could visit only countries in the Socialist bloc.

I travelled the world with football. We weren't as famous as Dukla Prague, for example, but we also received two invitations to go to America. It was a historical moment for Bohemians: we were the first Czech side to play in Honduras, Haiti or Nicaragua. It was an amazing experience.

⟳ The trips usually lasted three or four weeks. What were they like?

I remember we stayed there once throughout Christmas and New Year. It was in Colombia. One Czech-American businessman invited the whole team for Christmas dinner to his house. We had a guy in the team who had been an apprentice chef and he prepared *svíčková* [roasted sirloin of beef with traditional cream sauce] and dumplings. We prepared dumplings in a bath, bought almost a whole bull and cooked it in his garden. We had never experienced such a Christmas before, in 30-degree heat.

⟳ Karol Dobias, your former teammate, once told me that when Czechoslovakian teams went abroad, players took with them crystal souvenirs and famous Czech glass items to sell and earn some extra money.

The problem was that if we travelled abroad, we didn't get money. So if we wanted to make our trips more comfortable or buy any gifts for our families we took some things which we could sell. I remember that in Haiti, we bartered as they didn't have money either. So we exchanged some shirts, shorts or trainers for their handmade wooden artefacts which were really nice. One of the players even got one for a bandage. I also remember that before one trip we bought a six-arm crystal chandelier but we had a problem how to get it onto the aeroplane. So we had to dismantle it into small pieces. The problem was that when we wanted to put it together against we couldn't do it properly. We created a five-arm chandelier and sold it with a spare part.

Not many people have such experiences.

The trips were really interesting. Once we stayed in a castle, once we slept in houses without roofs. I don't remember if it was in Martinique or Guadaloupe, but they took us to the 'school in nature' for children from outside of the city. You could hear noises from the jungle; half of the team was afraid of it. There were lizards running about in our rooms; a lot of us didn't want to sleep there but we were told to be happy for the presence of the lizards as they caught poisonous spiders.

You left Bohemians for Rapid Vienna when you were 32. Why did you choose them?

If you wanted to go abroad, the Communist officials would allow you if you were older than 32 and had more than 50 international caps. I had an offer from Belgium but it was two months before my 32nd birthday. Then there were others from Spain, Sweden, Belgium again and Austria. If I'd considered only money, the Spanish offer from Real Murcia was the best one. But it wasn't easy for me to go to Spain at 32, and into a team that was in a relegation battle. It was too far in comparison to Vienna. I'd heard good things about Rapid from Frantisek Vesely and Pepi Bican who played there.

It turned out to be a good choice.

It was. I can't complain. They treated me like I was one of them. I still have a very good name there, maybe even better than here in the Czech Republic.

You were close to success in the Cup-Winners' Cup final against Everton in 1985. Why didn't it go your way?

I didn't start the game because of problems with my knees. I had an agreement with the coach that I would play in the later stages so I went on for the last half an hour. We couldn't compete with an Everton squad that was full of international players. Despite a 3-1 defeat, we left a good impression, I guess.

Apart from penalties, you were famous for taking free-kicks. Do you know how many goals you scored from that position?

I scored more than 70 goals for Bohemians and half of them were from set pieces. And it was the same for Rapid. You have to have a skill for it but it's not enough. I practised it an awful lot between the ages of 15 and 19. We used to play football on the street or in the park, mainly against older boys who were taller, stronger and faster than I was. So I had to find a way to play and relied more on technical skills. I kicked most of my free-kicks over the wall so a few goalkeepers tried to surprise me and didn't prepare the wall. Of course, I wasn't stupid so I told my players to make a wall. I sent the free-kick over the wall and that was the end of the story [laughs].

Since your retirement, you have never been main coach; only short periods as an assistant. Why?

I didn't have the ambition. If you want to do something well, you have to have some skill for it. As a main coach, you have to communicate with the team and have to be hard and demanding. I used to be more of a friend to the players. And it's wrong for this job. Players will not appreciate such kind of treatment.

 But you've stayed close to football and few years ago you helped fans to save Bohemians which was on the brink of disappearing.

Bohemians were bankrupt and they asked me to join the project of fans who had decided to save their club. I am happy Bohemka are still alive even though there are still big problems.

 You are honorary president. What are your duties?

My role is more representative than executive. I look after the relationship between the club's partners, sponsors and media, trying to improve the image of the club. There is a nice word for it in English football: an ambassador. Someone like Sir Bobby Charlton for Manchester United or Eusébio for Benfica.

 Apart from your penalty, you are famous for your moustache. Have you ever shaved it?

Never. I've been waiting for an offer and if someone gives me a million, I'm ready to shave it immediately [laughs].

"...the largest, the least casually racist,
the most furiously drunken fan-zone
populations in recorded history."

The Essential Backdrop

Euro 2012 raised major questions about the nature of fandom and what comprises a tournament

By Jonathan Wilson

Go on any football message-board, look at the comments under any football article, engage for long enough about football on Twitter and somebody will assert that "there's nobody more important than the fans". It's one of those truths held to be self-evident, but it isn't true, not really, neither in theory nor in practice.

Anybody who slogged around Poland and Ukraine, who paid a fortune for inadequate accommodation, who struggled with multiple flights or desperately slow and overcrowded trains will know that fans come pretty low on the list of priorities for Uefa. The corporate totalitarianism — only pay with the right credit card, only drink the right branded water, only wear underpants branded with the right betting company — makes clear that fans now are seen as little more than a herd to be milked for as much cash as they'll yield. Major tournaments these days are designed largely for corporate yield. Fans are there to provide a backdrop and little more; they are essentially extras expected to contribute to the cost of the major production.

Perhaps it's as a defence against that marginalisation that so many subscribe to the idea that the fans are what football is all about even as they are systematically exploited by football's authorities and their sponsors. It's the belief in that supposed fact that gives so many fans a sense of entitlement, the belief that they are there to be entertained. But actually, the most important thing about football is the game itself. Then come the players, coaches and referees. Then, some way behind, fans, journalists and club administrators. And some way behind them the agents and businessmen, the sponsors and marketing wonks who seek to turn football into a great reserve of cash.

The idea that "there'd be no game without the fans" is commonplace. There would; it's just it would be small-scale, played out on parks with nobody on the touchlines but the subs and a couple of bored players' girlfriends like most Sunday football. Sport doesn't need crowds to thrive; the likes of hockey, angling and rock-climbing get by perfectly well without thousands of people roaring encouragement or abuse at the participants. Football wasn't set up to attract crowds — unlike, say, WWE or cinema; it was organised and structured because people enjoyed playing it and wanted a standardised set of rules and regular opponents. People then came along to watch because they found the sporting struggle fascinating. The entertainment came from finding out who won.

It's important always to remember that crowds are secondary. The game itself must come first. During the 2010 World Cup John Barnes, working as a pundit for South African television, complained about the number of red cards being shown, using the familiar line that "fans have paid to see 11 against 11" and arguing that an early sending off could ruin a match. Yes it can, but the wider point is that if you don't punish lunging challenges in the opening minutes of matches, players get injured, which is far worse for the game as a whole than if even 100,000 fans end up watching a mismatch.

This is true of all sport, not just football. When Pakistan refused to return to the pitch after tea at the Oval Test in 2006, angered by the umpire Darryl Hair's decision to award five penalty runs against them for ball-tampering, they were deemed to have forfeited the match, leaving thousands of fans with nothing to watch. Perhaps Hair was a stubborn, publicity-loving stickler who could have handled the situation better but by protesting in such a way Pakistan had gone against a fundamental of any sport; the law and its application must be left in the hands of the officials or anarchy ensues. The former England bowler Angus Fraser suggested a compromise should have been found so there was cricket for paying fans to watch — even though that would, effectively, have legitimised the practice of teams stopping play to protest about umpiring. Of course there was a need to compensate those who had bought tickets but, as Richard Williams wrote of that incident in the *Guardian*, "sport is about the contest between its participants, and no decision affecting that contest should be taken with the motive of pleasing, placating or otherwise satisfying the people who have bought tickets to watch. Entertainment is a by-product of the contest, and not an end in itself, no matter how greatly the box-office income contributes to the wealth of the game and its players and officials."

The game itself is key and that means the contest. And the contest means two teams both doing their utmost to get the most they can out of a game. Defensive football can be good football. You might not like the way Chelsea played against Barcelona or Bayern Munich, and football would be a much poorer game if every side played like that, or even if Chelsea played like that all the time, but it's hard to deny that they produced thrilling, memorable matches. This is one of the beauties of football; teams can beat sides that are ostensibly better than them by dint of organisation, resolve and good fortune. "Football," as the former England manager Walter Winterbottom said in 1950, "is a game where superiority in match play can't always be indicated in goals, because of the difficulty of scoring."

In basketball, say, or rugby, the better team almost always wins. Giant-killings are all but unheard of. It's just not possible for teams to defend for the whole game and nick a try or a basket on the break. But that fascination can lead to an odd dynamic: for a stronger team, when it takes the lead, and is faced with a massed defence, it may not make sense to keep attacking. It may make more sense to sit back and simply hold the ball. At the Euros, particularly in the knock-out stage, Spain's aim was not to go out and blast as many goals past their opponents as possible; it was to control the game. Vicente del Bosque said that again and again.

Perhaps the defeat to Switzerland in the group stage of the last World Cup stung them. Perhaps it is simply that success itself leads a side to adopt an increasingly cautious mindset: battling to win a trophy is exciting, an aspiration; battling to cling to status is about holding off loss, about postponing the moment of decline for as long as possible. Whatever the reason, Spain have changed over the past four years from a side that sought to create 25 chances a game even if it meant allowing the opponents five, to one that preferred to have five chances and give the opponent none. The former will bring a lot of 3-0s and 4-1s and the occasional 0-1; the latter a lot of 1-0s and the occasional 0-0. It may be that in a league format the former is more effective but in knock-out games, the latter is preferable: the worst-case scenario is a penalty shoot-out.

In each of the past three tournaments, Spain's average share of possession and number of passes per shot has gone up. They've increasingly settled into the rhythm of holding the ball, wearing their opponents down and then, having gone ahead, keeping the ball from their opponents. In part, of course, the change in their approach has been conditioned by a change in their opponents' approach. The USA showed a way to beat Spain in the semi-final of the Confederations Cup in Bloemfontein in 2009 when they ended their record 35-match unbeaten run with a 2-0 victory. They sat deep, kept the midfield narrow, ceding the flanks, and left two players forward to strike on the break. Let

Spain cross, ran the logic, because they have no significant aerial presence. Again and again in that match, Jay DeMerit beat Fernando Torres to balls looped in from wide. Other sides might have responded by playing a tall, muscular centre-forward such as Fernando Llorente (although he apparently turned up for the Euros so exhausted after a tough club season that Del Bosque effectively regarded him as unselectable); Spain simply stopped crossing. The reason they so often played a midfielder in the centre-forward role was to enhance their capacity to retain possession; playing a centre-forward to whom they could have crossed risked squandering possession — and thus control.

In a sense, that is the logical endpoint of possession football. When Ajax won their third straight European Cup, in 1973, they took a fourth-minute lead through Jonny Rep and then kept the ball. It was commonly said at the time that they were intent on humiliating Juventus, of emphasising the victory of their style over *catenaccio*. Perhaps they were, but the end result was the same: a way of playing that stifled the opponent, only achieved by proactive rather than reactive means.

When I first said that "goals are overrated" I was responding to a question from James Richardson on *Football Weekly* about who would be top-scorer at the World Cup. My point, not that I expressed it particularly coherently, was that it didn't matter who scored the goals because what was important at the highest level of the modern game was control of midfield. In fact, in a way, the number of goals was less important than the completeness of the control; better a

1-0 lead and domination of the ball than a 2-0 lead with chances being created at either end. The goals, or goal, came as a result of that control — which, once a lead had been established, becomes an end in itself — and, truly exceptional talents like Lionel Messi notwithstanding, tended to be shared around. As though to prove the point, Fernando Torres won the Golden Boot at the Euros despite being so far from a regular starter for Spain that he probably wasn't even one of their best 11 players in the tournament.

That Spain are exceptionally good at playing their way and that their method is exceptionally effective can hardly be doubted. They are prodigious, a phenomenon. No other side since the Second World War has achieved such a run of success; arguably, depending how seriously you regard those inter-War Olympic Games, no side has ever won three major tournaments in succession before. In their last 10 knock-out games at major tournaments, they haven't conceded a goal. They haven't just achieved an unprecedented level of success, they've done it without ever really being threatened: there have been no frantic scraps for a late equaliser, no games in which they've held out only thanks to brilliant goalkeeping or desperate defending. Even in an era in which the quality of the competition they've faced has been questionable, that is some achievement.

It also means that they aren't particularly exciting to watch. They don't produce a thrill a minute and that led many to proclaim them boring. Now of course viewers are quite entitled to find watching Spain matches boring; it's a subjective judgement and different things will stimulate different people. The oddity of the reaction was twofold, though. For one thing, nobody ever seemed to blame Spain's opponents for sitting deep, defending in numbers to deny them the *profundidad* [depth of field of play] Del Bosque kept insisting they needed to be at their best. Not that their opponents were wrong; Italy's 4-0 defeat in the final was evidence of the dangers of giving Spain any space at all in the final third. And for another, there was the level of anger. There seemed to be a feeling that Spain's responsibility should be to entertain rather than to win and hostility towards them for not doing so.

At the same time, the majority of people seemed enraptured by a fairly ordinary Germany. I'd been critical of them at the World Cup, pointing out that, discounting the third-place play-off, although they'd scored 13 goals in six games, 12 of those goals came in three matches — against Australia, England and Argentina. In each of those games, they scored in the opening 10 minutes and then picked off opponents who pushed too high. On the break they were superb, the intermovement of Thomas Müller, Lukas Podolski and Mesut Özil behind Miroslav Klose magnificent. But they were essentially a reactive team, a little one-dimensional. When they didn't find an early goal they struggled: games against Serbia, Ghana and Spain brought a single goal in total.

When I wrote that in a *Guardian* piece, though, I was savaged by commenters. I was accused of being anti-German. I'd like to think that's ridiculous — in fact, I do think it's ridiculous — but it was an allegation that unsettled me. Pointing out that I revere the West Germany sides of the 1972 European Championship and the 1990 World Cup sounded horribly like the "some of my best friends are gay" defence of casual homophobes. It's very easy for British people to be anti-German.

In qualifying, Germany were imperious, winning 10 games out of 10. Jogi Löw seemed aware of the limitations his side had demonstrated at the World Cup and made them a proactive team. I was seduced. Partly because I couldn't believe Spain could retain their hunger and partly because both Barcelona and Real Madrid looked exhausted in their Champions League semi-final defeats, I tipped Germany to win the Euros, ignoring the evidence of the five friendlies they played between the end of qualifying and the start of the tournament. In those games they conceded 10 goals and, while a 5-3 defeat to Switzerland could be written off because of the absence of the large Bayern contingent, a 3-3 draw against Ukraine was harder to explain.

Germany won all three games in the group stage but even then there were warning signs. They struggled to break down Portugal and, although they never looked like doing anything other than beating the Netherlands, the goals they scored both stemmed from Dutch sloppiness coupled with moments of individual excellence from Mario Gomez. Gomez, though, is an old-fashioned forward; if he isn't scoring goals he tends not to be doing much and that, in the modern game, places great strain on the midfield. The goal the Dutch scored, Robin van Persie accelerating through the space in front of the back four that should have been filled by Bastian Schweinsteiger and Sami Khedira,

raised further concerns. Schweinsteiger, inconsistent for Bayern after his return from injury, had played well, from an attacking point of view at least, but his form deserted him as Germany laboured against Denmark.

Löw changed three of his front four against Greece, bringing in Marco Reus, Andre Schürrle and Klose for Müller, Podolski and Gomez. Some saw it as arrogance, resting three players in a quarter-final; others saw it as a reaction to the specific problems caused by a Greece side that would sit deep and deny Müller and Podolski the space they need in front of them to be at their most effective. That hinted at doubts on Löw's part but the problems were actually at the other end. Germany won comfortably enough, 4-2, but they were open at the back.

Although the defence featured three of the Bayern back four, only one of them, Holger Badstuber, played in the same position he does for his club. More significantly, the Khedira-Schweinsteiger axis had stopped working. At the World Cup, Khedira had sat very deep, allowing Schweinsteiger to break forward and link with the creative trident. He has developed as a player at Real Madrid, though, becoming far more adventurous, not merely a stopper and a spoiler in front of the back four but somebody comfortable breaking forwards to make late darts into the box – as he did in volleying Germany's second goal against Greece in the quarter-final.

The problem with this is that it means either Khedira must curb his forward surges, or Schweinsteiger, whose form has been uncertain as he feels his way back from injury, must be prepared to sit deep when Khedira goes — and, as England know all too well from the eternal Gerrard-Lampard debate, that is not an easy balance to achieve in the limited time available at international level. "He's very important as a player for me," said Schweinsteiger. "He opens up spaces going forward, is always available, scores goals but we both can't be up front during a game. We have to make sure we know where our positions are and what we have to do."

The problems weren't rectified against Italy, while a new one emerged: Mats Hummels, so impressive until then, was undone by Mario Balotelli and Antonio Cassano. Composed in possession he may be, but defensively he was made to look deeply suspect. Podolski, restored to the starting line-up, was ineffective. Özil seemed bewildered to be shifted to the right as Toni Kroos was brought into the middle to combat Andrea Pirlo. And, in the first half at least, Cassano and Balotelli found space again and again in front of the back four, in the area Khedira and Schweinsteiger should have been patrolling.

Yet still people seemed positive about Germany. Löw, having failed to solve a major tactical issue, was given a remarkably easy ride. Writing anything about Spain, though, particularly anything positive, would draw a barrage of Tweets or below-the-line comments complaining about their supposed boringness. I sat opposite a hollow-eyed Sid Lowe in a Georgian restaurant in Donetsk as he muttered repeatedly, "Don't they understand I don't pick the team...?" There were suggestions that they were destroying football, that they

had to be stopped. That would have been hyperbole even for a team that spoiled and time-wasted and cheated like Osvaldo Zubeldía's Estudiantes at their worst, but Spain's only crime was to have mastered one of the key arts of football: control of the ball. Nobody has to like it but the desire to destroy it was odd; TS Eliot didn't like *Paradise Lost* but he never suggested all copies should be burned. The real problem was that Spain's opponents were unable or unwilling to come out, win the ball from them and then do something with it themselves.

And the oddest aspect of the hostility was the perverse sense that to admire anything other than hell-for-leather, hammer-and-tongs, up-and-at-'em, get-it-in-the-mixer football is to mark yourself out as a pseud, the equivalent of Louis Balfour, the John Thomson character in *The Fast Show* who sits in smoky bars listening to the most preposterous avant-garde jazz and proclaiming it "nice".

Football has changed dramatically over the past two decades. Given how, for many of us, football was a central strand of our growing up, the theatre in which dramas of our relationships with parents and friends, our coming of age, our acceptance of failure and loss, was played out, there's an understandable nostalgia for how things used to be. There is a quite reasonable unease at the transition of those who watch football from fans to consumers, at the so-called gentrification of the game, but what is odd is how that anxiety seems to underlie so many debates about the game that seem ostensibly to have little to do with it.

One of the weirdest criticisms directed at my tactics pieces is that I'm "clearly a post-Euro 96 fan". It's not a common line of attack but it's come up often enough to make me ponder the rationale behind it. My dad took me to my first Sunderland game in 1982 when I was six, I went to Roker Park regularly after that and I had three seasons in a row in the early nineties when I missed no more than three games a season home and away, so I feel quite secure in rebutting it, but what if I hadn't? What if I had first started following closely at Euro 96? Would that somehow invalidate what I was writing?

There's an obvious point, of course, which is that somebody who got into football in 1996 and is still talking about it has followed it for 16 years, which seems a long enough apprenticeship to assume their commitment is relatively serious. Equally, I grew up in Sunderland and had a dad whose idea of an ideal Saturday involved watching *Football Focus*, standing in the cold on the Roker End and falling asleep while reading the paper in front of the fire; the chances of me not liking football were pretty remote. Not everybody can be so lucky: not everybody grew up in football-loving families or football-loving cities (or countries). If it took a major event like Euro 96 to nudge them into recognising football's appeal, so what? The issue surely is not what prompted them to start watching football but how they have done so since: if, 16 years on, they're still enthusiastic, isn't that enough?

But there's another side to this, which is what is implied by the "post Euro-96" criticism. The suggestion is that the post-96 fan is somehow ersatz, a middle-class posturer who probably over-analyses or over-intellectualises the game; by extension that implies that 'real fans' are working-class and 'passionate'. The problem with that argument is that it is so close to having validity that it's very difficult to combat.

The issue of ticket-pricing and the way a certain type of fan, the fans who formed the core of football's support for the majority of the twentieth-century, has been edged out is very real. Given the way the age profile of supporters is rising, it may even become a major financial problem for some clubs. Certainly it's become harder and harder for fans to get into the habit of going to matches the way I did, simply by paying £2.50 every other week.

But it doesn't also follow that the only true fan is the old-school working-class fan, whatever that generation's incarnation is of the miners or steelworkers or factory-men who initially swelled crowds in the late nineteenth-century. Fans have never been drawn from one class and one class only. One of football's strengths has always been the broadness of its appeal, across classes, across cultures, across nationalities. Equally it can be enjoyed and appreciated in a multitude of ways. There seems to be an assumption that, because I often write about tactics, I can only appreciate a game as a series of coloured dots forming patterns across a magnetic board, that I'm some sort of analytical cyborg with binary code for blood.

But football at times moves me on a visceral level. Sometimes that's because of its beauty or brilliance; when Balotelli thumped in his second for Italy in the semi-final against Germany, for instance,

I snorted at the ridiculous wonderfulness of it all and my mind instantly went back, presumably because of the way the ball sat up and was then smashed, to a goal Tony Yeboah scored for Leeds against Wimbledon at Selhurst Park in 1995 to which my dad and I had both reacted with similar throaty chuckles and disbelieving shakes of the head.

Sometimes it's for the storyline, for sport's tremendous capacity for moments of sentimental coincidence or redemption. When Zambia won the Cup of Nations earlier this year in Libreville, the city off the coast of which a plane crash wiped out their squad in 1993, for instance, their players singing a song of remembrance throughout the penalty shoot-out as Kalusha Bwalya, who had been part of that team but had not been on the plane, looked on from the touchline, I couldn't speak for the size of the lump in my throat.

And sometimes it's for Sunderland, whether misting up over the glories of 1973 or anxiously counting down the seconds to a goalless draw against a big side. Nobody who saw me during the Manchester City game on New Year's Day as I passed from resignation at inevitable defeat to hopeful fretting at the possibility of a draw to half-crouching expectancy in the final seconds of injury-time as Ji Dong-won wasn't called offside, stumbled round Joe Hart and kept his balance to roaring but disbelieving release as he poked it in — "He can't miss that. He *can't* miss that. It counts. It counts!" — could think football was 'only' an intellectual pursuit for me.

But again, what if it were? Why should there be a 'right' way to appreciate football? If you don't like my way of looking at football, fine, don't read me. If I make a mistake or you think I've missed a key point or you disagree with my conclusions, fine, engage and join the debate, but why insist my entire way of interacting with football is somehow wrong or insidious? It's the aggression I don't understand.

This is something Brian Phillips touched on in his piece about the use of the term 'real fan' in *The Blizzard* Issue Five. His argument was that a fan is a fan no matter where he or she lives and no matter whether he or she consumes their football at the stadium or on television. And here again we enter tricky territory. On a rational level I agree with him, particularly when it comes to online debates. The argument that "I'm right because I've been a season-ticket holder for 20 years" is no more valid than the "You've never played the game" argument spouted by so many ex-pros. The answer to both, of course, is, "Yes, so use your superior experience, that advantage you have, to explain why I'm wrong."

But on another level, it seems to me sad that clubs that were once beacons of their communities are now effectively franchises for the whole world. "There's something spectacularly silly about fans policing other fans for their adherence to the laws of fandom, as if not having one favourite club, or preferring to watch from a seated position, is a "VERY SERIOUS INFRACTION that should be SWIFTLY AND MERCILESSLY DEALT WITH," Phillips wrote. "Because, you know, the economic recovery can't gather steam if Kyle in Ohio thinks it's fun to watch Chelsea on television." Put like that, of course, his argument is hard to refute and yet equally, at least from the point of view of a fan conditioned to British notions of what a club is, it's not to think that Kev from West Brompton, whose family have been season-ticket holders at Stamford Bridge for four generations, shouldn't somehow have more of a say than Kyle.

Perhaps the reason for the difference of opinion is revealed in Phillips's assertion that football "has no real importance beyond its ability to add some enjoyment to our lives." Again, on a rational level that's hard to dispute. It is just some men kicking a ball in a game that is probably derived from an ancient fertility rite. And yet, on an emotional level, I can't help thinking he couldn't be more wrong.

I actually wish I didn't care as much about Sunderland. I wish I didn't feel nauseous when they go ahead. In his entry in *Life's a Pitch*, an anthology of pieces by journalists writing about the clubs they support published in September 2012, Mike Calvin writes of envying his mother's "detachment" watching Watford lose the 1984 FA Cup final while he went through agonies. I wish I had the detachment of Brian Phillips, but my support for Sunderland is deep-rooted. As somebody who moved away in 1999, fandom links me to home, to old friends and, most particularly, to past generations of my family. I didn't choose Sunderland; it just was.

I hesitate to say that my form of fandom is the right one, or better than other modes, but equally it seems to me that to ignore that cultural aspect of football, the fact that it is more than an entertainment or a business, is to miss something profound. And that is why

Manchester United's flotation on the New York stock exchange and its move to be controlled by a company based in the Cayman Islands is so depressing. It's not like we couldn't see this coming and to an extent this is the logical outcome of a league in which the majority of players, coaches and owners are foreign, but if United's holding company isn't even paying tax to the British government then they have become effectively an international franchise that happens to be based in Manchester.

Which brings us, oddly, back to the Euros, which was less a Polish tournament or a Ukrainian tournament than a global tournament that happened to be based in Poland and Ukraine. When the announcement that the tournament was to be held there was made in Cardiff in 2007, I was torn. On the one hand I was delighted that Uefa was reaching out to the east and that, after a 36-year hiatus, eastern Europe would again stage a major championship; on the other I was deeply sceptical about their capacity to do so. This, though, is the new logic of football's governing bodies, that, as they break new frontiers, having the infrastructure to host a tournament is itself a reason you will not get to host it.

The stadiums, in the end, were excellent. It's hard to draw any definitive conclusions but, anecdotally at least, most people who went to Poland and Ukraine had a good time. English fans in Donetsk, in fact, were made to feel so welcome and were so infuriated by *Panorama*'s scaremongering that they staged a demonstration mocking Sol Campbell's assertion that black fans risked "coming home in a coffin". So in that sense the tournament was a success.

And yet there was also a feeling, common at tournaments these days, that the real story was happening in the margins, in the spaces between the antiseptic, homogenised stadiums and fan zones. Were so much of the BBC these days not obsessed by populist sensationalism, they might have looked in more detail at Ukraine's president Viktor Yanukovych (the man, who 'lost' the Orange Revolution of 2004) and his treatment of the former prime minister Yulia Tymoschenko. They might, had they not been so busy scaring black fans and the families of black England players from travelling to watch matches, have looked at the human rights record of the Ukrainian police.

An Amnesty International report released shortly after the tournament revealed that Ukrainian police had been told not to touch fans from eastern Europe while carrying on intimidating and abusing their own citizens. On 8 June in Donetsk, for instance, three women were allegedly beaten and sexually molested by police in an attempt to compel them to confess to a theft from a Swiss national; when they protested, the father of two of the women was threatened, the third woman was attacked in her home and the man who helped them file their complaint was accused in a police statement of being a pimp. On June 15, three members of the feminist group Femen were detained by security forces in Donetsk and held without charge for several days. On June 17 a man arrested for drunkenness was allegedly sexually assaulted with a baton while his brother was forced to pay $20 for his release. He subsequently required surgery to repair internal organs.

"Before the European championship, Amnesty had raised a number of human rights concerns in the country, noting particularly that an often violent and corrupt police force posed a significant threat to affluent Europeans visiting for the football," the organisation's Ukraine campaigner Max Tucker said. "We detailed numerous cases where police used electric shocks, suffocated or savagely beat their victims in order to extort money, extract a confession, or simply because of the detainee's ethnicity or sexual orientation. In the event, Euro 2012 fans were spared such treatment thanks to police orders not to touch visiting fans. So how did the Ukrainian authorities manage to bring this brutal, ill-equipped and underfunded force into line to effectively police a major sporting event? The answer, of course, is they didn't. Officers were simply ordered not to touch foreign fans while police business continued as usual for ordinary Ukrainians."

Panorama might even, heaven forbid, have looked at the conditions that led, two weeks after the tournament, to hundreds of Ukrainians taking to the streets in protest at moves to give regional status to 18 languages spoken by minorities. If a bill were passed, it would mean the languages being taught in schools and used in official documents, prompting fears that Ukrainian may be sidelined, particularly in the east of the country, where Russian is commonly spoken. Under the proposed measures, Russian would be taught in schools for the first time since the collapse of the USSR. The language issue crystallises the more general divide between west and east in Ukraine that also underlay the Orange Revolution.

In terms of the tournament itself, there was the fact that the transport and hotel infrastructure simply wasn't good enough. Prices for the most modest guest houses reached £300 or £400, beyond the reach of major media organisations, let alone ordinary fans. It became common for journalists to sleep on each other's floors, something I've never known even at African Cups of Nations. Ukraine, unfortunately, became notorious for its rip-off culture. "Don't you care that people will form a bad impression and won't come back?" the Bloomberg journalist Tariq Panja despairingly asked one taxi-driver. "People aren't going to come back to Donetsk," the driver replied, and he is probably right. For an industrial city, Donetsk scrubs up pretty well, and the long thin strip of parkland, bars and restaurants that makes up Pushkin Boulevard is a delight, but it is an industrial city; it's not somewhere people are going to go on their holidays. At the other end of the scale of cynicism, one driver waited two hours for Tariq at Boryspil airport after his flight was delayed and, in a pantomime of apology, explained he had business to attend to on the way to the hotel. Which is how Tariq ended up helping a Ukrainian taxi driver buy a cat.

In the chaos that followed the Spain v Italy game in Gdansk, my first-class ticket back to Warsaw earned me a strip of corridor floor about four feet by 18 inches, where I tried to sleep with a laptop bag for a pillow as people going to the toilet whacked my legs with the carriage door. There was no agreement to allow people to take hire cars from one country to the other which, given that taking the train meant a minimum six-hour wait at the border as the carriages were lifted from one gauge of wheels to another, meant that flying, despite the cost, was the only realistic option. The quickest possible route to get from one semi-final to another by scheduled flights was six hours. The absurdness of people's journeys became a badge of honour: "How did you get here?" "Via Vienna." "That's nothing; I came through Copenhagen." "I missed my connection in Antalya so I ended up being routed via Istanbul and Athens." I read a couple of John Le Carré novels during the tournament; frankly his spies' efforts to disguise their intentions by flying from Berlin to Hamburg via London came to seem half-arsed.

When Michel Platini, in one of his off-the-cuff policy announcements, commented that it's easier to get from London to Paris than from Kharkiv[1] to Gdansk as a justification for his idea of hosting Euro 2020 in "12 or 13" European cities, he was right. If you are going to host the tournament so that it requires journeys of five or six hours to get from one venue to another, where is the advantage of hosting it in one or two countries? South Africa at the 2010 World Cup was much the same, Brazil in 2014 will be and so too will Russia in 2018. If cities that far apart really are the preferred option, then the logical end point is multiple hosts. It's widely expected that the centenary World Cup in 2030 will be hosted by Uruguay, which staged the first tournament, and

---

[1] *Not "Cardiff", as was widely reported; a mistake on the part of the translator.*

Argentina. Given Montevideo is an hour's flight, or a short ride on the ferry, from Buenos Aires, that makes sense. But in that case, would it really hurt to hold some games in Asunción as well, given there's no way Paraguay could ever host a tournament alone?

That's the logic; whether it's right or not is another issue. There needs to be a debate on what a tournament is. Up to 1976, the European Championship consisted of home-and-away, round-robin qualifiers, followed by two-legged knock-out games, with the last four meeting in one country to play the semi-finals and final; until the last four, the format was not unlike that of the Champions League. In 1980, the format was changed so that seven sides qualified to play in the finals in Italy, who qualified as hosts. The World Cup had always had a finals tournament, logically given the difficulties of travel in 1930. Europe in 1980 didn't have those restrictions but there was presumably a sense that the tournament should be a festival at which fans, coaches, scouts and journalists could mix, watching as much football, sharing as much information, as possible. That has been lost.

In Sopot, near Gdansk, it seemed that Irish, Spanish, Croatian and Italian fans mixed happily and there was a sense of festival, but very few of those fans bothered with the five-and-half-hour train ride to watch games in Warsaw. If that's the case then, as Platini said, does it really matter whether the cities are in the same country or not? The only problem presented by a London-Paris tournament as opposed to a Warsaw-Gdansk tournament is immigration and even that could readily be solved by

the issuing of an EU-wide visa for the duration of the tournament.

Sentimentally, I'm still drawn to the idea of one nation hosting. I like the sense that each tournament has an identity. The ideal still seems to me a tournament in which you could, say, watch England v Ukraine at Wembley today, Germany v Portugal at Villa Park tomorrow, Italy v Croatia at Old Trafford the day after and Russia v Poland at Anfield the day after that, before returning to London for Ukraine against France at the Emirates. But if I'm going to be asked to flog about by plane, it might as well be efficient international flights to cities with a wealth of hotels rather than Aerosvit to a duvet on the floor. Maybe hubs are the answer — a tournament hosted by four major cities (or nearby pairs of cities), each providing two stadiums: Wembley and the Emirates in London, Hampden and Parkhead in Glasgow, the Amsterdam Arena and De Kuip in Amsterdam and Rotterdam, the Stade de France and the Grand Stade Lille Métropole in Paris and Lille, for instance.

But then again, given the vast majority of viewers consume their football on television perhaps this is a minority concern. The rush to build new stadiums for every finals coupled with Uefa's insistence on taking over grounds and their surroundings completely and making them over so they become just another part of football's corporate homogeneity, means there's next to no local colour at games, unless you count the cringe-inducing mini-opening ceremonies at each match in the Euros. Matches may as well be hosted on vast floating stadiums in the middle of the ocean, which would have the added benefit of getting Fifa and Uefa round the awkward issue of local tax regimes. CGI crowds would cut the policing bill as well.

And perhaps the issue of consumption on television helps explain the hostile reaction to Spain. In a stadium a fan is much more a part of the drama, much less a consumer. The sense of effort and struggle is much more tangible. Sitting in an armchair in front of the television, the temptation must be far greater to disengage, to flick over to see how the golf's going, or to catch the last 10 minutes of *Neighbours*, or to check if you've seen that episode of *Murder, She Wrote*. There must be a greater sense that football has to compete for attention.

But that's to make a category error: football is a sport, not an entertainment. It's about finding a way within the rules and spirit of the game to get the best result possible. It's about who wins and Spain are unprecedentedly good at that. If other teams aren't good enough to compete, that's not their problem. It may not produce the most thrilling spectacles, but history will deem us fortunate to have seen a side this masterful. Ⓑ

The First Twitter Tournament

In Euro 2012, newspapers were very rarely first with the news as social media came into its own

By Barney Ronay

"Yeah we're really happy with the way the lads FUCK OFF!!! in the second half when Sweden scored we didn't panic FUCK OFF!! just kept our heads and FUCK!! OFF!! Welbs took his goal so well he made it look NO!! FUCK OFF!!"

The tape of Theo Walcott's mixed zone interview after England's 3-2 Euro 2012 defeat of Sweden in Kyiv makes for interesting listening. Albeit, it should be pointed out, it isn't actually Walcott telling everybody to fuck off in between offering an expertly anodyne summary of England's rousing Group D victory. In fact, Walcott is such a pleasant, archly well-mannered young man that even while the reporter in front of him is — following well-established professional protocol — elbowing a Norwegian TV presenter in the chest and yelling "FUCK OFF!!" he still looks like he'd struggle to find it in himself to swear at anyone.

It is a rare ability to continue speaking in calm, well-modulated sentences in such circumstances and perhaps Walcott might harbour realistic hopes of a post-football career in parliamentary politics or supply teaching. More likely, though, he's just used to it. Scenes like this are not uncommon in what is a precarious, high-stakes business, every gobbet wrung from an England player the end point of a gruelling process of travel, expense,

forward planning and plenty of basic hard graft. Careers hang — or, at least, have in the past hung — on the ring-fencing of this basic product, the quotes pieces with star players that are still the staple of print media football coverage.

And yet at Euro 2012 there was still something unexpectedly poignant about the sight of the grand old battle-hardened English newspaper pack — of which I was fortunate to be a minor part-time member — huddled in the bowels of some new-build stadium: elbows primed, besieged on all sides, and defending to the last the unwritten protocols of reporting the news to vigorously persevered print-run deadlines, like Sid James and Roy Castle settling down to eat a six-course colonial lunch amid great plumes of shattered plaster, chandeliers shelled from the ceilings, the marauding Burpas machine-gunning the gates outside.

Because things have definitely changed. If Euro 2012 demonstrated anything away from the pitch it is the way in which the central relationship between reporter and spectator is now fundamentally altered. Not that this was immediately obvious at the time. Instead there was a sense throughout the tournament of a mass groping for the correct superlative, the precise, the apt measure of footballing ultimacy for an unusually absorbing month of football. What was it, exactly, about these Euros?

Even before Spain's bravura performance in the final, one newspaper had already gone straight for the jugular with "the greatest tournament of modern times". Uefa had trotted out its own party line: the largest, the least casually racist, the most furiously drunken fan-zone populations in recorded history. But none of these seemed to chime precisely with whatever it was about Euro 2012 that seemed so startlingly novel.

Perhaps the real difference was simply in the sheer level of reverb. This was undoubtedly the most *involved* tournament of all time: the first real Twitter tournament, the most aggressively blogged, the most widely commented on sporting event in the short history of mass new media opinion overload.

If Euro 2012 seemed unusually vibrant it was in part because of those echoes, the resonance of a million instant verbal salutes, a million demands for a retweet for this fascinating piece on the Czech Republic's mildly innovative use of the attacking long throw-in. No wonder the men at the centre of this opinion whirlpool — paid media with its full-time convictions, its editorial framework, its deadlines — might have looked a little besieged. There is a simple reason for this: they are besieged.

At Italia 90 Pete Davis wrote the landmark book *All Played Out*, shedding light on the rise of the football press as a self-aware and aggressively interventionist entity. Coupled with the subsequent newspaper-led assault on

Graham Taylor, it had become clear that when it came to England the press wasn't just content with reporting any more. Instead the press now wanted to gate-crash the main stage, to stalk the touchline, a player in its own right.

There is a pleasing synchronicity to the fact that 20 years on it is the press itself that has the air of being hunted. Menaced by declining revenues and tried and convicted on a daily basis by the unfenced self-publishers of the internet, it is now the football press that must face its inquisitors, obliged by decorum to explain and equivocate and bite its tongue. Being the England football manager is no longer the impossible job: we're all fairly sanguine about that now. But reporting on the England football manager — well, that looks like a pretty tough gig from here.

It turns out it is the last 20 years of football journalism that have been the historical aberration here. Prior to the late 1980s covering football was a one-person job. A lone brown-suited man with a notebook would share plane trips, hotels and sun loungers with England players on tour. It is only in the course of football's furious expansion into a mainstream "leisure product" that the itinerant mob-handed pack has become a fixture, diffuse beneficiaries of football's fiscal explosion, and fortunate to be in the right place at the right moment to experience en masse the fascination of following the national football team through the nine England-flavoured international tournaments that have followed Italia 90.

It has been an excellent period to choose to become a sports reporter. But how many British newspapers are really going to be bankrolling this same portable feast in the years to come, as the rise of new media and the decline of old transform decisively the notion of how their readers consume their football?

Albeit there were no obvious signs of a diminution of influence — in fact quite the opposite — as England's players appeared on the pitch in the Donbass Arena to play France in their opening Euro 2012 match. The Donbass has a wonderfully central low-slung press box, a multi-tiered section of high-spec thrones close to the halfway line. And three days after the tournament opening, there was instead a palpable sense of relish among the assorted chief sports writers, senior correspondents and austere executive scribes at finally getting the chance to watch some actual football after the peripheral delights of reporting on preparations in Krakow.

Admittedly in the end the most notable aspect of the night was the general lack of atmosphere in what was perhaps the most low-key match of the tournament. During the second half the players could be heard quite clearly shouting to each other as England wilted back into their fearful one-bank-of-eight defensive formation, one particular howl of pain from Scott Parker after being rather gently hacked down from behind echoing with chilling immediacy around Eastern Europe's grandest glass and steel football dish.

Perhaps the 47,400 spectators present were simply fiddling with their phones instead. It is a mark of the disjunct between the live and televised experience that the match was also the first really notable example of footballing Twitter-power at Euro 2012, an early spike in what would become a consistent background timpani. According to Twitter's own figures, Euro 2012 was the most digitally discussed sporting event ever, with a record 15,000 tweets per second published during the final. There were 873,000 mentions of Spain during the tournament, with England second-placed in the popularity stakes on 849,000 (no figures are given for the proportion of these concerned solely with expressions of spittle-flecking fury, head-wringing anguish and so on). Cristiano Ronaldo was mentioned more than any other player, although again of 268,000 Twitter references no figures are given as the exact ratio concerned solely with mocking his excessive upper body musculature or attempting to describe the precise consistency of his densely-pomaded hair.

Of course, it is very easy to take all this far too seriously. Twitter is in the end just so much chaff, the most highly evolved expression yet devised of the basic human need to gossip, moan and generally bullshit. It will not last: something else will emerge, something even more beautifully simple and persuasive. Plus of course mainstream journalists, while apparently menaced by this new technology, are among the current big Twitter-hitters, stockpiling their own follower armies.

But still, there has been an impact, a sense of basic chiselling away. Instant, often furiously abusive accountability has had an effect on the way many journalists write. For some there has been a tightening up, a curtailment of adornment, an awareness of the mocking chorus of pedants and malevolents that shadows every piece. The fact is nobody works well under constant browbeating suspicion and there is a genuine unpleasantness in the way the mob can round on its chosen targets. At least one recently-installed broadsheet football reporter considered giving up the career altogether in his first week, shocked at the level of abuse directed his way, before cautiously raising the subject with his fellow writers and being reassured that this is all entirely normal.

How did this happen? And is it ever going to stop? Perhaps it is simply an effect of opening up journalism to all, the swishing back of the curtain that previously shrouded the professional writer in mystique. The key attribute of the reporter has always been his access. He is there. You are not. He brings you his experience, funnelled back from some gloom-shrouded footballing outpost and accepted as a kind of interpretative truth.

Except, this privilege has now largely dissolved at the top level. These days everybody has access, via ever-widening blanket television coverage. The reporter has access to players, but then so does the fan at home via Twitter and via the instant news wrap of the internet. Moreover, the viewer at home and the man on the train with his mobile minute-by-minute have access to a conversation that happens beyond the grasp of the reporter urgently honing his print-deadline copy in the press box, with opinions dissected, cast aside and resurrected with fevered haste. And so the newspaper man appears bang on cue 90 minutes later, star-jumping in through the front door with his flowers and his

bottle of wine, his box-fresh 900 words, just as everybody else is leaving by the back door.

It must be said that if this is the way things are heading few would mourn the disappearance of some of the more arcane practices. For example there is no doubt new media has undermined the primacy of the dreaded 'huddle'. For years it has been common practice for journalists at press conferences to hatch their own mutually agreed 'line' on whatever it is they've just witnessed, parcelling out a version of events that, on the plus side, is most likely to get itself in the newspaper and, less appealingly, is both a form of internal self-preservation, ensuring unanimity and no awkward questions from editors the following morning, and of writerly laziness. There are few tasks less demanding than the simple quotes piece, which often skates along simply on the novelty of its own virgin *obiter dicta*.

Hence the elbow-jabbing fuck-yous and the roping off of the Dictaphone-thrusting mob, as exported once again to the media zones of Euro 2012. This is the meat of football newspaper coverage, a form of journalism at which tabloid newspapers in particular excel but which is increasingly undermined at major events by the bandit presence of outsiders, and the deadline-free rhythms of the internet. Often press conferences are tweeted or broadcast or covered by foreign writers who operate outside the parochial huddle. Embargos — a mutual agreement not to publish material before a certain time or date — have oiled the wheels of quote-journalism. But to those wedded to the notion of digital media embargoes increasingly look rather dinosaur-ish, an artificial brake tied in to old-school print deadlines and often ignored by news wires and websites, leading to occasionally violent internecine disputes.

First — and to date alone — among traditional newspapers the *Guardian* recently declared itself a digital-first medium, turning its back on the traditional rhythms in favour of a rolling, web-based news operation, which will inevitably involve the trimming of embargoes, the overwriting of the old behavioural codes. There is an unseen friction here. Careers ride on such matters and voices and fists have already been raised around the subject, press-conference bans threatened and even — drama! — the odd laptop swept off a desk in intimidatory rage.

At which point it would also perhaps also be appropriate to dim the lights, insert a CD of sombre piano music and announce in a croaking voice something else many have been wearily predicting for years: the lingering death of the match report. Poor old match reports. You were where it all began, rising up out of the soup of primordial football journalism, a sole record of events provided by a pork-pie-hatted man with a train ticket and a notebook. Over time the report evolved into the central hub of all football writing, to which generations of writers have added their mediations on raking passes, cynical fouls and fulminating drives from fully 30 yards.

At times during Euro 2012 the match report almost felt like an irrelevance, as is often the case with the grand shared televised event. The difference now is the sheer level of alternative analysis.

By the time that most newspaper reports of England's final group match against Ukraine had been published the ghost goal incident involving John Terry's goal-line clearance had been so widely Twittered, YouTubed, parodied and generally over-digested, it seemed to have been put to bed entirely. It is perhaps the first time an instant match report has looked quite so dog-eared, so prematurely aged by the rolling digital conversation.

On the other hand, there are aspects of the experience of being there that remain irreplaceable, and which are perhaps also in danger of being lost in the rush to disregard the match reporter. For example, only inside the stadium was it really obvious that Danny Welbeck's lovely drag-back finish for the winning goal against Sweden was entirely intentional, evident from the wider view of his body shape, the swiftness of his movements. Twitter disagreed, but Twitter was wrong. Similarly, the atmosphere within a ground cannot be accurately conveyed via television, while a really decisive tactical analysis remains incomplete without the broader vision of the spaces that appear away from the action, rather than simply those captured by the framing of the camera.

Perhaps the answer to this is simply to resist the disorientating confusion, to be unafraid of offering a more impressionistic, less formal kind of reportage. Football journalism will continue to be reconfigured by the competing gravity of these orbital voices, but there are many brilliant new things to come out of this altered state. For a start, it is easier than ever before to emerge from beyond the traditional avenues and find an audience simply through a talent for writing, a distinctive voice or a communicable football intelligence. New media gives equal gravitas to the novice and the grizzled multi-tournament veteran. If you're good enough, people will read you. Take away the anxiety and the animosity and this is above all an exciting process, a reordering of a century-old industry that is no doubt long overdue.

For England's footballers Euro 2012 ultimately congealed into a rather exhausted stasis. After the early encouragements — absence of complete humiliation; rousing defensive negativity; Wayne Rooney not sent off — things unravelled rapidly into a familiar mixed bag of physical willingness and technical inadequacy, captured best over 120 minutes of high alert caution-football against Italy in Kyiv. So much so that perhaps the only really novel developments around England belonged to the press-thronged periphery. Before the quarter-final at the Olympiyskyi Roy Hodgson could be seen talking happily to Italian journalists, waving at his old Uefa friends, smiling his way through training and appearing entirely at ease as England's tournament wound down. This is of course how it should be for a man newly installed in a job that remains at least semi-impossible. And for now it is instead the trailing pack who return from a major tournament looking if not exactly menaced, then perhaps a little uncertain, elbows raised, ears tuned to the competing voices, still fighting an ever-diminishing corner. Ⓑ

72

Theory

"To a considerable extent, Brazilian football was able to develop in harmony with the dictatorship."

Directing the Pianists

Brendan Rodgers discusses the importance of possession football and what he's learned from José Mourinho

By Philippe Auclair

It's not every day that the manager of a Premier League football club cuts short a lunch with the queen to accommodate a journalist's request to interview him. But this is what happened when, shortly before the end of last season, Brendan Rodgers made his excuses and left a Diamond Jubilee civic banquet held at Swansea's City Hall in the presence of Her Majesty to drive back to the Liberty Stadium as quickly as he could. A rather embarrassed *Blizzard* contributor had explained that, his train ticket being non-exchangeable and non-refundable, not mentioning First Great Western Trains' pitiless fare policy for late bookers, changing the date of the agreed rendez-vous would entail gigantic costs neither he nor his employer could justify.

The remarkably friendly press officer of the Welsh club ("remarkably friendly'" being words which, judging by this visit, could be used for all members of Swansea's staff, players included) passed on the message to Rodgers, who skipped the royal pudding and ushered the *El Mundo* correspondent Begoña Pérez and myself into his office, first apologising for his lateness, then offering water, coffee and biscuits to his guests. It was very difficult to watch Swansea's following game with neutral eyes after such a welcome. Since then, of course,

Brendan Rodgers has moved on to what he hopes to be bigger and better things, which doesn't mean he has moved on to a different way of thinking about the way football should be played. What he believed in and preached in Wales is what he will still believe in and preach at Anfield. Fortunately, that's precisely what we talked about that afternoon.

One of the most striking aspects of your work at Swansea was the adoption of a possession-based type of football that many people thought was unsuited to British players — and with a playing staff that was overwhelmingly British... How did you achieve that?

¡Muy facil! All players, whether they're Spanish, French, English, Welsh, want to *play* football. To play. We were favourites to be relegated but our biggest success has been our philosophy, our identity of football. The players have been incredible in their capacity to play our style of football. Of course, you've got to be effective, win games, but the starting point is the football. We have an idea of the 'ideal football' we want to play and we work on making it a reality. All players want to attack — and our way of defending is to have the ball. Of course, you want the players to believe

and you get to this by working on it every day on the training ground, with the ball at their feet. We've spent a lot of time at Swansea polishing this idea of football by working on tactics. Every way of learning is used. By working on the field, by watching videos… everything we did on the training pitch, we did with the ball. You'll never see a pianist run around his piano. People ask me: "why don't you run through the forest, through the trees?" Well, I've never seen a tree on a football field. Our philosophy was to feel confident in a possession game and keep improving the players through video analysis, through talking, communicating…

⊕ *Where does this 'philosophy' stem from? Barcelona?*

I've been a follower of their model for many, many years. I was so enthused by it. Van Gaal… I just loved their way of playing. It goes back to my life as a young man. My father loved European football; he also loved the Brazilian team. His own dad loved the Brazilian team. So I grew up loving the technical game, and when I played as a young boy, I played in teams that were not technical. So I spent more time without the ball than with it. I always wanted to change that. But I had a very short career as a player, from 16 to 20 [for Ballymena United in his native country, Northern Ireland, then, very briefly, Reading]. So my ideology then was, "Ok, I'm not going to have an influence on the game as a player, technically or tactically. Can I do it as a coach?" My objective was to show that British players could *play* football. That was the challenge.

⊕ *To take up that challenge, from a very*

young age, you spent a great deal of time in Spain. How did that come about?

The experience of travelling, getting familiar with other languages, other cultures definitely helps. It makes you a better person. You respect more, you understand more what a foreign player is going through, you experience new ideas. There's no doubt that my spending time in Spain made me a better person. I worked very hard to learn Spanish. Every day, I studied with a teacher who came from Madrid… but my Spanish is not perfect. And my French, *muy, muy mal!* [laughs] My Italian, not so great… I went to Barcelona, Valencia, Sevilla, clubs which had that tradition of playing and youth formation. I wanted to see the connection between the first team and… the child. I wanted to see from close how the club worked on developing the under-9s, how they put that ethos of technical continuity into practice. I didn't just turn up at the gate of those clubs, of course. I made contact through coaches who'd been there. At Valencia, for example, there was a former player called Juan Sol, who also played for Real Madrid, who was a good friend of mine, and with whom I stayed when I went there… There was also José Luis Albiol — the uncle of Raul Albiol, the Real Madrid central defender — Alex Garcia, who was youth coach at Barcelona… I had loads of contacts. I wanted to see for myself how this model worked.

⊕ *Is there any particular reason why you didn't try to do the same thing at Real Madrid?*

No. I'm not sure why. My feeling was more for the *canteras*, the Dutch influence…

⊕ *You worked with José Mourinho for three years at Chelsea and often speak of him as a major influence. One thing, though, is that, in many respects, as a manager, he's the complete antithesis to the 'model' you love. He relies on established players, he's not that keen to integrate youth players into his starting XI. So how can he be such an important figure for you?*

He's a different man from the one portrayed in the press and the media. He is a good man. He was a fantastic educator. What he gave me was responsibility and opportunity. I was very young then [Rodgers was 31 when he joined Chelsea]. I was brought in in September 2004 — José had joined in June. They wanted to put his tactical ideas in practice throughout the club — his two favourite systems — the 4-4-2 diamond, the 4-3-3 — and I was one of the few British coaches who walked that way. We connected straight away. From the moment I arrived, he always looked for me. No question: he put me under pressure. He took me to the big players. If it hadn't worked, he wouldn't have given me a second chance. But he gave me that opportunity to work with the big players. He guided me. He told me how it had been for him when he was a young coach coming through. Of course he wants to win, but our ideas about football are not radically different. The personalities are.

⊕ *Almost every single player who's worked with Mourinho has insisted on the exceptional quality of his training sessions. In what respect were they so good and what did you get from them?*

José prepares hard and in great detail — but loads of coaches do. I'd say

that one of his biggest attributes is his ability to respect. He respects every player, whether they're playing or not. You cannot be another person — but one of the biggest things I got from José was respect, and seeing how he respects everyone. As to the details of the exercises... I can use a black pen as well as José! [laughs] Or a red pen. Or an orange pen! There are many colours in the world and they're for everyone...

⊕ *What about his attention to detail in planning training exercises?*

I spend a lot of time preparing my sessions. My staff totally understands the training. And the images that they see... [He rummages through folders, looking for drawings of training exercises.] I've left them at the training ground. But everything's drawn here, the colours, the details. What goes on the field goes on here [showing a diagram of a football field].

⊕ *But what did you take from him?*

He's a great man... but I take from myself. You cannot be anyone else. I've learned from many good people. I worked with some fantastic British coaches. When you're clever, you learn from everyone. The good things and the things that are not so good. My philosophy was already formed before I even went to Chelsea. What I was able to do at Chelsea was to experiment with some of the best youth and senior players in the world. By the time I finished at Chelsea, I had 15 years working as a coach from five-year-olds to the Ballacks, the Decos, the Shevchenkos, the Lampards. Then it was my time to go alone. You cannot take man-management from Mourinho: it has to be from you.

⊕ *Are you still in touch with him?*

Yeah. Every week. Real Madrid were fantastic last season. But look at José: the defeat against Bayern was his, what?, was it the fourth, fifth Champions League semi-final that he'd lost? He's also learnt to lose. He's not just a serial winner, he's adapted to losing as well.

⊕ *Talking about losing, seeing what happened to Barcelona and Bayern in the Champions League, are people starting to find ways to counter possession teams?*

[Interrupting] No.

⊕ *Well, with Swansea, you had 77% possession against Newcastle and still lost 2-0.*

I will always defend the right to play attacking football: you'll win more games than you will lose. You just have to keep finding solutions, yes, but the intent of my teams will remain the same. If you look at Swansea last season, it's been incredible, not just the possession and the number of games we've won, but also the fact that we have learnt as much from the games we have lost. You mention the game against Newcastle: they were chasing a spot in the Champions League and we killed them here. But we couldn't score. They have a £10m striker [Papiss Cissé] who gets two chances and scores two goals. Well done, my friend! If teams defend like that [against Swansea], they show the ultimate respect they can pay to our way of playing. As a coach, I'd never say: we play the right way and Newcastle the wrong way. All coaches want to win; I'm a coach: I want to win,

but I want to do it in a certain style and I will never come away from that. I will have to try to find the solutions. For a club like Swansea, when we came to the Premier League, people said we were like Blackpool. Seven months later, they were comparing us to Arsenal. It shows how much we had grown.

⊕ *Could a Swansea ever step to the next level and play in Europe?*

No sé. Football is such a short-term thing. It's not by accident that the teams with the big money are there every year. Manchester City and Chelsea came to where they are now because they have money. A coach is not a magician.

⊕ *What type of player do you look for? What is the first thing you look at when you evaluate a potential recruit?*

Technique. I like to know that they can play football. Then, intelligence and, at this level, personality, the capacity to play at the highest level, but they also need to have the capacity to have the ball for nearly 75% of the game. Some players would rather not have the ball than have it. I need players who want to have the ball.

⊕ *...and have the humility to accept constant drilling on the training pitch?*

Big ego, *¡hasta luego!* It's a question of DNA, of a certain culture of football. I spoke with some players last summer. Big players. I was asking them to become part of our system, telling them I could help them be big players again. The first question one of them asked me was, "Where's the nearest airport?" So he tells me straight away he wants to be away more than here. Then I ask another one, "What's your training like at this other club?" And he says, "It's fantastic, we normally get three days off!" Straight away, they tell me they don't want to work. The personality is vital. I push my players every day, big demands, big pressure.

Would you agree that you also place big demands on the supporters of your teams? In England, most of them seem to prefer a high-intensity, box-to-box approach…

At Swansea, when we played back, they clapped. Normally, in England, when you play back, phew… Because they understood the football, that we had to go back to go forward. It's education. In England, it's difficult at times. But that's ok. It's education. Life is about educating and improving. This is my journey, from the time when I was a young coach, working with young players and telling them, "You can play like that." "We don't play that way in the first team." "I don't care, this is what I want, the way I work."

Do you sometimes feel that your philosophy, as you say, makes you a lone ranger among British coaches?

I don't worry. I used to want everyone to play football, bam-bam-bam, but I respect other teams, players and managers. But it's very short-term nowadays, people will play as they see fit to survive. My way of working is different. It doesn't make it right. It doesn't make it wrong either. **B**

On the new-look Cult Zeros website, you can now mock-up the t-shirt or hoodie online.

So you can view before you buy!

 For exclusive offers follow us @cultzeros

www.cultzeros.co.uk

Ivan the Reasonable

Ivan Jovanović explains his philosophy and how he hopes to build on Apoel's success last season

By Antonis Oikonomodis

It all began with an agreement. The kind that is often made between parents and children. "We'll allow you to... only if you..." Božidar and Danica Jovanović had nothing to do with football. But they lived next to the ground of Loznica and that led them to make an agreement with their son, who was so fascinated by it that he spent many hours there. At first, he was just trying to catch a glimpse of training sessions, then he summoned up the courage to return balls that had been kicked off the pitch and, finally, it was his turn to put on a pair of boots. It was then that he made the deal with his parents: he could play football, so long as he attained excellent marks at school.

He did, all the way through to university. Only when he had to make a choice did he break the agreement. Academic studies and a professional football career did not go together and he chose the latter. Božidar and Danica never forgot, perhaps because as a football player their son never did enough to vindicate his decision. He drifted as an average midfielder through Loznica and Rad Beograd before ending up playing for Iraklis in Thessaloniki. Perhaps that's why Ivan Jovanović chose to remain in football, why he was so driven to win titles and recognition as a coach. He did that but his parents still would not be

won over. Only in January, when he was named Serbia's coach of the year, did they forgive him. It might not have been the most obvious benefit derived from Apoel's run to the Champions League quarter-final but its significance to the 50 year old was real enough.

⬅ *Have you fully digested exactly what you achieved last year? How would you describe it?*

Everything happened very quickly in terms of the magnitude of the success. In the summer, our main goal was to play again in the Champions League group stage but our successive qualifications led to the biggest success in the history of Apoel. We have surely gained a great deal but it's too soon to predict what this achievement may mean in the future. In practical terms, it means acknowledgment for the team, but also for the country, because it surely cannot be attributed to chance that a club from Cyprus twice participated in the Champions League group stage in the space of three years and actually managed to reach the quarter-finals the second time. The financial benefits are obvious but what is more significant is the greater recognition that we have received as a team despite coming from a country that is not among the strongest in terms of European football.

⊕ *When referring to Apoel, Uefa characterised its achievement as "a football revolution". Do you believe that you did indeed 'rebel'?*

It can obviously be regarded as a revolution in terms of the size of Apoel in relation to the opposition we faced in the group stage and knock-out games. The differences are enormous and the fact that we succeeded in getting to the last eight is a football phenomenon. My interpretation of the term "revolution" is that my team brings hope to countries and teams that may not have the football capacity and tradition of other nations and that that hope allows them to dream and follow a path similar to my team's.

⊕ *Do you believe that Chelsea's victory in the Champions League and Apoel's progress to the last eight provides teams who are lacking technically with a model for how to compete with teams of higher stature?*

We knew that we were confronting better teams, so we had to compensate for the difference in quality by being more compact, by running more. Apoel are a quality team and rely very much on the passing game in the Cypriot championship. We wanted to keep that up in the Champions League. We knew, however, that our opponents would control the rhythm of matches as well, perhaps for more time than we had estimated. So we needed much more running, a great deal of competitiveness, discipline and dedication in everything we had agreed to do before every game, bearing in mind also that, regardless of our opponents, we would have our own time to play our own game. Therefore, that was the time we had

to take advantage of, not only to keep the ball or to rest, but to score and to create, because that was the only way to achieve the results we wanted. And the reason why we also scored in most of our games is obvious. It isn't chance that Apoel consistently ran, on average, 5-6 km more than their opponents.

⊕ *What elements of Apoel's play will you be looking to maintain in the new cycle the team is beginning?*

I don't know! In essence, I'm also learning through my team. We have a common journey. I had no Champions League experience before Apoel and Apoel had not previously taken part in the competition. My team and I are growing together and the experiences we are acquiring, we are gathering together. For me, the two participations in the Champions League are very important experiences. We attempted to learn from the teams we played against: the way they function, their facilities, their organisational charts, everything we can utilise in the future. This year, we are renewing the roster with new players, who may possibly not have the same experiences but they are helping us to acquire the right mix to create new dynamics and to find new incentives — which is a difficult task after our last year's success.

⊕ *Which opponent played most effectively against Apoel?*

Real Madrid were the only team that understood us very well because they had obviously devoted more time than the other teams to analysing our game. They managed to give form to the difference in quality that existed between our teams by using that knowledge on the pitch. And they did so by showing patience in their game. They did not treat us like a team from Cyprus that they had to do away with quickly. They had prepared differently, ran as much as we did, allowed us to exhaust ourselves [in the first game in Nikosia] and, in the end, they got what they wanted. They were by far the best team we played against and we were perhaps fortunate in the misfortune of that draw because we were given the chance to play against a top team, so we could see, in practical terms, what we are really made of.

⚽ *But even so it must have been disheartening to draw Real Madrid in the quarter-final. Was that how your team reacted?*

It's completely normal! We qualified top of our group [above Porto, Zenit and Shakhtar Donetsk] and we played in the last 16 in Lyon, where we were lucky that we lost just 1-0 in the Gerland. But in the second leg at home we played an exceptional game and went on with even greater confidence than before. We knew that teams such as Real, Barcelona and Bayern are in a different category, one that doesn't offer many possibilities. And that's why the first feeling after the draw with Real was one of great disappointment as we realised that our journey would be coming to an end. On the other hand, when the disappointment subsided, we thought that if our tournament was to end there, at least we were being given the opportunity to challenge the best.

⚽ *If you were to change something that happened last season, what would it be?*

I truly don't know! Everything happened — in football time — very quickly. I don't think I could expect anything more from myself and my players, given the spirit we had during the entire year. No one else could know how we dealt with each game, because, for us, each game was not a simple matter; it was unique. And what we strived for, and what we did to the point of excellence, was at least to learn as much as possible. We knew that we could not take advantage of our opponents' shortcomings, so we had to focus more on adjusting our game to their strengths and preparing to limit them. Up to a point in our first games, there was a certain enthusiasm. After the first results, we felt pressured to qualify for the Europa League and then to qualify for the last 16 of the Champions League, something that was historic for Apoel. It's not an easy task to manage, going from enthusiasm to fulfilling an obligation. And at the same time always trying not to get carried away and go to the other extreme, believing that we've reached the level of our competitors. What I certainly didn't want to happen in the course of pursuing something truly wonderful was to harm the egos and the spirit of my players, whom I knew had given me all they had to give.

⚽ *As a football player you won nothing. Did this determine your coaching philosophy?*

I believe I was a good football player but it's true that I didn't win anything. I didn't change clubs and environments easily. I only played for three teams throughout my career: that of my city, Loznica, playing there from 12 to 21, in Rad Belgrade from 21 to 27 and Iraklis Thessaloniki where I played until I was

37. The truth is that as a football player I didn't achieve much. And when I began to do this job, that of coach, I remember saying to myself over and over again that I had to make an effort to win at least something, since I didn't make it as a football player. And thank God, I was lucky that the players themselves had goals and that others who came to Apoel realised that this team gave them the right to hope that they could achieve something special. And this is because in a team everything does not depend only on you but on your teammates as well and the spirit with which they desire and attempt to succeed.

Jovanović's career was shaped by a fight at the end of an InterToto Cup tie between Rad and Carl Zeiss Jena in 1988. He wasn't even on the pitch, having been substituted 10 minutes from time but, although he played no part in the brawl, his role as captain was taken into account and Uefa banned him from European competition for two years. That led to Metz pulling out of a deal to sign him and he went instead to Iraklis, who qualified for the Uefa Cup on three occasions. The first two seasons, Jovanovic could not play. The third time, in 1996-7, he did but Iraklis were eliminated in the second qualifying round — by Apoel.

⊕ *Consequently, the focal point of your professional career as a football player and a coach must have been that InterToto game in East Germany...*

Perhaps so. Football is very unpredictable. For good and for bad, you can only judge its every moment after your career is over. For example, that Uefa punishment forced me to go to Iraklis instead of Metz without the right to play in European competition. This changed my entire career. It determined my subsequent activities in football, since I began my coaching career from Iraklis. Even here, at Apoel, you see the unpredictability. Before I came, it was normal for Apoel to change coaches frequently [as he knows, having been sacked by them in 2005 after two years in the job]. I am now, however, completing the fifth year of my second term, something unprecedented at the club.

⊕ *What future do you see for yourself at Apoel?*

The only reason I would leave would be to join a team with similar goals — not just for a good contract. What is important to me is to create a new team and through that effort to find a new incentive, to pursue something similar to last year's success. Very carefully, however, because we can't allow ourselves to get carried away by what happened last season. It should serve as a guide, not be an end in itself. We are not a Champions League quarter-finals level team because we got there last year. We reached the limit of our potential and I don't know if this can be an objective standard for setting the team's future goals. We must start over, with an awareness of our abilities and our potential, because I think it is difficult for a team, for any team whatsoever, to repeat such a feat in such a short time. That said, we realise that the expectations on us, our obligations, have now increased.

⚽ *And what about the Serbia national team? After you were named Serbian coach of the year you were mentioned as a candidate for national coach...*

I have been away from my country for 22 years. It was fascinating and touching for me that Apoel's success received so much publicity in Serbia. It's the greatest recognition I could hope for, especially in light of the fears I may have, never having worked in my country. The national team is something else. It would be a great honour. But you must also feel ready because it's very different from the work done at a club and I don't know if I am ready for something like that. I'm a coach who is on the training pitch on a daily basis and I'm not yet sure that the job of a selector is something I could do well.

⚽ *How long can you coach like that?*

You can't place boundaries on coaching. As long as you are willing to learn, as long as you are willing to be informed, as long you feel that something is missing and that there is something you haven't accomplished, you continue. And as long as I have this feeling I believe that I can do this job in a dignified manner. When I judge and when I feel that I have no desire to reach for more, I will know that this cycle has closed for me, even though I know that football will always be a part of my life.

Jovanović keeps his passion alive through his two sons, Nikola and Nemanja. Having lived alone in Cyprus for two years, he has brought them — together with his wife, Tania, who is, he says, the only positive to arise from his time at university — from Thessaloniki and they are now in the Apoel academies. The 15-year old Nikola, who is a central defender, has yet to experience his father as a coach. Nemanja, an 18-year-old winger, got his first taste in Apoel's summer preparations. This coexistence creates a strange feeling ("to say the very least" according to Jovanović). But his strictness during coaching will seem even stranger. Following the standards his own parents set for him, he has made exactly the same agreement with his sons. "I will allow you to... only if you..."

"I want them to derive pleasure from what they do, but their studies are my priority," he says. "This was the only way to keep them devoted to their school obligations when they began playing football."

His reconciliation with his own father came through bees. They are Božidar's passion. Even before retiring — and almost exclusively since then — Jovanović's father supplied the family with honey he produced from breeding thousands of bees. Ivan followed him — just as he has done in (almost) everything. Even now, during every summer visit to Loznica, he and his father collect the year's honey. This is the honey that he supplies his own home with, the honey he shares with a few good friends in Cyprus. And even though Ivan has not embraced his father's love for beekeeping, not even as a hobby, in his industriousness he has perhaps accepted the logic of the bee in his career, his work, his team and even his family. Ⓑ

The Rise of the Technocrats

How attitudes to the dictatorship shape Brazil's change of approach in the seventies

By Tim Vickery

Last December Jordi Mestre, the director in charge of Barcelona's famed La Masia youth development structure, addressed a conference of Brazilian coaches. It made for a fascinating clash of cultures. To an audience that greeted his words with a mixture of admiration, envy and bewilderment, Mestre explained how, right from the start of the process, Barcelona aimed to groom stars who do not behave as stars, and how from the youngest junior side all the way to the B team the priority was never on results but always on developing a style of play.

In the debate that followed, the Brazil national team coach Mano Menezes argued that Brazil's clubs count on a good structure in which to develop young players, but, especially in contrast to Barcelona, were lacking in any philosophy of formation. There was no long-term, collective vision, he said. The project is always an individual one — usually the quest for the youth team coach to do well enough to gain promotion to the more lucrative senior ranks. "In Brazil," he said, "even in youth football, we are not able to live without giving priority to results." The tendency was always for youth teams to be prepared for short-term victory, not long-term player development. As Fluminense's youth specialist Marcelo Teixeira (who spent four years at Manchester United) pointed out, this almost inevitably led to premature physical strength being preferred to pure footballing talent.

The fascinating exchange of views inside Brazil's footballing community would have come as a huge surprise to those who continue to imagine the game in the country as some kind of *carnaval* in boots, a '*jogo bonito*' of joyful expression for as long as the samba drums can pound. It is the standard myth of Brazilian football. Many intelligent people have fallen for it. Some have set out to slay the dragon, but it is a resilient foe, sure to raise its head again. There is also a new counter-myth, a sophisticated mutation of the original. This one argues that there is no such thing as the *jogo bonito* and that the biggest trick Brazil ever pulled was to persuade the world that such a thing existed. The existence of this strain of thinking should come as a salient lesson to the advertising executive. Do not oversell your product: it can bring short-term rewards, but always at the expense of long-term problems.

There was a time when, with rare exceptions, the Brazil team only appeared to a global audience once every four years. Before the USA World Cup in 1994 the average British fan was not familiar with any of the side that went on to win the trophy, not even Romário. By France 98, all that had changed. The first team and even some of the substitutes were household names, stars of commercials skilfully put together to a scorching soundtrack. Nike had got involved, with the aim of establishing Brazil as a permanent presence in the European mind, all with the aim of shifting shirts. Brazil were marketed as the dream team, a kind of Harlem Globetrotters of football. But as the years went by, even when they won trophies, waking up from the dream left people feeling disappointed. Compared with the advert set in the airport lounge, the performances on the field seemed lacking in joyful sparkle. "Where was the show?" Brazil's players were asked after every win in a World Cup game. "For us the show is the victory," was the standard response, as if 'winning' and 'spectacle' were somehow mutually exclusive. The side that Dunga coached in the South Africa World Cup carried the theory to the limit. Two parts pragmatism, one part individual brilliance and one part plain truculence combined to form a team that would not have been remembered with great fondness even if it had gone home with the title, rather than falling in the quarter-finals. But that does not mean that it was ever thus.

Some things do not change. There are two characteristics which have been part of the essence of Brazilian football ever since the game became a popular phenomenon. One is the emphasis on individual ability. As in Britain, football began with the elites and spread down the social scale, colonised by its own people — but it has done so in very different ways.

As a mass sport British football is obviously the child of the world's first industrial society, of necessity labour-intensive. Physical strength and reliability were as valued on the football field as they were on the factory floor or down the mine. In this collective context the gifted individual has often been mistrusted, seen as a wayward figure, worryingly undependable. When the Colombian striker Faustino Asprilla joined Newcastle he was struck by the way the fans celebrated when the team won a corner. But it makes perfect sense. The corner is the ultimate collective moment — the ball stuck in the mixer for the team to attack, while the fans behind the goal try to suck it in.

In Brazil it is a moment of individual magic that is guaranteed to get the crowd going. To this day Brazil remains semi-feudal in a number of ways, left in limbo by the contrasting aims of the president between 1930 and 1954 (with one interruption), Getúlio Vargas: develop the country while preserving the existing social structure. Rich and poor are often treated almost as different species and, an industrial game in a semi-feudal setting, football is a powerful mechanism for subverting traditional hierarchies. The gifted individual player is the pawn who becomes king. He can be indulged beyond all European understanding. Normal rules do not apply. And when he does a little shimmy and an opponent clumsily falls to the ground the roar from the crowd can be almost as loud as a goal. Even if the opponent is quickly back on his feet and doggedly performing his marking duties, he has been publicly humiliated for that split second — a hugely significant moment.

That is because Brazil is a society with a self-esteem problem. It was identified by Nelson Rodrigues, one of the country's great writers and a football fanatic (the Maracanã stadium is named after his brother), as "the mongrel complex". Some see this as racial. In truth it is more likely social. In a land once described by the historian Eric Hobsbawm as "the world champion of economic inequality", it was all too easy for people to fall to fatalism when contemplating their lack of prospects of advancement. With its unmatched power to make people feel represented, football took on extra importance in this context, which brings us to the second characteristic of the essence of the Brazilian game — the importance of victory.

Of course, winning is important everywhere. But here it reaches new heights. I have heard the same line time and time again from many in the Brazilian game. Deep down, they say, Brazilians don't really like football. They like victories. Crowd figures certainly bear this out. Attendances for the same club can oscillate wildly; the big clubs can comfortably fill giant stadiums when the team is doing well. But in times of disappointment there are so few people in the ground that it is possible to count them individually. It's as if the supporter is saying, "When the team is doing well it is my team. When it's struggling it's not my representative and I refuse to be humiliated by identifying myself with it."

I had the good fortune to know some of the stars of Brazil's 1950 World Cup team, a great side that put their country's football on the map when the country hosted that year's tournament. I knew Flávio Costa, a hugely important coach,

and Zizinho and Jair Rosa Pinto, two magnificent inside forwards. If I had the capacity to go back in time and watch any side from football's past, then the Brazil of 1950 may even top the list. But in the newly built Maracanã they lost the title to Uruguay. Nearly half a century later I could still feel how much it hurt them, especially the two players. They had extraordinary careers but at home they were always remembered for that one game. A recurrent theme was the reaction of their countrymen to the defeat: elsewhere, they said, a side can lose and still be respected but in Brazil it was if all their triumphs did not exist. All that counted was that one game in 1950. Decades afterwards they would still be pointed out in the street as men who had let their country down. In Brazilian football, victory is a serious business.

The question, then, becomes one of how to win. Over time, the answer is not always the same.

That fateful game against Uruguay seemed to confirm many of the doubts that Brazilians had about their own self-worth. But in purely footballing terms, a more solid diagnosis was made. Needing only a draw to win the World Cup, Brazil had led by a single goal until they were undone by Alcides Ghiggia, Uruguay's right-winger, who laid on the equaliser and scored the winner himself. The Brazil coach Flávio Costa went to his grave blaming the centre-half Juvenal for hiding from the action and not supporting his overworked left-back Bigode. But the problem was at least as much collective as individual. As England were soon to find out against the great Hungarians, W-M was a system that did not guarantee sufficient defensive cover.

The back four was another matter. As the 1970 coach (and a player in 58 and 62) Mario Zagallo explained at length in *the Blizzard* Issue Three, the key drive behind Brazil's wholehearted adoption of the back four was that of always having enough defensive cover. Brazilian clubs had been experimenting with back fours — withdrawing an extra player alongside the centre-half — since the early to mid-1940s. The disaster of 1950 gave an extra push to the wheel. And so the template was born for the glory years, for the three World Cups won in four tournaments between 1958 and 1970. The sides all defended with a back four and increasingly brought more men behind the line of the ball when possession was lost, from the 4-2-4 with Zagallo shuttling back from the left wing in 58, to Zagallo's own prototype 4-5-1 of 70.

In possession, Brazil's secret was to have top individual talent in enough positions to have a range of attacking options; fast and tricky wingers capable of reaching the by-line, quick brave centre-forwards who could thrive off crosses or balls played over the top — and, of course, Pelé as a superhumanly talented support striker. And to organise the play from deep and choose from the many options, a central midfielder capable of closing down space and marking, but mainly there for his intelligence and magnificent range of passing — a kind of coach on the field, such as Danilo Alvim in 1950, Didi in 1958 and 1962 and Gérson in 1970.

Then came Holland in 1974. Brazil's central midfielder was Rivelino, who had improvised as a false left-winger four years earlier but in that tournament operated in his true position. The game against the Dutch in the 74 World Cup, effectively the semi-final, was probably never going to be his night. Rain had left the Dortmund pitch heavy, which didn't suit him. But he hardly had a chance to get himself into the game. His predecessors in the position had been used to having time on the ball. In Mexico four years earlier, Gérson had appeared able to pick up possession, wander about chatting to all around him, glance at the newspaper to consult his star sign and only then decide what he was going to do. By way of contrast, Rivelino looked up to find half of Holland charging at him.

Aesthetes saw in the Dutch side the liberating possibilities opened up by the changing of positions — the right-back Wim Suurbier nearly scoring, for example, after cutting in from the left-wing. Pragmatists were more concerned by the difficulty of playing against a side that pressed with such intensity. And South Americans were alarmed by seeing their continent's football rendered obsolete by one team in the course of a single tournament — before ending Brazil's golden period Holland had overcome Uruguay and Argentina with contemptuous ease.

The signs had been there for a while. Northern European football was on the rise. In the previous decade the game in Holland and West Germany had gone fully professional. England had abolished the maximum wage and carried forward the idea of polyfunctionality with the adoption of 4-4-2 in 1966. In 1967, Celtic became the first northern European side to win the European Cup, starting a regional stranglehold that, with the exception of 1969, would last until the mid-80s. Brazil had received a taste of what was to come as far back as April 1963, when, much to their surprise, a team full of world champions was overpowered 5-1 by Belgium; part of a tour on which they also lost to Holland. That could be shrugged off as a lapse: after all, the previous week they had beaten Argentina 4-1 in the Maracanã. But 11 years later in West Germany it was no longer possible to hide from the challenge posed by the dynamism of the northern Europeans. A response had to be found.

It is at this point that elements of football in Brazil and Argentina move off in very different directions. The same challenge provoked contrasting responses because it was viewed through different perspectives — much of which had to do with the relationships between the game and the military dictatorships which ruled the two countries in the mid-70s. So politically polarised it had become virtually ungovernable, Argentina succumbed to a brutal military coup in 1976. There were no doubts or niceties. This was like a heel smashing down on the face of a society whose national football team was coached by a left-wing bohemian intellectual, César Luis Menotti.

Menotti conceptualised Argentinian football, both as a natural talker, but also in response to the circumstances in which he found himself, representing a nation whose regime was killing some 20,000 of its citizens, in many cases the brightest and most courageously idealistic youngsters. Prior to the final of the 1978 World Cup in Buenos Aires, Menotti is supposed to have told his players, "We are the people, we come from the victimised classes and we represent the only thing that is legitimate in this country — football. We are not playing for the expensive seats full of military officers. We represent freedom, not the dictatorship."

The coach defined Argentinian football in cultural and philosophical terms, as the true manifestation of the country's working class. In purely football terms, his response to the new challenge from across the Atlantic was a gesture of faith in the traditional passing style of the Argentinian game. The modernisation came in the emphasis on upping the rhythm — hence the importance of the dynamic, fetch-and-carry midfield work of Osvado Ardiles. The observation that "the point of training is to increase the speed at which one can be precise" is Menotti at his wise and succinct best.

"Before when we wanted to study and progress we had to read European books," said the legendary Uruguay-born coach Ondino Vieira, "because the Europeans wrote down what they knew in order to pass on knowledge and we didn't. But with Menotti, for the first time a theorist of our football appeared, and guided by his books we were able to transmit our way of playing."

And one of the things that has stuck, with a certain romantic school of Argentine coaches, is the idea of football as a cultural and philosophical manifestation. Apparently there are none of Menotti's pavement café politics in Marcelo Bielsa, but his commitment to attacking play, to seeking to impose the game in the opponent's half of the field, is rooted in a philosophical code, a way of living one's life in all circumstances. It is all but impossible to think of a

Brazilian equivalent.

But then the only question in Brazilian football was how to win. It was not called upon to define itself in philosophical and cultural terms against its military regime. The situation in Brazil was very different — to a considerable extent, Brazilian football was able to develop in harmony with the dictatorship. The establishment of the National Championship in 1971, for example, was an explicit part of the regime's plan to unify the giant country.

Ashamed, the military government limped slowly away during the 1980s and is now remembered as an unsavoury and difficult period. But it has been forgotten (conveniently for many) just how much popular support it enjoyed for over a decade after the coup of 1964. Much has been made of the late-60s student resistance, with the famous March of 100,000. A new generation of historians is now pointing out unpleasant truths — such as the fact that in the mid-60s there were marches at least five times as big all over the country in support of the regime. One of them, David Aarão Reis, goes as far as to attack the term "military dictatorship". He looks at those who supported the coup — "business, political and religious leaders, entities of civil society such as the lawyers organisation and the council of bishops, the right-wing in general" and comes to the conclusion that "civil-military dictatorship" is a more accurate term for what actually took place.

The renowned economist Celso Furtado, one of the regime's most lucid opponents, was more specific. He described the dictatorship as "military-technocratic", an alliance between the armed forces and middle-class technical specialists, such as economists and engineers involved in the plethora of huge construction projects. Football, too, became the preserve of the technocrat.

The roots were already there. As far back as 1958, the Brazil team was supported by a back-up staff including doctors, physical preparation specialists, a dentist and even an early (and unsuccessful) experiment with a sports psychologist. Increasingly the coaches, too, became technocrats, physical education graduates instead of the traditional ex-player. And the tactical revolution of the Dutch in 1974 appeared to make redundant the hands-on knowledge of the ex-player. Clipboard in hand, only the technocrats had the answer.

They worked with models which were culturally alien. In 1978 under Cláudio Coutinho, Brazil set out to imitate what the Dutch had done. There was an attempt to turn the clock back under Telê Santana in 1982, especially, and 1986. But in 1990 under Sebastião Lazaroni the model was an Italian-style sweeper system. And like all technocrats, these new coaches lived in a world of numbers. What they could not measure they could not manage.

Their conclusions were based on the physical evolution of the game. According to Murici Sant'anna, one of the country's leading physical preparation specialists, the ground covered by players doubled between the mid-70s and the mid-90s. So if the old-style midfield elaboration had not worked against the Dutch in 1974, there was no chance of going back to the attacking template of 1958-70. Physical evolution meant less space on the field and more contact. This led to two conclusions. Firstly, Brazil's players had to be able to match the northern Europeans in physical terms. Assuming parity in strength, size and speed, Brazil's technical advantage should be enough to tip the balance. Secondly, there was little point in grooming players to work the midfield patterns of old. There was not enough space for such relics and the numbers appeared to prove that the greater the number of passes in a move, the lower the chances of it ending in a goal. And so, where once there was Danilo Alvim at the heart of the side, or Didi and Zito, Clodoaldo and Gérson, Falcão and Toninho Cerezo, come 2010 there were Gilberto Silva and Felipe Melo — central midfield was closed up, freeing the flanks for fast breaks from wonderfully athletic full-backs, in the hope that the ball could be delivered to the talented front men quickly enough for them to do some damage.

For a while the model worked — between 1994 and 2002, Brazil played in three successive World Cup finals, winning two of them. But it was not always easy on the eye. In 1985, Zizinho penned his autobiography, no ghost writers involved. The closing words were something of a lament. Brazilian football, he said, "has given the central midfielder, the man who has 70% of his team's possession in his hands, the specific function of destroying, when it should be to set up the play." The technocrats would argue that he was living in the past. And then along came Barcelona.

In the four years of Pep Guardiola's reign Brazil had to accept that spiritual guardianship of the beautiful game had passed to Barcelona. This has led to outbreaks of jealousy. Andres Sanchez, the former president of Corinthians and currently the director of Brazil's national teams, recently described the idea that Barcelona have some sort of school of footballing thought as "a load of nonsense". The basis for his outburst seems to be that a few years back he took a Corinthians Under-17 side to play Barcelona and they apparently won 2-0. This, if nothing else, is proof that science needs to apply itself to the task of inventing the one-ended stick so that people like Sanchez cannot get the wrong end of it.

Wiser heads have watched in awe. The little midfielders, the likes of Xavi and Iniesta, and the possession-based game — all of this was not out of date after all! The technocrats' path to victory was not the only road! With elegance and a dose of venom, Guardiola stuck the knife in last December, after his Barcelona side had swept Santos aside with astonishing ease in the final of the World Club Cup. His team played the ball around, he said, in the manner that his father and grandfather told him that Brazil used to do.

And may start doing once more. The future is a fascinating place. But Brazilian football is an oil tanker that will not turn round quickly. The former Barcelona player, and one-time teammate of Guardiola, Rivaldo points out that contemporary Brazilian players are easily bored by training aimed at retaining possession. "Everyone wants to get the ball under control and dribble at the opposition," he said. It has been apparent in some recent performances by Brazilian clubs and national teams just how little grasp the players have of working

triangles through the midfield.
But they do not need to copy Barcelona or anyone else to get it back. It is there in their own tradition if they can be bothered to look. One of my favourite pieces of football writing is the eyewitness account of the Argentinian coach Ángel Cappa, almost crazed with joy at the chance to watch Brazil in the 1982 World Cup, their last attempt to do things the old way. "The ball arrived in one part of the field and then disappeared — to appear again in the form of a rabbit and also of a dove, and was then hidden again from opponents who, in their anguish, looked for it in the most unlikely places without being able to find it... The ball had not enjoyed itself so much for ages, or received so much affection... And the crowd, myself included, glanced at our watches in the hope that time could stand still because we wanted the game to go on for ever... Every game Brazil played in the tournament was a kind of magical, beautiful dance."

He saw it, and wrote it all down. It is not possible to read his account and believe that the *jogo bonito* is nothing but a myth. It existed! And if we are lucky, it may exist once more.

The Second Coming

Zdeněk Zeman talks about attacking, romance and his challenge after returning to Roma this season

By Federico Farcomeni

The Italian singer-songwriter Antonello Venditti once composed a song called *Zeman's Conscience* that included the line, *"Perche' non cambi mai... "* ["Because you never change..."] For Zdeněk Zeman himself, old habits die hard. During the course of this interview, he smoked, on average, one cigarette every six minutes. We shouldn't be too surprised. He once said, "I don't count how many cigarettes I smoke every day, otherwise I would become nervous and would smoke even more."

At Roma, though, Zeman has changed a habit of a lifetime. Usually he signs contracts for only a year at a time; in the summer, when he moved from Pescara, he agreed a two-year deal with an option for a third. Zeman is back, looking to do what he does best: nurturing young talent and bringing crowds and enthusiasm to cities that previously lacked them. This, at least, is what he did at Foggia and Lecce — in 2004-5, for instance, the *giallorossi* scored 66 goals, just one fewer than the champions, Juventus — while he has also coached Parma, Lazio and Napoli. Last season, he led Pescara to promotion from Serie B. He is wedded to a 4-3-3 formation and prefers to use young players whose unrelenting energy burns up the pitch and exhausts opponents. No rival team ever runs faster or for longer.

The Czech took the policy of focusing on young players from his uncle Cestmir Vycpalek, his only positive link to Juventus, a club he has repeatedly and publicly criticised, alleging, among other things, systematic drug use in the 1990s. Vycpalek led Juventus to consecutive titles in 1972 and 1973 and was noted for his capacity to develop young talent. Zeman visited Italy in the summers of 1966 and 1967 and, in 1968, he stayed four months because of the Soviet invasion of Prague. He settled in Palermo in 1969 and graduated from the ISEF, the pre-eminent sporting institute. Uncle Cestmir passed on his passion for sport. The young Zeman played ice hockey, volleyball, handball and baseball, before becoming a swimming coach. In his book *Una vita a testa alta* The Juventus legend Giampiero Boniperti tells a story about an unexpected meeting. While walking in Prague before a European Cup tie in 1985, a woman recognised Boniperti and took his hand. "Please say hello to Cesto from me. I'm his sister," she said tearfully, before swiftly disappearing into the crowd. That was Zdeněk's mother, Kweta Vycpalek.

Zeman unwittingly helped produce new coaches. Eusebio Di Francesco, who moved to Lecce last summer, is one of the lucky few to have understood his methods. "No one has ever died because of them," is how Zeman defends himself.

Aron Winter had a spell as coach at Toronto FC in MLS. Francesco Baiano, now an assistant manager at Siena, shares his views on attacking football. Other players perhaps were just too tired out to follow his footsteps.

Let's start with the present: why did you feel the desire to go back to Roma?

In 1999 I said that eventually I'd come back and this is exactly what happened. And I thank the club for giving me this chance. I read in the papers last summer that I might join the academy, yes. But in fact with all the young talent we have in our first team, I think that we can really entertain people this season. We want to move our fans emotionally. And we'll also try to win, why not?

Is it true that you could have come back before?

It's written in some transcripts from the 2006 investigation but 'somebody' had decided that I could not come back. [In 1998 Zeman accused Luciano Moggi and Juventus of using illegal drugs to enhance performance, leading to a trial that lasted nine years. In return, according to Zeman, Moggi prevented the Czech manager from joining certain teams, deliberately hampering his career. Moggi was subsequently implicated in the Calciopoli scandal that led to Juventus being stripped of two *scudetti* for influencing referees]

Could you describe your relationship with Luciano Moggi?

I'm happy I've never had any relationship with Moggi, to be honest. Of course I don't regret having said those things in the past. I'm not a *pentito*. I've been in sports for so long, that I've always felt the duty to defend their spirit and football in particular.

What was so special about Pescara last season?

I chose Pescara because the sea entices me. Besides, they had their golden age 20 years ago and almost 3,000 supporters came to greet me at my first press conference. These things normally don't happen elsewhere. I like their passion and we lived up to the expectations despite bigger clubs like Torino and Sampdoria being clear favourites at the beginning of the season. Expectations were an extra motivation for my players. We developed some good football and brought many people to the Stadio Adriatico to watch us.

In your last season at Foggia, in 2010-11, you regularly fielded 11 Under-21s and had 12 more players coming from the reserve team in your squad, but still could not match the success of your first Foggia, when you entertained thousands, played three consecutive seasons in the top tier and nearly qualified for Europe [Marcelo Lippi's Napoli defeated Lecce on the final day of the season in 1993-94, preventing them from qualifying].

I think that this Foggia played even better than the one in the 1990s. We competed at the same level against more experienced players. They set up better goals and we were as good as the teams that eventually reached the play-offs.

Foggia had the best attack but also the worst defence, which cost them promotion. What went wrong?

We had a better goal difference, though, and we gained 10 points out of 12 against Atletico Roma and Juve Stabia, the play-off finalists. We didn't go up because we blew too many chances at the end of the season.

⊕ *Although Foggia were not promoted, at least some of your kids went onto better things...*

I brought Lorenzo Insigne [on loan from Napoli] and Simone Romagnoli [on loan from AC Milan] with me to Pescara, but if I could I would have taken even more players. Marco Sau, for instance, scored 20 goals last season.

The problem with Foggia was exactly this: you couldn't buy any players, only have them on loan. And then you would have to start everything again every season. In any case, many of those players have the opportunity to play at a higher level; to me that's another achievement. Perhaps it's because I'm getting older, but I feel good with youngsters. I hope I can keep teaching them things for some more time.

⊕ *Did you develop this ability while at Palermo at the beginning of your career when your uncle Cestmir Vycpalek arranged for you to join the academy of the club?*

I was at the Palermo academy for nine years and it was constructive. But not just for me: when I left, 60 youngsters had become professionals during my time there. In my last season, in 1983, six local boys broke into the first team in Serie B and to me that was a great achievement. Back then, only two Palermo-born players were playing with the *rosanero*: Tanino Troja and Ignazio Arcoleo (who then went on to become Marco Materazzi's manager at Acireale, deploying him as a full-back). And for more than 10 years nobody else had made it. So that was a great result, especially because we didn't buy players; we grew them. Then, the mafia killed Roberto Parisi, the president, and the club didn't believe in my project anymore. I went to Licata, where we won the Serie C2 title with a squad completely made up of players from the academy in a season in which the number of foreign players in Italy had considerably increased.

⊕ *Still in Sicily, Salvatore Schillaci became Serie B top-scorer in 1989 while playing for you at Messina, bagging 23 goals, and joined Juventus right before those 'notti magiche' at Italia 90...*

Totò always scored against me when he was playing with Messina and I was coaching Palermo youngsters, so I tried to persuade him to go west and join the *rosanero*, but it was never to be. Such was the rivalry between the two clubs. To see him reach those heights was, for me, a big success, though.

⊕ *What's the team you were happiest coaching and why?*

Roma. And not just for the team itself, but also for the passion of the supporters. In my heyday Roma had more supporters than nowadays perhaps and they were so passionate that you felt you really wanted to do everything to make them happy. Football would be meaningless without people coming to attend the games. My best game for Roma was that 3-3 against Lazio in

November 1998 when we pulled back two. *"Che m'hai annullato!?"* ["What have you disallowed!?"] as Carlo Zampa [a commentator noted for his support for Roma] shouted. The derby is the best game you can go through. Not because of the things you see on the pitch — because generally they're quite rough — but because of what supporters do in the stands. If you lose, you smart over your defeat for days, but for the fans it's even worse. Most of them take the mickey out of each other, but some others don't just take it as a joke.

The new Roma with American owners chose Luís Enrique as coach. The new board had even considered you for a while last year...

I read this in the papers, but they never personally contacted me [last summer]. It's difficult to make it just through ifs and buts.

On his first day in the job, Luis Enrique sounded very much like you...

I consider myself more focused on the opponents' goal, to be honest. But last season I was curious to see that new Roma in action. I also thought back then that it was easier said than done. Luís Enrique seemed to have the will to change. Nowadays it's fashionable to choose young inexperienced managers. This is the presidents' choice. They believe in it and I don't feel like I want to criticise it. In Italy there are 1,500 professional managers for 70 teams — it's difficult to find the right people.

What about Lazio instead?

We could say that my best moments at Lazio were all in the 1994-95 season: the

4-0 win against European Champions AC Milan [when even the usually impeccable Franco Baresi looked uncertain and scored an own goal], or the 7-1 against Foggia [when Beppe Signori scored a hat-trick and Lazio scored four goals in the last seven minutes of the game], or also the 8-2 against Fiorentina [when Gabriel Batistuta missed a penalty, Pierluigi Casiraghi banged in four and Marco Di Vaio scored]. In a sense even the 3-0 hammering of Juventus, who were the eventual league champions, was special but I felt ashamed after that. That was Luca Marchegiani's match — he saved everything. We didn't win because we deserved to, but just because our goalkeeper was superb.

What's the best game of your career?

The best memory has to be our debut with Foggia at the San Siro against Inter: we even took the lead through Baiano on 52 minutes. Players like Salvatore Matrecano were playing in the old Serie C2 a few months before and were now facing a debut in Serie A in Milan. And they performed well. Also beating teams like Lazio or Juventus was good.

There are some memorable games in your timeline, for example when Lazio drew 4-4 in a pre-season friendly against Ajax in 1994, when they went on to be European champions, or when your Parma defeated Butragueño's Real Madrid in 1987 after they'd won seven pre-season games in a row...

I arrived in Parma when Arrigo Sacchi had just gone and there was no-one left. We had to build up from the foundation and changed as many as 22 players. People like Enzo Gambaro, Amedeo

Carboni and the 17-year-old Alessandro Melli all broke into the first team. But winning against Real Madrid was good not for the scoreline, but because of the way we managed to win that game.

⊕ *How would you describe yourself as a coach, and what is your coaching philosophy?*

My philosophy comes straight from the Danubian school of football, where concepts such as short-passing and team play were widespread. I've only changed the rhythm. My idol was [the Romanian] Stefan Kovacs [who succeeded Rinus Michels at Ajax, winning the European Cup in 1972 and 1973]: he used to say that you have to defend by going forward. You don't have to run after the opponents, because you have to face them front-on. In Italy, managers are afraid that losing a game might mean losing their job. That's why most teams in Italy tend to not make the opponents play, rather than play themselves. You have to make every effort in order to win and not in order to avoid defeat or not to lose. That's miles away from my mentality. I'm happy because everywhere I went people loved my style of play and even those players who were sceptical about my methods at the beginning in the end surrendered and happily adapted to them. In order to work with my idea of football, a high amount of work is needed. In general though, I think that a coach must try to convey some ideas to his players and persuade them to follow him.

⊕ *But sometimes the attacking mentality has also brought memorable set-backs. The 5-3 loss to Tenerife [when they surrendered a 1-0 first-leg lead*

despite going ahead after 14 minutes of the away game] or the 8-2 to Capello's Milan after leading 2-1 at half-time at the end of the 1991-92 season are examples of this.

I hate when people say that Serie A table is split into two — those who fight for 'something' and those who fight relegation. I've never fought to reach safety. In fact, I've never been relegated apart from the year I was in Serie B with Avellino, where politics and the system were mainly responsible. This demonstrates that my approach pays off. Although when I see other teams winning, I must say that it always depends on how you win. If there are teams around that are able to spend €150m and others like Foggia who have to stick to €2m, then it's normal that you are outclassed. But I believe you can still play good football and be competitive, even spending just a little money. To achieve what we've achieved with my teams means that we did better than the others who have spent more than us. Our rewards were bigger.

⊕ *Will financial fair play smooth over the gaps?*

It depends on if and how it will finally be applied. If, like many other things, there won't be any way to get around it, then yes, financial fair play could finally reward those who spend less and play better.

⊕ *Why have you not coached more teams outside of Italy? What did go wrong when you were abroad?*

At Fenerbahçe we didn't understand each other. I don't speak Turkish and I wasn't able to communicate properly with the players. It's difficult to develop an understanding with your players through translators. The president wanted to extend my contract but I chose to leave because I didn't feel fulfilled. At Crvena Zvezda, the club was almost bankrupt when I came so we could not put together a strong team. Of course, losing on away goals after two draws against Apoel in the second qualifying round of the Uefa Cup was decisive, although I believe that it was even too much to reach that stage of the competition and take that second leg to the very last minute of extra time. Progressing in Europe was the only source of income for the club and they sacked me.

 Would you consider coaching abroad again?

I've never said I would not go abroad again. It depends on the league and on the club. I would certainly join a league where I can understand the mentality and, after the experience at Zvezda, an economically balanced club.

 How do you regard English football these days?

I love the Premier League. It has always been important and recently they have changed mentality. Many European coaches have crossed the Channel in these years. Once, the English league was well known for two things: long ball

and 4-4-2 from the beginning to the end. Now many teams play continental football and I think they have raised their level. I would say Manchester United are world football legends and they are the team I watch with most pleasure. They keep on winning despite the number of opponents increasing every season. Besides, I believe that the Premier League is far more competitive than the other major European leagues: they've got the two Manchester teams and the others from London which are ambitious. And this makes it more interesting by far. But to me Spanish football is the real football. Every team comes out to play and entertain people even when the minnows face the heavyweights.

 What does the future hold for Zdeněk Zeman?

I'll keep going until I enjoy myself and the clubs will want to choose me. If they do, then I'll be happy. If they don't, I won't think they are wrong.

Antonello Venditti in his song also sang *"il pareggio mai / non lo firmerai"* ["You will never take a draw beforehand"]. Last season Pescara were knocked out of the Coppa Italia by Triestina. The Dolphins missed a penalty and then pulled back two goals in the last six minutes to take the game to a penalty shoot-out that Triestina won 12-11. Venditti was right: at heart, Zeman never changes. The immediate future for Roma should at the very least be exciting.

SPIRIT.STYLE.QUALITY
WHOEVER YOU FOLLOW... LOOK SHARP THIS SEASON.

GOALSOUL
KEEPING THE GAME BEAUTIFUL

SEE THE FULL COLLECTION AT WWW.GOALSOUL.NET

THE ICEMAN'S JOURNEY
DENNIS BERGKAMP
ARSENAL

BLUE SUNDAY
FACT 1-6
MANCHESTER CITY

BE SEEING YOU
DUNCAN FERGUSON
EVERTON

HAIRDRYER TREAT
ALEX FERGUSO
MANCHESTER UN

99

Photo Essay

River's Return

Images of River Plate's battle to win promotion from the purgatory of Nacional B

By Aníbal Greco

"Que se vayan todos" — "All of them must go" — they chanted. In 2001, it was the cry of the Argentinian protestors as the country was mired in a political, economic and social crisis. In 2011, it was the cry of the River Plate supporters. On 26 June 2011, one of the world's great clubs was relegated for the first time. 110 years of history — over 80,000 members, an estimated 14 million fans, an Intercontinental Cup, two Copa Libertadores and a record 33 league titles — had not been enough to protect River Plate from relegation.

They had fallen just one win short of safety — one win over the course of three seasons. Three points from a total of 342 on offer. Ultimately, the points averages that decide relegation in Argentina played against the type of club they were meant to protect. The year River went down, they ended the season in sixth place, yet they faced a relegation play-off.

With Mariano Pavone's penalty miss against Belgrano, towards the end of the return leg, any remaining hope of survival vanished. River were down and the Monumental was soon in flames. Once the smoke had cleared came the realisation that the return would be long and painful, even if it took just one year. In the end, it took 363 days.

They would travel thousands of miles to tiny lower division grounds where they had never played before. They would be greeted with abuse from opposing fans who delighted in River's plight. "RiBer" was scrawled on bridges and buildings: they will never live down having played in the second division — *la B Nacional*.

Yet there was a groundswell of support — some fans saw the club play for the first time in their lives, others travelled south to Patagonia, west to the Andes and north to the border with Bolivia to follow the side. All the while, the Monumental was packed for home games. Alejandro 'Chori' Dominguez and Fernando Cavenaghi turned their backs on contracts in Europe and offered to play for whatever the heavily indebted club could afford. Midway through the season, the World Cup and European Championship-winning striker David Trezeguet ripped up a lucrative contract in the Middle East to join the club he supported while growing up in Buenos Aires.

Yet despite the formidable attacking trident available to Matías Almeyda, who had taken over as coach just hours after relegation, it would not be easy. Opposing teams turned their 15 minutes of fame into 90 against River. They never managed to build up the comfortable lead at the top of the table that fans were convinced they should have. The boardroom civil war that centred on the club president and World Cup-winning captain Daniel Passarella grabbed as many headlines as the results and a sense of paranoia replaced the trauma of relegation — what if they didn't win promotion? After relegation, they reasoned, anything was possible.

Aníbal Greco's photos wonderfully capture River Plate's journey from relegation to tiny provincial stadiums, to the tension in the Monumental as the team stuttered, through to the final day of the season, when River returned to the place they should never have left.

Joel Richards

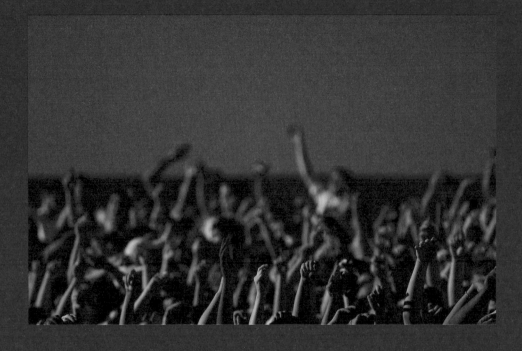

114

The Lost

"What about doing press
conferences in my head?"

The Paper Tiger

How politics and society have stood in the way of a Chinese boom

By David Bartram

Beijing, 1978

Deng Xiaoping has a decision to make. Since the death of Mao Zedong two years ago, Deng has been busy outmanoeuvring his political rivals, finally emerging as the de facto leader of the Chinese Communist Party, and by virtue of that, China as a whole. With his own position now secure, he has more pressing issues to deal with: China is in crisis. Still reeling from a generation of Mao's capricious rule, the country is starving. The chaos unleashed by the Cultural Revolution, a mass purge of Mao's enemies — real and perceived — has not been forgotten. How could it be, when barely a man or woman in all of China was left unaffected by the brutality?

But Deng has a dangerously simple idea to cure his country's woes. Almost 60 years earlier, while still a teenager, he travelled to France to work and study. Living in France, Deng joined the local Communist Party, but began to reach different conclusions when it came to his homeland and what would make China great. If China were to catch up with the West, Deng supposed, first it needed to learn from the West. And where better to start than the West's two greatest exports: capitalism and football?

So, more than half a century later, Deng is finally in a position to implement what he learnt in Europe all those years ago. He proposes a series of reforms: decollectivise farming, giving individuals the power to sell their excess produce for profit. Begin to denationalise some industry to increase production. Encourage foreign investment in the country as a way of stimulating trade. And for only the second time —the other being for the 1958 World Cup — enter a Chinese national football team into World Cup qualifying.

China don't qualify for Spain 82, losing 2-1 to New Zealand in a play-off in Singapore after the two countries finish level on points and goal difference in their group. But Deng's great 'opening up' of China produces more immediate, economic successes. Within a few years, China no longer needs to import food to feed its population.

As wealth increases throughout the eighties, more and more people move to the cities. Beijing grows into an unwieldy metropolis. Televisions become commonplace in households and with it a new generation of Chinese grows up watching football. Many support Liverpool, a team with appeal beyond their success — like China, they play in red.

Their new fans cheer enthusiastically — with a new found confidence, even — for their adopted team. China survived its century of humiliation at the hands of the colonial powers. It survived Mao too. Now with an economy growing at an unprecedented rate, dragging millions out of poverty, people across the country are daring to dream of a future in which China takes its place alongside the world's great powers, both on and off the football pitch.

Beijing, 2008

Something's wrong, but no-one's quite sure exactly what. The 90,000 strong crowd in Beijing's Bird's Nest Olympic Stadium are hushed in a confused silence. Liu Xiang's long march to a second 110m hurdles gold began the moment he crossed the finish line four years ago in Athens, instantly becoming a national hero, the national hero. Victory in front of his adoring fans will be the defining moment of the Beijing Olympics. So why the hell is he walking off the track?

It must be some mistake. A false start isn't unexpected in a sprint heat, all you need to do is return to your blocks for the restart. But Liu is heading out of the stadium clutching his leg. The defence of his gold medal hasn't even reached the first hurdle.

The crowd begins to stir. Some jeer, others burst into tears. Within minutes the recriminations begin not just in the stadium but across China. "We cannot accept that Liu Xiang quits! Liu Xiang dispels the passion of Chinese people," reads a government blog posted minutes after his withdrawal. Others propose conspiracy theories: Liu's sponsors were demanding too much of his time, he wasn't focused on preparations.

Liu himself appears publicly the next day. His coach is in tears next to him. "So many people have been worried and caring about me. I feel sorry," says Liu. "I could do nothing but pull out of the race."

Why should any of this matter? China aren't struggling for gold medals elsewhere. By the end of the Games, the country will top the medal table with 51 golds. And it's not even as though these Olympic Games are about medals anyway. That China has put on the most visually stunning, perfectly choreographed Olympic Games in history has made the main point: China is back at the world's top table.

Yet as the days after Liu's withdrawal turn into weeks and the Olympic flame is extinguished, something still nags. China didn't win a single medal in men's track and field; even the Japanese managed one. The women fared little better with two bronzes. And the football team! Well, the less said about that the better.

Sure, China topped the medal table, but most of its medals came in fringe events: shooting, diving, weightlifting. Just as those critics were arguing that China's economic growth was without true foundation, a product of artificial exchange rates and government interference, so some dissenters began to question China's sporting achievements, in spite of the hefty medal haul.

Six weeks before the Beijing Olympics, China recorded an impressive 1-0 win against Australia in Sydney in qualification for the 2010 World Cup. The only problem? The game was a dead rubber, China already eliminated.

Could China really claim to be a sporting superpower while crashing out of the World Cup two years before the main event, at the same stage as Turkmenistan, Lebanon and Syria? It couldn't say it didn't care; China was home to hundreds of millions of football fans. And anyway, that other world superpower that 'didn't care' about football still managed at least to qualify on a regular basis.

So as the world departed from Beijing, amid the fanfare lingered a sense that there was still something left to prove. National pride — the importance of which might only be appreciated by those who have experienced a recent history as tumultuous as China's — had not been restored quite yet, but maybe football was the place to start trying to put that right.

First some questions needed answering: why could China win 51 gold medals at an Olympic Games but not get anywhere near the World Cup? How hard could it be to find 11 decent footballers among a population of 1.3 billion? And could it be that China's new-found wealth was actually hindering the development of football in the country?

This is the story of Deng Xiaoping's China; how one man's vision transformed a country from failed state to global superpower, but — despite all his efforts — left it trailing behind on the football pitch.

It seems strange that the man who laid the foundations for the most remarkable transformation in modern economic history was unable to fix Chinese football. Perhaps building economies is easier than building football teams.

Deng fell in love with the sport while living in Paris. He moved to the city as a teenager in search of adventure. When it hosted the 1924 Olympic Games, Deng was an impoverished student, but scraped together any money he could find to attend the football tournament. It was won by a magnificent Uruguay team that would go on to lift the inaugural World Cup six years later. Although Deng never specified the games he attended, he could very well have been part of the 45,000 crowd packed into the Stade Olympique Yves-du-Manoir to watch Uruguay dismantle the hosts 5-1 in the quarter-finals. It was the type of display to spark a lifelong passion.

China did not participate in the 1924 Games — from the fall of the Qing Dynasty 12 years earlier to the establishment of the People's Republic under the Communists in 1949, invasions and civil wars all but precluded international participation of any note. It wasn't until 1957, under Mao, that China first entered a team into World Cup qualifying, going out to Indonesia on goal average after a play-off in Burma finished 0-0. By then Deng was one of China's most senior leaders, a confidante of Mao and the man in charge of the country's sports policy.

Deng was devastated by the defeat. It had been his idea to enter the World Cup, a way of reaching out to the international community. He personally visited the national team on several occasions during the 1950s. With the civil war behind them, he not only believed this was the moment for Chinese resurgence, but that football was a way to show off China's newfound independence to the world.

On one visit to the national team in 1952, just three years after the revolution, he commented that he hoped China would soon become an excellent side. But by the end of the decade optimism had been replaced by frustration. "Football is my favourite game," Deng said, "but when I watch China play, I feel like I'm suffocating."

It was an apt simile. Deng wasn't the only person in China who felt like he was suffocating. As the fifties gave way to the sixties, so the optimism of the revolution turned into the choking reality of life under Mao's cult of personality.

After a series of failed attempts to kick-start China's faltering economy, Mao[1], fearing for his own position, launched the Cultural Revolution in 1966. He mobilised China's rural youth against anyone or anything that might be considered a threat. Teachers were murdered, property seized from those deemed to own too much, religious and historical sites pillaged. Millions were killed.

Deng, ever the pragmatist, suggested an alternative to the chaos: reform China's economy to encourage growth. But Mao had chosen his path and, even as a long-time ally, Deng was not immune from the persecution. He was condemned as a capitalist sympathiser and, in 1969, purged and sent to work as an ordinary labourer at a tractor factory in the remote countryside of Jiangxi. His family was also targeted, the Maoist Red Guards torturing and defenestrating his son, who is still confined to a wheelchair.

Yet Deng's fall from favour was matched only by the speed of his unexpected return. By the mid-seventies, with the true horror of the Cultural Revolution only beginning to become clear, a politically-weakened Mao allowed Deng back into a senior position. When Mao died in 1976 and voices within the Party began calling for reform, Deng's objections to collectivism — the same objections that had got him purged and crippled his son just a few years earlier — now played in his favour.

Among the confusion and power-wrangling post-Mao, it took a football match to secure his place as leader of China. In the summer of 1977, Deng made his first public appearance since being exiled seven years earlier at Beijing's Workers' Stadium during a match between a Chinese youth team and Hong Kong. As the loudspeaker announced his arrival, the crowd burst into a spontaneous standing ovation.

The significance of the crowd's reaction cannot be underestimated. With no clear successor to Mao yet emerging, as Deng accepted the applause he must have considered that this was the moment to

[1] Mao was, allegedly, a talented footballer in his youth, playing in goal while studying in Hunan. It has been claimed he once went an entire season without conceding a goal, although as anyone who saw Kim Jong-il chip out of a bunker will know, official accounts of despots' sporting prowess cannot always be trusted.

make his move. The show of raucous public support — rare at a football match in China at the time, where crowds usually watched on in near silence — proved that Deng had the support of the ordinary Chinese worker. Within a year, he was leader of China.

Hong Kong, 1997

Fireworks erupt over Victoria Harbour but not many people in Hong Kong are celebrating. Certainly not Prince Charles, aboard the HM Yacht *Britannia* as it sails away from the neon skyscrapers and into the South China Sea. This wasn't how it was supposed to be — another piece of the Empire gone before he's even on the throne. After more than 150 years of British rule, Hong Kong has been returned to China. Charles scrawls in his diary, "The Great Chinese Takeaway."

This was the moment that Deng had worked so tirelessly for throughout the 1980s. He'd met with Margaret Thatcher to negotiate the return and attempted to allay Hong Kongers' fears by guaranteeing that their way of life would not be altered for at least 50 years. He called the compromise "one country, two systems"; it had been formulated initially during discussions with the International Olympic Committee as a way of justifying Taiwan and China competing at the Olympics under separate flags, despite China's persistent claims that the island is rightfully theirs[2].

Deng's determination to see Hong Kong returned to China was made all the more resolute by an incident in 1985. As soon as Deng had become China's paramount leader in 1978, he moved quickly to improve the country's football team. That year overtures were made towards the FA in an attempt to persuade the England team to tour China. When England failed to qualify for the 1978 World Cup the proposal collapsed, but an unlikely compromise was struck — West Bromwich Albion would instead embark on a four match tour of the country.

The tour was captured by the BBC for the documentary *Albion in the Orient*. The footage includes the team, managed by Ron Atkinson, visiting the Great Wall where an unimpressed John Trewick muses that, "Once you've seen one wall, you've seen them all."

After narrowly missing out on qualification for Spain 82, Deng was confident that China would qualify for its maiden World Cup in 1986. They topped their first-round qualifying group going into the final game, requiring only a draw against Hong Kong in Beijing to progress.

Everything was set up for a huge celebration. The Workers' Stadium was packed — 80,000 football fans expecting China's passage into Asia's final World Cup qualifying round. The game also held added personal significance for Deng: it was in this very stadium eight years earlier, also during a match between China and Hong Kong, that he

---

[2] *"One country, two systems" is not so dissimilar to how the Football Association and the Premier League co-exist. In theory the Football Association holds total power over the sport; in practice, the Premier League is left to its own devices.*

had first dared to believe he could lead his country.

Although China had only managed a 0-0 draw in Hong Kong, they had won all their other games convincingly, notching up 22 goals without reply in the process. Needing just a single point, few believed China wouldn't get it. But Hong Kong shocked China early on, taking the lead 19 minutes in through a Cheung Chi Tak free-kick. China responded well and equalised on the half hour. With the score at 1-1, China were heading through.

Hong Kong opened up in the second half, in search of the most unlikely of winners. Then it happened, defender Ku Kam Fai popping up with the goal that would silence the 80,000 crammed into the Workers' Stadium. Not that they would stay silent for long. At full-time the angry crowd took to the streets, rampaging through Beijing in what would be remembered by its date, 19 May 1985, as the 519 incident. Deng's own disappointment soon turned to anger and armed police were sent in to quell the riot.

Had the rioters known China would have to wait another 17 years to play at a World Cup, things might have been even worse.

So as Prince Charles sails out of Hong Kong and Ku Kam Fai raises a wry smile remembering that night 12 years ago, 2000km north in Beijing government officials celebrate. Many gather in the Workers' Stadium, which hosts an exhibition marking the handover. But as the party goes on into the night, there are just two regrets. Firstly, that "one country, two systems" means that China hasn't fully regained control of Hong

Kong. In fact not a great deal changes; Hong Kong retains its Fifa recognised football team, hoping one day to repeat the heroics of the 519 team.

And the second regret? That despite a lifetime of struggle for this moment, the moment that China might put years of colonial humiliation and civil strife behind them, Deng Xiaoping had died five months earlier. He never saw China at a World Cup.

Gwangju, South Korea, 2002

This is the moment that 170 million people have bought TV sets for. As the players line up for the national anthems, particularly enthusiastic cheers go up in households across China when the camera pans past Li Tie and Sun Jihai. From next season, China's best two players will turn out for Everton and Manchester City respectively.

People are realistic. Chinese football fans know their team won't win this World Cup, but it barely matters. The most important thing is that they are here, finally, and that they don't embarrass themselves. The last part shouldn't be a problem: China's opening game in eminently winnable, against the World Cup's customary Concacaf whipping boys, this time Costa Rica.

The circumstances are far from ideal. Few have paid much attention to China in the build-up to the World Cup. Instead the focus has been on Japan and South Korea — the old enemies — but then they are hosting the event. Still, what does that matter? China are at a World Cup!

Deng is no longer around to watch but the country is feeling his impact more than ever. For one thing, those 170 million televisions have been bought by people who would never have dreamed of affording such a thing a few years earlier. Most of them have been manufactured in the country as well; since China was finally admitted to the World Trade Organisation last year the country has cemented its place as the world's leading exporter.

As *Yiyongjun Jinxingqu* ("*The March of the Volunteers*") plays in Gwangju, it is clear that the Chinese team appreciate the weight of the moment. The defender Fan Zhiyi, recently transferred to Dundee, sings along, hand on heart. The goalkeeper Jiang Jin lets out a roar. On the bench, the Serbian coach Bora Milutinović smiles nervously.

It takes just 61 minutes for the dream to be dashed, the ball falling to Rónald Gómez who side-foots in from the edge of the area. It is to be the first of nine goals China concede in their three matches.

They don't score any and return home disgraced. China haven't come close to a World Cup since.

Beijing, 2009

Phil Brown is enjoying a well-earned pint, sitting in Danger Doyle's, an Irish pub in the centre of Beijing. Just a few months ago, it didn't feel like he'd be

here — China! — preparing his Hull City side for a second season in the Premier League. Double training sessions along the Humber seemed more likely, ready for a trip down the road to Barnsley next season. But Newcastle capitulated, Hull survived and now Brown is dreaming of what might be possible next season.

He can barely believe his luck. Surely China is where big clubs go for their pre-season? Where Real Madrid and Internazionale and Manchester United tour, picking up millions of fans — is it even hundreds of millions of fans? — along the way. Where shirt sales alone will buy you a Champions League-ready squad. Where billionaire tycoons lurk around every corner, just waiting to buy your club. China! Phil Brown has taken Hull City to China.

But just like the fake iPhones or Louis Vuitton handbags being hawked down the road, not everything in this country is as it seems. As he gazes out of the window, just across the street he sees the Workers' Stadium, where his Hull City team have just beaten Beijing Guo'an on penalties in the Barclays Asia Trophy. The Workers' Stadium is known as *Gong Ti* by the locals. It is a heartless piece of brutalist architecture. A rickety, sprawling stadium with about as much atmosphere as the moon which inexplicably continues to be used despite the sparkling new Bird's Nest Olympic stadium lying vacant down the road[3].

The Workers' Stadium was one of the Ten Great Buildings, part of an initiative

[3] *In fact this isn't quite inexplicable. An executive at Beijing Guo'an turned down the chance to move to the Bird's Nest on the grounds that his club weren't worthy to play in such a prestigious stadium..*

undertaken by Mao and the Communists in 1959 to commemorate the tenth anniversary of their takeover of China. It was hoped that the construction of vast public works would not only elevate the status of Beijing but also help spur on the Great Leap Forward, Mao's attempt to fast-track China's global economic rise during the late 1950s and early 1960s.

To say the Great Leap Forward did not go to plan would be an understatement. Between 1958 and 1962, as historian Frank Dikotter put it, "China descended into hell." Mao, by this time drunk on power, introduced initiatives on whim. He famously called on all Chinese peasants to kill sparrows, on the grounds that they ate grain and robbed people of the fruits of their hard labour. But as sparrow populations dwindled, so locust populations increased, no longer kept in check by their main predator. The locust swarms grew, destroying crops across the country. Millions starved.

But this was more systematic than ill-advised. "Revolution is no dinner party," as Mao himself said, and of course there would be casualties on the path to his communist utopia. An estimated 2.5 million dissenters were murdered, many tortured to death. Others were deliberately deprived of food for being too old, too educated, too anything. By the time this murderous imbroglio of neglect, incompetence and state-sponsored killing — Mao's Great Leap Forward — was abandoned, it had killed something like 45 million people.

Yet the Workers' Stadium remains and as Phil Brown glances across the street perhaps he feels an affinity with it. Perhaps he senses that in a few months

time, Hull's own Great Leap Forward will have cost him his job. Premier League football did not come cheaply and with debts mounting he knows that anything less than a repeat of last season's survival will be disastrous for the club. Because this is what happens when the pursuit of growth is put above everything else. It becomes unsustainable and eventually ends up killing the thing you wanted to grow in the first place.

So as Phil Brown looks at the Workers' Stadium, occasionally interrupted by an expat asking for an autograph, perhaps he starts to wonder whether Hull City in Beijing is such a good idea. He watches the final trickle of fans returning home after the match. And a trickle is all it is. Just 15,000 fans showed up to watch Hull's victory. Even fewer will show up in two days time to see his team lose 3-0 to Spurs in the final. The Workers' Stadium — *Mao's* Workers' Stadium — was barely a quarter full.

During the fiasco of the Premier League's proposed 39th game one of the more nuanced arguments against the proposal ignored what the extra game might mean for domestic fans or the integrity of the league and instead focused on its financial viability. Given that the idea of the 39th game seemed wholly driven by money, it was a clever tactic. The argument went as follows: sure, Manchester United versus Liverpool will go down a storm in New York but is anyone going to turn out to watch Hull City versus Wigan in Kuala Lumpur? Hull's visit to Beijing in 2009 suggested not. It also hinted at a reason why China have struggled to build upon their sole World Cup appearance in 2002 despite the remarkable economic development during this period.

Talk to a young Chinese football fan and they will enthuse about Manchester United or Barcelona; ask them about their national team or which Chinese club they support and they will likely go quiet. More worryingly, ask them if they'd like a kick-about at the weekend and they will probably tell you they are busy.

When European clubs look at China, an equation flashes before their eyes. It generally includes some of the following inputs: second largest economy on earth, population of 1.3 billion, hundreds of millions of football fans, increasing disposable income. What it generally excludes is any understanding of China's history or its society.

This is a country where the nature of support is different. The British ideal of the loyal fan supporting a team of no-hopers through thin and thinner does not apply. Instead Deng's 'opening up' of China has turned it into a society where success is paramount and failure, even when combined with heroic effort, is rarely respected.

Football is suffering from this mentality for a number of reasons. For one, people are giving up on the sport. Walk around Beijing or Shanghai or Guangzhou and you are more likely to see kids playing basketball than football, even more so than five or six years ago. Why? Because Chinese basketball has had success stories, most notably Yao Ming who became a top player in the NBA. There is no similar precedent for football.

As a result, kids who display talent at a young age are not generally encouraged to pursue a career in football. What prospects are there for a Chinese footballer, the thinking goes, when the sport is in such disarray in the country? Instead young people are told to focus on their schoolwork; with the economy growing at the rate it is, study hard and there is every chance you will be rewarded with a well-paid job.

People often ask how a country with such a massive population cannot find at least a few decent players. But even if millions across China would call themselves football fans, football is not a sport people actually play. In fact, the Chinese Football Association (CFA) itself estimates that only 100,000 teenagers across the entire country are involved in any form of organised football. (Exact equivalent figures are hard to come by, but roughly 3million adults regularly play football in the UK, the population of which is around a twentieth of that of China.)

Even for those who are keen to play, there is no established grassroots structure through which talent can rise. The CFA does not even have a department for amateur football. Such an approach is typical of the wider distrust the Chinese government has for grassroots organisations. A top-down approach has brought success to China in many fields and kept the country united for more than 60 years — no mean feat given its past.

It has also worked in other sports, notably those at the Olympics. By plucking promising athletes at a young age and providing specialised central training in more obscure sports, China has converted population and economic advantages into sporting success. Yet the approach struggles against the depth of worldwide competition provided by football. Perhaps more so than any other sport, world-class footballers are created from the bottom, not the top. They are rarely anomalies either. For every world-class player, there almost always exists another 10 solid internationals, a few hundred professionals, a million or more playing on a muddy pitch every Sunday morning.

Is there an answer to China's football problem? Yes, but it is one unlikely to be pursued any time soon. Instead of investing in the grassroots structure needed to encourage growth, China's billionaires have started to throw money at ageing stars looking for a final big payday. Some will argue that Nicholas Anelka's move to Shanghai Shenhua might inspire a new generation to take up the sport. Others will point out that his £270,000 a week salary would be better spent building pitches on which people can actually play.

Even a recent government crackdown on corruption in football will do little to get people out and playing. When trust is lost, it can only be rebuilt from the bottom, not by government declarations that football is now clean.

With the right organisation general Olympic success can be bought, but football is different. It must grow organically, with governments only lending support where it is needed. Even while lurching from Mao's forced collectivism to Deng's open economy

in little over 30 years, one thing has remained constant: the unquestionable control of central power. Unless the government learns to let go, to allow people more space to breathe, then watching China play football will always feel like suffocating.

Beijing, 1990

There may not be an individual who played a greater role in forging the modern world than Deng Xiaoping, although even he probably never envisaged the pace and extent of China's rise.

By 1990, Deng had retired from senior politics, just in time to settle down to watch Italia 90 that summer. In an interview in 2004 to commemorate the 100th anniversary of his birth, Deng's younger sister Xianqun revealed that her brother had watched all but two of the 52 matches of the 1990 World Cup. "He could then visit places as freely as he liked," she said. "What's more, he could spend more time watching football."

Lin, Deng's eldest daughter, spoke of how her father would become irritated when told the score of games he had recorded. "He tried to watch them live," she said. "Those he could not, he asked his son Pufang to record. He did not let us tell him the result, as it was less exciting if he knew the final score."

As Deng watches the tournament unfold he has time to reflect on his career. Just the previous summer, in his final act as leader of China, he had ordered the army to clear Tiananmen Square of pro-democracy protesters using whatever force was necessary. Deng had learnt a thing or two about the danger of an unruly crowd four years earlier when that mob rampaged through Beijing following China's 519 defeat to Hong Kong.

He told himself that his actions were justified; that he had done what was needed to keep China united. Let the protesters get their way, and before long China would once again descend into hell. All that progress wasted. The prospect of another Mao, or even worse? He couldn't let that happen.

Yet as he watches another World Cup — China as ever conspicuous by their absence — he can't help but think that the players on the television are the same age as those students massacred on his orders in Tiananmen the previous year.

Halfway around the world another elder statesman of international affairs is also watching the World Cup. Henry Kissinger met Deng on several occasions, describing him as the "doughty man with the melancholy eyes". Both share a love of football.

Four years earlier, Kissinger wrote a preview of the 1986 World Cup for the *LA Times*. He made the point that communist nations had consistently underperformed at World Cups, the USSR only once progressing beyond the quarter-finals. "Too much stereotyped planning destroys the creativity indispensable for effective soccer," he posited.

Was this why Chinese football was not improving? Had Deng picked the right path for his country? Could he still visit the national team as he had back in the 1950s? Who scored that marvellous goal for Uruguay at the Paris Olympics all those years ago? Were there to be other unforeseen consequences to his 'opening up' of China? Would he ever see his country at a World Cup?

But this is too much to think about for Deng, who by now is an elderly man. So with a shake of the head he gets up to insert a VHS of the next match. **Ⓑ**

The Coach on the Couch

Is being addicted to Football Manager a medical condition?

By Iain Macintosh

Sometimes, I worry about the effect that Football Manager has had on my life. I've had girlfriends I haven't loved as much as my Uefa Cup winning Southend United side (CM97-98) and friends that I haven't seen as much as I saw my Nottingham Forest reserves (CM01-02). Why is it that I've never stayed up until 3am to write a book, but I did it on numerous occasions to guide Welling out of the Conference South (FM07)?

I decided that it was time to go and see a man who could give me some answers: Dr Simon Moore, Principal Lecturer in Psychology at London Metropolitan University and an expert in the effects of gaming on the human condition. If anyone can tell me whether or not I've got a serious, serious problem, it's him.

Me: Hello, Doctor. Thank you for seeing me at such short notice.

Dr: No problem at all, Iain.

Me: You see... Actually, should I be lying down for this?

Dr: If it makes you feel better.

Me: You know, I really think it will. [Lies down] Oh yes, that's lovely.

Dr: Now, what seems to be the problem?

Me: Well, Doctor, it's like this. I've been playing the Football Manager games for 20 years. Since the very first one, the one with the picture of an angry man on the box, came out I've spent hours and hours and hours of my life tinkering with make-believe football teams, playing with tactics, scouting and recruiting new players. When I think about what I could have achieved in my life, the languages I could have learned, the places I could have seen, it really does break my heart. At some point, I'm going to be on my death bed, surrounded by family members, gently ebbing away into the next plane of existence and all I'm going to be able to think about is the fact that I must have spent a cumulative total of six unbroken months playing a computer game. But you know the worst thing?

Dr: Go on...

Me: I'm actually a football journalist. I have a press pass and everything. Within reason, and dependent on travel budgets, I can watch any football match in the country and get paid to do so. I'm basically spending all of my free time doing something which is pretty much an extension of my day job. Am I weird?

Dr: Eeeeerm.....

Me: Oh dear, that's not a good start.

Dr: You're not playing the same one are you? The same one with a picture of an angry man on the box?

Me: Oh God, no. No, I've bought every new one when it's been released. I'm not locked in 1992.

Dr: But you like the concept, you like the micro-management?

Me: I do, I really do. I love taking over a team and assessing the squad. I like to assemble a backroom staff, prepare a coaching routine, get the youngsters mentored by senior pros, practise set-pieces, deploy scouts, everything. And then I never just play with the first team. I'll always control the reserves and the youth teams, just to make sure that there's progression in the club. And that's the strangest thing. I'm not a precise man in any other walk of life. My tax records are all over the place, my diary is written on my arm in biro, I'm forever losing notepads. But when I get on Football Manager, suddenly I become the most meticulous man in the world. Everything is planned and prepped, the future is mapped out.

Dr: When you play the game, how do you feel?

Me: Genuinely?

Dr: Genuinely.

Me: I feel like a god.

Dr: Really?

Me: I feel like a god, sat astride a mountain, staring down at the mortals as they scurry like ants, desperate to do

my bidding, fearful of my wrath. Is *that* weird? That *is* weird, isn't it?

Dr: Eeeerm....

Me: I don't like the way you draw out your 'erms'.

Dr: Sorry. It's not weird that you don't do these things in real life. Control freaks don't control every part of their lives. If you think about work, for example, some people are not control freaks at work because they are unable to manipulate people in that sense. But they might be in their own home, with cleanliness, or where the remote control is kept. But if you change the environment, you can change the behaviour. You must feel you have more control in this Football Manager environment.

Me: But I'm a football journalist and I have been for six years. You'd think I'd have no need to immerse myself in this pretend world of football because I'm in the real one.

Dr: Yes, but only to a certain extent. You're not in it, you're alongside it. You're on the outside looking in. Your influence is limited.

Me: Ah, you've seen my contacts book. Well, I say book. It's more of a pamphlet.

Dr: You don't really control the day-to-day mechanics of real football, or the way the real teams perform. But you do in the game.

Me: Do you think that's why my need to play has intensified in recent years?

Dr: Maybe.... Maybe that's a function of

what you do. Perhaps influence is what you feel you lack and this game gives it to you in great quantity.

Me: OK. What is it about always wanting one more game, always wanting one more match? Why am I sometimes sat downstairs on my sofa at 1am, my living room illuminated only by the glow of my laptop as I push deep into the night in pursuit of a pretend trophy?

Dr: Well, that's the same with lots of gamers and indeed lots of addictions. Think about horse racing fans always wanting one more race, gamblers unable to walk away from a fruit machine.

Me: God, is it that bad? Is it that closely linked with other addictions?

Dr: Yep. Some people are addicted to basic principles or linear relationships. You press 'a' and 'b' happens. You have a drink and you feel good. They like that simplicity. Then there are lot of people who like the complexities of other relationships. With this sort of game there are so many possibilities, so many permutations. You could literally play Football Manager a hundred times and have a different result every time. You are also obviously addicted to this kind of 'deity' analogy that you alluded to earlier. Your addiction is built around a 'what happens if I do this to them?' principle.

Me: So not only do I think I'm a god, but you also think I'm also a vengeful, wrathful god?

Dr: Well, not entirely. You want your team to perform well. That's your aim.

Me: But if I was the kind of person

who dropped players repeatedly, fined them, transfer listed them, then I'd be a vengeful god?

Dr: Exactly. Your personality is going to come out somehow in the game itself. Are you impulsive in the transfer market?

Me: No. I'm quite impulsive in real-life markets, especially if cheese is involved, but not on Football Manager. I always make sure that my signings are the result of thorough scouting and extensive deliberation.

Dr: You see, you're very concerned about how you do in the game, that's your motivation. You can't talk about personality without talking about motivation. You want to perform well but it's also integral to the fact that you enjoy it so much. You don't want to spoil the enjoyment by failing to put in the investment. If you're not winning, you're not having fun.

Me: Is it not a little concerning that in real life I'm reckless and impulsive, but in Football Manager I'll micromanage and plan?

Dr: Well, it just goes to show that you're not stable in your personality, doesn't it?

Me: Really?

Dr: Yes. Don't worry, that sounds a lot worse than it is. It's a good thing.

Me: It is?

Dr: Instability is good. Not reckless instability. You don't want to be murdering someone with an axe one day and then acting normal the next day.

Me: I'm not an axe murderer.

Dr: I didn't say that you were.

Me: I just want to clarify that.

Dr: Of course, of course. What I mean is that your personality is flexible. It's going to be linked to greater issues of survival. If you adopted the same persona, the same characteristics, you wouldn't be able to adapt to changing situations. If I wired you up for the day, I'd be able to show that you had spoken differently to different people, that you were acting differently, more or less confident, according to different scenarios. You're simply adapting your personality for survival in the game. In real life, you can behave as you do because the ramifications are not especially dramatic. You're untidy, but the world doesn't end because of it. You're impulsive, but I assume it hasn't caused your life to break down in any way? But you know that if you don't plan in Football Manager, you'll be less likely to win and winning is what gives you pleasure, which in turn is what drives the addiction.

Me: Oh.

Dr: It's a reinforcement, a positive reinforcement. Your work only pays your bills, Football Manager delivers hits of pleasure. So it's not a surprise that you'll act differently.

Me: This isn't going to look good to prospective employers, is it?

Dr: It's perfectly normal. You're going to get more motivated by things that make you feel good than things that you have to do.

Me: Do you think it's a little sad that micromanaging a pretend football team gets me off more than, say, a big fat line of cocaine?

Dr: Not at all. That's just how motivation works. It's like the way that money motivates some and not others, it's personal. Football Manager is what appeals to you. Not big fat lines of cocaine. Which is probably a good thing on balance, I'd say.

Me: OK. But is it a bad thing that I occasionally imagine conversations with my players?

Dr: No, because that's integral to the whole experience. It's the immersion that appeals to you, that's what draws you in. I've heard of people giving speeches in empty rooms, shaking hands with doorknobs and pretending it's a member of the Royal Family. You're just keeping the situation alive, doing what you need to do to keep the dream going. As long as you're not hurting anyone else, it's fine.

Me: What about doing press conferences in my head?

Dr: That's fine too. In fact, for you, it's even more normal because that's an environment that you know well, so you can easily imagine it.

Me: Well, this is all very encouraging. Have you ever encountered people who aren't normal? People who have taken these things too far?

Dr: Oh yes. You have people who have seen their health fade, whose personal relations have broken down, who haven't been able to break away long enough to do work. But these are extremes. There are always going to be some people who struggle with addiction, but that's the same with any kind of stimulus.

Me: Isn't it worrying that there are so many similarities between Football Manager addiction and, say, alcohol addiction?

Dr: Addiction is addiction.

Me: So my 'addiction' to Football Manager is actually a genuine, 20-year addiction?

Dr: Yes.

Me: Wow... I think that's actually longer than Eric Clapton did cocaine.

Dr: The health risks aren't as great with Football Manager.

Me: Someone should have mentioned that to Clapton.

Dr: It's possible that his music may have suffered.

Me: [sings] Layla. You've got me on my knees, Layla. Distracted from friendlies, Layla. I'm begging, darling, for you to do my coaching routiiiiiines!

[SILENCE]

Dr: Please don't EVER do that again.

Me: Sorry.

Dr: [shudders] Anyway, anything like this, anything that you enjoy will get your endorphins flowing. That will amplify the positive feeling. It's all down to cognition; whatever you believe is a positive stimulus will have that effect. Your subconscious enjoys Football Manager, it enjoys winning, it enjoys the alternative reality that you create. This, for want of better phrase, is your drug.

Me: Gosh. So, is admitting that I have a problem the first step to recovery?

Dr: Is it a problem? Or is it just something you enjoy? Is it negatively impacting anything in your life?

Me: Well, sometimes my wife gets offended if she's watching a Jennifer Aniston movie and I play it on my laptop on the sofa next to her.

Dr: Well, you've got a problem.

Me: I have?

Dr: Yes, Jennifer Aniston movies are almost exclusively awful.

Me: It's not just me, is it?

Dr: Nope.

Me: Every film is the same. She's a gorgeous singleton who, for inexplicable reasons, just cannot find a man and she has a friend who is also gorgeous, but in a less obvious way, and she is mostly there to make sardonic jokes. Then she meets someone who is *absolutely* unsuitable for her and they have arguments that become increasingly heated until something draws them together and they kiss, only swiftly to jeopardise the whole affair on a point of principle before a race against time brings them together forever.

Dr: I've actually got real work to do, you know.

Me: Sorry.

Dr: So, Football Manager isn't causing you any real problems? You play it up until a certain point and then you stop playing it?

Me: Yes. But sometimes that certain point is 1am and I'm up again at 6am.

Dr: Well, you know what you can and can't do. I take it that you haven't failed to get up at 6am, that you haven't failed to do what you've had to do the next day?

Me: No. I've just been a bit tired.

Dr: Well, that's fine. The point is that you're still doing what you need to do. In fact, your brain might be thinking, "I had lots of fun last night playing Football Manager, now let's do some work."

Me: It usually tells me to make a cup of tea and bacon sandwich first, but yes, I see your point.

Dr: That's fine as well. If you cut the fat off.

Me: That's a good tip. So basically, if it's not a problem, it's not a problem?

Dr: Essentially, yes. I mean, if you're denying it to yourself and it is a problem, if you're not meeting people, if you're not eating properly, if you're not doing any work, then it's a different matter, but this isn't the case, is it?

Me: No! This is wonderful news. I feel like I've had a great weight lifted off my shoulders!

Dr: I'm happy to have helped. You know,

games are often demonised, especially the violent ones, but that's not fair. We know what they're about, gamers know what they're about. You do what you must to progress in the game.

Me: What is it that sends some people to fighty games and some people to football games? Why do some people want to slay a dragon, while others just want to win a pretend trophy?

Dr: All games are about play. We don't stop playing at the age of 12. Play is integral to psychology. It lets you rehearse, it gives you enjoyment, it lets you do things you wouldn't ordinarily do. Video games are extensions of stories.

Me: But what is it that attracts some people to fighting a dragon and some people to a statistic-loaded football database that is essentially an exercise in human resources? Surely we'd all rather fight a dragon?

Dr: Would you?

Me: Well, yes.

Dr: I wouldn't, I'd rather coach a football team. It's safer.

Me: Not if it's Millwall. What I'm trying to say is, are there certain personality types that will be drawn to Football Manager?

Dr: No, I wouldn't say so. I've done some research on this and personality types don't necessarily pick specific games. There's more of a relationship with their personality and how they play the game. Do they use melee weapons or spells, are they reckless drivers or careful drivers? These traits can correlate with personality. How that relationship manifests itself is completely random. Some cautious people are reckless in games, some reckless people, like you, are cautious. It's possible that you're living up to an ideal that perhaps you can't achieve in real life.

Me: Woah. That's pretty deep.

Dr: That's what I do.

Me: So, to recap: I play Football Manager because I like it and my subconscious likes it. I'm cautious because that's what my subconscious believes is the best way to prosper and therefore how I'll like it more. I hold press conferences in my head because it adds to the enjoyment and the best bit, it's not a problem because it's not a problem. My life is still very much intact.

Dr: Precisely.

Me: Well, that's great. Now, can you do me a favour? Can you call my wife and tell her everything you've just told me?

Dr: Get out.

This is an extract from the book Football Manager Stole My Life, *by Iain Macintosh, Kenny Millar and Neil White, published by BackPage Press*

The Far Corner

How football in the north-east of Brazil struggles to keep up with the giants of the south

By James Young

On summer afternoons in the Brazilian *nordeste* temperatures rarely dip below 35 degrees. Some think such heat too intense for football. Others say days like that, when the temperature in the middle of a big standing crowd seems to rise another five or ten degrees, are perfect. Shirts stick to wet backs, the heat rises with the ebb and flow of the game and the aromas of the grilled cheese on the barbecues and the peanuts on the braziers mingle with the smoke from the firecrackers. Flags and ticker-tape and the green of the pitch and the players' shirts all look brighter — and better — against a blue sky, too.

In Recife — a sprawling, chaotic city of close on four million people (in the *nordeste* Recife trails only Salvador in size) — on just such a sweltering Saturday in November 2005, Santa Cruz defeated Portuguesa from São Paulo by two goals to one. The official crowd at Arruda was given as 60,000, though most observers put it at 70,000 or higher. The result, the last in Serie B that year, clinched Santa's promotion, making them the first team from the state of Pernambuco to play in the first division since 2001. The game took place on the same day that Gremio won the infamous 'Battle of Aflitos', also in Recife, beating the home side Nautico 1-0 (Anderson, now at Manchester United, scored the winner) to clinch their own promotion, with Nautico missing two penalties and Gremio finishing the game with seven players.

But Santa barely lasted a year in Serie A, a memorable run of victories over Flamengo, Corinthians (boasting Tevéz, Mascherano and Nilmar) and Fortaleza being the only bright spot in a miserable campaign. The year after that, in Serie B again, the team flirted with the promotion spots for a few months before going into a tailspin, and by the end of 2007 they were relegated to Serie C for the first time in their history.

Worse was to come in 2008 — the Brazilian third division's convoluted regional group system (planned for economic reasons; to ask generally impoverished teams to travel halfway across such a huge country 19 times a year for away games would be impossible) meant that after hobbling through the first phase Santa were eliminated in the next (losing to such obscure opposition as Icasa and Potiguar, and failing to beat their state rivals from the vast, and largely empty, interior, Salgueiro) and relegated for the third time in three years, this time to the newly created Serie D.

Fiercely contested local disputes take place in each of Brazil's 28 states prior to the start of the national championship, and things weren't much better in the Pernambuco state championship that year. Santa were left trailing not only their big city rivals Sport and Nautico but also several teams from small towns in the backlands — in fact, things went so badly that in the second phase the team were placed outside the 'championship hexagonal' six-team group and floundered instead in the 'hexagonal of death' in which the only prize is avoiding relegation to the second rank of the *Pernambucano* — the equivalent of a parks league.

Other major teams in other countries have suffered declines, but Santa's demise is probably the most spectacular. And, like so many others, the constant throughout the club's collapse (aside from bad luck, bad management, lack of investment and players of questionable quality) has been the fierce loyalty of the fans. In 2010 and 2011 Santa, still mired in Serie D, pulled in the biggest average crowds in Brazil — around 35,000 per game.

It's a tale that resonates among supporters across Brazil's deprived norte and *nordeste* regions. From Belem at the mouth of the Amazon to Salvador on the Atlantic coast, *norte* and *nordestino* football is a story of squandered hopes and dreams. The love people in the region have for their teams is famous — local derbies in Salvador, Recife, Fortaleza and Belem can attract over 60,000 people and the average attendance of a number of sides can reach 40,000 in a successful year, which is more than many of the "Big 12" teams from Rio de Janeiro, the São Paulo region, Belo Horizonte and Porto Alegre. The *norte* and *nordeste* is an area that covers around 60% of Brazil's land mass and includes around 37% of its population, or approximately 65 million people.

Yet when Sport of Recife lifted the Copa Do Brasil in 2008 it was the first national trophy won by a team from the north or north-east of the country since Bahia won the national championship in 1988. Teams from the region struggle to survive for very long in the top flight of the *Brasileirão* — Fortaleza, Vitoria and Bahia have been relegated from Serie A in the last few years, although though both Náutico and Sport won promotion from Serie B last season; that may seem healthy but the prime objective of all three this season will be to avoid relegation. Of the six *nordestino* teams in Serie B in 2010, three were relegated.

Further down the league, the picture is no rosier. Of the seven *nordestino* teams in Serie B in 2011, two were relegated, while ASA, from Alagoas, survived by only a point. Remo and Paysandu (the two big teams from Belém), Bahia, Vitória, Santa and Náutico have spent time in Serie C in the last few years.

Remo, in particular, might be even worse off than Santa. Twice in the last four years the team that, according to local polls, boast over a million fans in the region, have failed to qualify for Serie D (achieved by finishing in one of the top positions in the respective state championship), meaning they did not play any competitive national league games. A spot in the bottom division was only achieved this year when little Cametá, the 2012 Pará state champions, gave up their place due to lack of funds.

Why should clubs with such popular support fail so consistently? Most obviously, teams from the region, more so even than most Brazilian football clubs, seem to enjoy shooting themselves in the foot — a constant merry-go-round of managers and players removes any hope of continuity or sustained growth, and behind the scenes frequent presidential elections and power struggles prevent any hope of stability.

As with much of Brazilian political life, corruption casts a long shadow and rumours of financial skulduggery in the boardroom are commonplace. Often it's more than just rumours: the Remo president Sergio Cabeca was recently sentenced to 16 years in prison for financial wrongdoing when in charge of a Belém educational organisation during the 1990s.

History plays a part. As well as huge fan bases in their home cities, the big teams from Rio de Janeiro and São Paulo claim nationwide support. The influence of early radio, and later television, broadcasting these teams' games, often to places with little organised football of their own, mythologised the great Flamengo, Vasco da Gama, Palmeiras and Corinthians teams of the past and ingrained their place in popular culture throughout Brazil. There are many sizeable states in the north and north east without a widely-supported local team — everyone there supports Flamengo, São Paulo or Fluminense. Even in the bigger football states of the region (Ceara, Pernambuco and Bahia), teams from the south-east enjoy wide popular support outside the metropolises.

Eduardo Campos, governor of Pernambuco, summed the situation up recently. "We know that football is an important part of our culture," he said. "In the interior, this means the presence of our supporters in the stadium. We need to bring this to the masses, because it reflects upon our own self-esteem. In the *nordeste*, only Pernambuco continues to mount strong resistance. We are in a trench, and we need to be an example with the growth and valorisation of local supporters supporting local teams."

Clubs from the region also face other problems. The political history of Brazil is the story of centuries of the abuse of power being slowly eroded by positive social change. Such a summation could apply equally well to Brazilian football — the first half of the phrase, anyway. Brazilian football is dominated by the previously mentioned São Paulo-Rio de Janeiro-Porto Alegre-Belo Horizonte axis, way down in the south and the south-east. Teams from these regions dominate the lists of title winners, national media coverage and, most importantly, money.

The infamous *Clube dos 13*, what began as a union of the 13 most powerful teams in Brazil now expanded to 20, for years divvied up the majority of TV and sponsorship money and shared it out largely among its own members. Common enough in the footballing world, except membership of the *Clube* was not based on league position, but by voting among existing members. And, as any expansion of the organisation would result in a smaller slice of the pie for member clubs, there was not usually much incentive to embrace newcomers.

São Paulo's Guarani, for example, a *Clube* member who spent 2008 in Serie C and 2009 in Serie B, earned around twice as much money from TV during these two years as Nautico, who spent the same two years in Serie A, but were not a *Clube* member[1].

Simple economic truth prevails. While Brazilian football as a whole has learnt to deal with the drain of the country's brightest talent to Europe (and today even to Japan and Arab countries), the *norte* and *nordeste* tries to cope with a different reality — that the region's best players go south to São Paulo or Rio first, often without even playing for a local team, and then on to other leagues (Hernanes of Lazio, is *recifense*, as are Rivaldo and Juninho Pernambucano, while Daniel Alves is from Salvador). Money from player sales is essential to the survival of every Brazilian club, whether *Clube Dos 13* members or not. And it is much rarer that a team from the *norte* or *nordeste* makes money from an overseas transfer deal than it is for, say, Cruzeiro or Internacional.

Regional financial inequality draws a line in thick black ink across the map of Brazilian football. Life in the *norte* and *nordeste* is often difficult — the region trails behind the rest of Brazil in every social and economic indicator — from per capita earnings to infant mortality and adult literacy levels — and its football teams are similarly impoverished. Clubs in São Paulo, the biggest and richest city in South America, can charge three or four times as much for tickets than can teams in Salvador or Recife, while local TV and sponsorship deals in the *nordeste* pay a fraction of what they might in the *sudeste*.

One of the reasons cited for the departure of the respected coach Nelsinho Baptista from Sport following the team's *Copa Do Brasil* triumph was that the wages of most of his proposed list of reinforcements for the coming season, many of whom were sitting on the substitute benches of teams from Rio de Janeiro and São Paulo, would have shattered the club's salary structure.

Over lunch in a restaurant tucked under the great grey bowl of Arruda, Sylvio Ferreira, advisor to Santa Cruz president Antonio Luiz Neto, tells me about some of the great *nordeste* teams of the past, such as the Bahia side that overcame Pelé's Santos to win the Brazilian title in 1959, and the Náutico team of 1967 that finished runners-up nationally and played in the Libertadores the following year. "The problem isn't as obvious as a simple lack of money," he says. "You don't necessarily need money to have a good team. But without money in the local economy, in the state, clubs can't sustain that success. Without money, success can only ever be ephemeral."

In 2009, fans of Santa Cruz had high hopes of an instant return to *Serie C*. But following a bright start, when they won 3-0 away at CSA (6,000 fans made the four-hour journey to Maceió), things quickly went awry. A 2-2 draw at home against the same opposition meant early elimination and another season in Serie D.

Yet the love of football runs deep in the region. Arguably those who suffer most

---

[1] *In 2011 the leading Brazilian clubs broke away from the Clube and negotiated their own TV deals. The long-term impact of this on clubs from the norte and nordeste remains to be seen.*

in the chaos are the fans and arguably the fans who suffer the most of all are the poor, of whom there are a great many in Recife, Salvador and beyond (37% of Salvador's population and 43% of Recife's live below the poverty line,). While a large part of the country's middle class has forsaken attending football matches, a result of fear of violence in the stadiums and easy access to pay-per-view live transmission, those with hardly the means to do so continue to do their best to fill the country's grounds.

In Recife, the state government has introduced the *Todos Com A Nota* programme, which allows anyone with a hundred *reais* of shopping receipts to claim a free ticket to a Sport, Nautico or Santa game (the programme, as well as protecting the area's footballing heritage, is a mixture of vote-winner and tax inspection scheme). As a result, the *Pernambucano* championship is Brazil's best supported regional tournament, pulling in around 9,000 people per game across the state, an impressive number when the size of some of the tiny towns in the interior is taken into account. The number of free tickets is limited, so plenty of tickets are sold in the normal way, but the scheme gives people who might not ordinarily be able to afford entry the chance to watch a game.

But when it comes to attendances the real story is Santa Cruz. The figures for 2011, the club's third successive season in Serie D, are remarkable. 60,000 watched the home leg of the *Pernambucano* final against Sport in May. A couple of months later, amid severe rainstorms and flooding, 16,000 followed the club to João Pessoa for their first

away game in *Serie D*. 45,000 showed up for the home *Serie D* opener against Guarani and 60,000 squeezed into Arruda for the decisive quarter-final against Treze of Paraiba. Santa's average league attendance this year was over 40,000, the highest in the country and the club is surely, by some distance, the world's best supported fourth-division side.

A central part of Santa's core support is the club's *torcida organizada*, the *Inferno Coral*. Much has been written and said in Brazil about the rise of the *torcidas organizadas* — in some ways a throwback to the hooliganism of British football in the 70s and 80s. This being Brazil, however, where violence is considerably more ingrained in society and guns are frighteningly easy to come by, things often become decidedly more bloody. There were 42 violent deaths inside Brazilian football stadiums between 1999 and 2009, and far more have died in football-related violence away from the grounds. *Torcidas organizadas* are often responsible for this — pitched battles are fought in the streets before *classicos*, dozens of city buses are destroyed and homemade bombs are smuggled into stadiums. And no Brazilian football season would be complete without at least one story of how *organizadas* have invaded the training ground of a struggling club, threatening or attacking the players and coach.

A major difference between the Brazilian *organizadas* and European hooligans is that in Brazil internecine rivalries (usually squabbles between neighbourhoods or gangs) mean that fighting among supporters of the same team is common. Before Sport played at Arruda in last year's

Pernambuco championship, one member of the *Inferno Coral* shot and killed another inside the group's headquarters. The local newspaper took advantage of the opportunity to publish an insider report into the murky underworld of the *organizadas*, complete with statistics about the percentage of members of *Inferno* who have been involved in violence, who use marijuana or sniff glue before games, who indulge in underage drinking and who rob and steal. It is a far from pretty picture.

But neither is it a complete picture. Unlike teams from the south and south-east (with the possible exception of Corinthians), the *torcidas organizadas* of teams from the north and north-east represent a huge percentage of the club's fan base — at any Santa game, for example, there are likely to be as many *Inferno* shirts on display as there are replica team strips. Including those who wear the organisation's colours but are not necessarily registered members, the *Inferno Coral* army can total between 10,000 and 15,000 for a big game. While some of these people, perhaps many, engage in violent and criminal activity, when looked at in the context of such numbers the percentage of troublemakers is not as great.

Samuel, Nel for short, is what many would consider a typical member of *Inferno Coral* — young, black and from the extremely poor, frequently dangerous neighbourhood of Coque. He is fiercely proud of his *recifense* roots, of being *tricolor* (Santa's colours are white, red and black), and most of all, of being *Inferno*. Now 32, he has been a member of the organisation since the age of 14,

when his brother took him to Arruda for the first time.

I meet him in a street corner bar in Recife's Beco da Fome, or Hunger Alley, on a Friday night. It has been a typical early summer day in Recife — temperatures hovering around a balmy 30 degrees, towering blue skies, white-tipped waves flickering out on the ocean. We drink beer and he introduces me to the other Inferno members sprawled around the table. With them is Diogo, a high ranking member of *Força Jovem Vasco*, up from Rio to press some flesh and firm up the bond between the Vasco and Santa *organizadas*. Everyone is wearing Inferno sleeveless shirts and baseball caps, and I wonder briefly if the sleeveless cut is designed best to show off bulging biceps and menacing tattoos.

Most of the people around the table are pleasant enough company. I ask Nel why he thinks young men like these feel the need to smash buses, to run onto football pitches, to fight with other young men they don't really know. Bright and articulate, he talks about the effects of growing up surrounded by poverty and violence. He tells me that he was often involved in skirmishes with both neighbourhood gangs and the police when he was a teenager and, once he discovered the *Inferno*, fighting with rival groups was a logical next step. Uncomplainingly, he describes his lack of opportunities — Brazil delivers only the most rudimentary of educations to people such as Nel, and university, and a decent job after it, is rarely an option. "If it had been," he says, "maybe I'd have had something else to focus on."

A voice from the end of the table mentions the group mentality — that you are with your mates, and when someone starts doing something, you follow them. *Adrenalina*, agrees Nel. The buzz. Everybody nods. It is a word that crops up a lot.

Like many such groups, there is a curious moral code at work. Violence is accepted as part of *organizada* life, but other forms of petty crime are frowned upon. Nel stresses firmly the organisation's commitment to rooting out criminality — Santa avoided punishment from the Brazilian football authorities a couple of years ago when an *Inferno* member ran on to the pitch during the game against CSA as Inferno leaders identified the culprit and then banned him from their headquarters and social events for six months. Nel has paid a heavy price for his attempts to civilize elements of *Inferno* — he shows me a scar above his right ear where he was stabbed after attempting to reason with one *Inferno* sect who had been attacking and robbing fellow *tricolores* after home games.

This demonstrates the greatest problem facing the members of *torcidas organizadas* who wish to bring some respectability to their groups—trying to find a way of controlling large groups of young men from underprivileged neighbourhoods who are extremely reluctant to recognise any kind of authority. Nel admits he has no idea, and says that of the 4,000 or so registered *Inferno Coral* members, he considers less than 500 to be 'core' members who take part in the decision-making processes, identify themselves completely with the ideals of the group and travel to every game no matter the distance. The rest, he says, shrugging,

just wear the shirt and make a lot of noise at home games.

2010 promised better for Santa. Lessons had been learned, everyone believed, and, boosted by the rambunctious performances of the striker Brasão (last seen at Vitória Setúbal in Portugal), the club did well enough in the Pernambucano, reaching the semi-finals before losing to Nautico. The first group stage of *Serie D* was negotiated successfully if not convincingly. That meant the little-known Guarany de Sobral, from the parched interior of Ceara, were next up.

On a sweltering August day Arruda heaved with 55,000 bodies for the first leg. Santa responded in traditional fashion, going 2-0 down inside 24 minutes, courtesy of two own goals from the hapless *zagueiro* Leandro Cardoso. A terrible silence settled over the big concrete bowl of the ground — could it be over again, so soon?

Not quite.

Santa roared back, scoring four without reply, with each goal, each attack, followed by huge, billowing roars from the crowd.

With the score at 4-2, Santa might justifiably have believed they had one foot in *Serie C*. But things are rarely so easy. Attention wandered towards the end and Guarany scored another away goal — one that would prove fatal.

A week later, 1000km away in the scorching heat of the northern backlands, Santa went down 2-0, leaving them to face their third successive year in *Serie D*.

I talk to Nel about what *Inferno Coral* means to its members and remember a night game I attended at Arruda a few years ago. The crowd was big and boisterous, and after Santa scored the winner an enormous flag was unfurled across the heads of the supporters. When fully open it stretched across a third of the huge upper deck of the stadium. "The biggest flag in the world, 175m by 45m", it says on the photo of the unfurled flag on the back of the *Inferno* membership card, though fans of Uruguay's Peñarol might beg to differ.

After the game that night I stood waiting to cross the road as an army of teenage *Inferno* members carried the flag into the group's headquarters. A full five minutes passed before the tail of the flag disappeared inside, and I remember wondering about the dedication of the boys (and the occasional girl) carrying the flag, and of the drummers who spend their Saturdays rehearsing and their Sundays at the game, pounding out hissing rhythms to accompany the chanting. It is clear that there is a tremendous sense of pride and of belonging felt by *Inferno* members — and for young men from disadvantaged neighbourhoods, often with absent fathers and with few positive role models, and without much hope of upward social mobility, any feelings of self-worth are welcome. There are few teenagers from Santa Amaro, to name just one of Recife's needier *bairros*, who are able to say they were once involved

with something which might feature in the record books.

We talk about the alliances between *organizadas* throughout Brazil — *Inferno* are allies with, among others, Bahia's *Bamor*, Palmeiras's *Mancha Verde*, *Força Jovem Vasco* and *Galoucora*. When the clubs of two allied *organizadas* play each other there is a great swapping of flags and T-shirts and often (as was the case in Maceio against CSA a couple of years ago) the two groups intermingle or carry each other's banners. And when one of the teams plays away it is obligatory for the allied *torcida organizadas* in that city to turn out in support. Of the few hundred people at Santa's recent Serie D semi-final against Cuiaba in Rondonopolis, Mato Grosso, 2000km from Recife, a couple of dozen or so were from the Rondonopolis branch of *Mancha Verde*, cheering on Santa.

We discuss the social projects that *organizadas* are involved in — Diogo tells me that *Galocoura* have set up more than 200 such projects, running from crèches to *muay thai* and *capoeira* classes and blood donation drives, and that many of these schemes are run in conjunction with the Minas Gerais state government, who recognise the social punch of the *organizadas*.

It grows late. Talk has ranged across subjects as diverse as the similarities in the origins of British and Brazilian football hooliganism, how the *organizadas* must change in what will probably be a very different Brazilian footballing landscape in the run up to the 2014 World Cup and when Santa might return to Serie A — if ever.

Towards the end of the evening I ask Nel if he has any friends in *Jovem Sport*, the *organizada* of Sport and *Inferno*'s hated rivals. He grimaces and admits that yes, he has one or two childhood friends who found themselves on the wrong path. We laugh. He points to another knife scar, this time above his left eye. "I got this one last year during the Sport v Goiás game," he tells me (*Força Jovem Goiás* are also *Inferno* allies). His eyes shine a little brighter and he leans forward in his seat, excited by the memory. His relish makes me feel a little uncomfortable, particularly given the knowledge that many young men have died in such circumstances (two Palmeiras supporters were killed early this year during a battle between *Mancha Verde* and *Gaviões da Fiel* in São Paulo).

Once again, I ask him why he does it. He shrugs. "Defending our territory," he says, "our honour." He gives me another example, this time from Santa's recent home game with Paysandu, whose *organizada* is allied to Náutico's *Fanáutico* gang. "We told Paysandu that if they came alone there'd be no trouble," he says, "but that if they came with *Fanáutico*, then it would kick-off." I ask him what happened, already knowing the answer. Another shrug. "It kicked off," says Nel, giving me a troublingly infectious grin.

Then it is time to pay the bill and go home.

This is a story with a happy ending. Following the disaster in Sobral, Santa hired a relatively unheralded coach for the 2011 *Pernambucano*. Zé Teodoro's CV is fairly standard among Brazilian football managers, boasting 21 clubs in 15 years, but he soon set about melding a group of youngsters and journeymen into some sort of a team.

The results were better than anyone could have hoped. São Paulo were defeated in the *Copa do Brasil* at a pulsating Arruda, with the 17-year-old local Everton Sena marking the highly-rated Lucas Moura out of the game. Their rivals Sport were beaten at Arruda and, remarkably, away at the Ilha do Retiro, where another youngster, Gilberto (since sold to Internacional) scored twice. Santa went on to win the *Pernambucano* title, their first in six years, beating Sport in the two-legged final.

But while the win against São Paulo, and even the *Pernambucano* triumph, were nice enough, the real focus was *Serie D* and a return to some kind of national respectability. With Gilberto gone, the team suddenly forgot how to score goals and the short *Serie D* season, in which elimination could come after only eight first-round group games, is no place to tinker.

Still, despite managing just 10 goals, Santa scraped painfully through their group, courtesy of a nerve-wracking final-day victory against Alecrim. Tiny Coruripe, from the neighbouring state of Alagoas, were next, and again Santa did barely enough, winning 1-0 at home before hanging on grimly for a 0-0 in the second leg.

All this meant the team were 180 minutes from *Serie C*, exactly as they had been the year before. And after 45 of those minutes it seems that the only thing that had changed in 12 months was the name of the opposition. Away in

João Pessoa, Treze quickly went 2-0 up, and were bossing the game. Santa heads dropped — the failure of the past is a heavy burden to carry.

Hope blossomed briefly when the Treze keeper Lopes tossed a Thiago Cunha potshot into his own goal, though Tigrão made it 3-1 soon after.

But the Santa of 2011 were a more resourceful bunch than in previous years. The team dug deep and two goals from Fernando Gaucho completed an unlikely comeback.

Needing just a home draw to go through, Santa lived on the edge at Arruda the following Sunday. The home team were dominant, but Treze, needing just a goal, looked dangerous on the counter-attack. 60,000 chewed their finger nails in the stands. Finally, with the score at 0-0, and after what seemed like a decade of injury time, the referee Marcelo de Lima Henrique blew his whistle for full-time and Santa could finally say *adeus* to *Serie D*, having taken one small step back on the road to redemption.

So for Santa Cruz, at least, 2011 was a good year. 2012 has gone pretty well too, with the *Pernambucano* retained after another triumph over Sport and a solid if unspectacular start to *Serie C*. As the Brasileirão season winds on, huge crowds will once again fill Arruda and transistor radios across the city will pour out the news of the game on Sunday afternoons. The *Inferno Coral* will be there, beating their drums and belting

out their ferocious chants. There will probably be windows broken and buses smashed, too, and young men arrested, and bloodied pavements, and this is something Nel and other *organizada* leaders must address, just as Brazil must address the violence that is rife throughout its society.

2011 was also a good year for Náutico and Sport, who made it back to *Serie A*. Alongside Bahia, they will try and hang on to their top flight status in 2012, while in *Serie B*, Vitória, Ceará and a clutch of other *nordestino* clubs dream of promotion. Fortaleza and Paysandu remain mired in *Serie C* and poor old Remo will be happy to have at least qualified for *Serie D*.

In the long-term things are looking up for the *nordeste* and *norte* of Brazil. The former president Lula is a *nordestino* (though, unforgivably, also a *Corintiano*), and did a great deal for Brazil's needier regions. Improved social welfare programmes and an increased minimum wage have meant a better quality of life for more and more of Brazil's poor. Public and private investment in the area has increased dramatically. This greater affluence is bound to be reflected in the financial fortunes of the region's football clubs, although parity with the *sul* and *sudeste* is a long way off. And until it comes, all there is to do for Santa and Remo and Paysandu and Bahia and Náutico and all the other clubs of the *norte* and *nordeste* of Brazil, is to keep going. It may be a vainglorious pursuit, but it is a pursuit. Ⓑ

143

Polemics

"The whole purpose is to consolidate
the link between a community and
its local team..."

Care for the Community

Could a radical rejig of television schedules help create a greater bond between clubs and their fans?

By Gabriele Marcotti

The path to fandom used to be pretty straightforward. An older family member — usually a father or grandfather, sometimes a sibling or uncle — took you to watch your local team. You were smitten and the addiction began. You went as often as you could, you read up on whatever there was to read about your team. When you were old enough, you started going with your friends. If you moved away, whether for work or study, you always caught the result in the papers and, when you were home for the holidays, you caught a game.

That was the blueprint for many years and it worked. It steadily churned out generation after generation of fan who knew and understood the game primarily as a live event. Anything on top of that was special occasion stuff delivered via television: FA Cup finals, World Cups, Match of the Day. It didn't really matter if your team was on or not, you watched because it was football and you liked the sport, but you were under no illusion: supporting your team was different and you lived your fandom in a different way.

Times have changed. For most, the introduction to football is via television and the internet. That's where you fall in love, that's where you become a fan. And even if are a young kid who is lucky enough to have a family member with the time and finances to take you to watch your local team, consider the circumstances and the competition.

You're ten years old, Dad takes you to the City Ground to watch Nottingham Forest, say, 20 times a year (most Saturdays, plus the odd FA Cup tie, but not in midweek, since you have school the next day). Beyond that, apart from Dad telling you about how they got on in their away matches, brief highlights on TV, consulting the league table every Sunday and maybe conversations with a couple Forest-supporting mates at school, this is pretty much the extent of Forest in your life.

Meanwhile, Manchester United are on the box — between league, European and cup fixtures — once or twice a week. Every week. Their players show up on Sky Sports News. The club are all over the papers. Everybody at school, regardless who they support, has an opinion on Wayne Rooney. Oh, and they're very good. Much better, in fact, than Forest.

Might you turn your back on your local club in exchange for membership of the Red Empire? Possibly... and that's with the cards stacked in favour of you being a Forest fan. Most kids don't have the privilege of football with Dad on

Saturdays. And yet they still have the lure of faraway clubs served up via television.

Some will argue that the only way to turn the tide is to rethink the way football revenue — especially TV money — is shared. They'll talk about levelling the playing field, giving everyone an equal slice and introducing salary caps to banish the Roman Abramoviches and Sheikh Mansours. That way, everyone will have a shot at winning, success will be shared around and, with it, so will fandom.

Well, this isn't about that. The harsh reality is that the ship has sailed on that front. The Premier League isn't going away any time soon and, for that matter, neither is the Champions' League. And, besides, the distribution of domestic TV money in England is already very equitable, at least in the top flight.

But there is another way. Television may have made life more difficult for those who believe in, above all, supporting their local club. Why watch Scunthorpe every other week when you can watch United just about EVERY week?

But what if football rethought its relationship with TV? What if you could come up with a plan that would, at once, revitalise local support, help smaller clubs market themselves better, boost attendances and, yes, increase the size of the pie for everyone? What follows is a modest proposal inspired by the NFL's approach to TV in the United States. It's a strategy that requires tweaks, sacrifices, cooperation between the Premier League and Football League and, perhaps, a leap of faith. But, hopefully, one worth exploring.

The first thing you do is get rid of the TV blackout rule, the one which prevents broadcasters from showing live football between 2.45pm and 5.15pm on Saturdays. It's a stupid anachronism dating back to the time when folks believed that televised football was a substitute for going to games. It's meant to protect attendances but, in fact, it does no such thing. It assumes that if you're a Liverpool fan in, say, Huddersfield, you'll watch the Reds at 12.45 pm on Sky and then set off for the Galpharm. In fact, you'll probably do no such thing. You'll pick one or the other.

Instead, divide up the weekend into nine "slots": 7.45pm on Friday, noon, 2pm, 4pm and 6pm on Saturday, noon, 2pm and 4pm on Sunday and 8pm on Monday. The Friday night game is reserved for a "Game of the Week" from the Championship. Sunday at 4pm, as is the case now, is for the pick of the Premier League games, as is the Monday night slot.

The other six time slots are reserved for local games to be shown on a regional basis. (For convenience, I'm referring to TV throughout this article but, in fact, the football would also be shown via the web but, again, using IP addresses and geo-location, with strict regional limitations.) For example, let's say you're in Rotherham. Here's what your weekend lineup might look like:

Friday, 7.45pm: Cardiff v Bolton (Championship Game of the Week)
Saturday, noon: Sheffield Wednesday v Brighton (local game)
Saturday, 2pm: Bury v Doncaster Rovers (local game)
Saturday 4pm: Rotherham v Aldershot

(local game)
Saturday 6pm: Derby County v Barnsley
(local game)
Sunday, noon: Chesterfield v Torquay
(local game)
Sunday, 2pm: Carlisle v Sheffield United
(local game)
Sunday, 4pm: Arsenal v Tottenham
(Super Sunday)
Monday, 8pm: Newcastle v Everton
(Monday Night Football)

And if you're in Portsmouth?

Friday, 7.45pm: Cardiff v Bolton
(Championship Game of the Week)
Saturday, noon: Sheffield Wednesday v
Brighton (local game)
Saturday, 2pm: Portsmouth v Oldham
(local game)
Saturday 4pm: Rotherham v Aldershot
(local game)
Saturday 6pm: Bournemouth v Walsall
(local game)
Sunday, noon: Southampton v Chelsea
(local game)
Sunday, 2pm: Leyton Orient v Crawley
(local game)
Sunday, 4pm: Arsenal v Tottenham
(Super Sunday)
Monday, 8pm: Newcastle v Everton
(Monday Night Football)

I could go on, but you get the picture. And I know what you're saying: if my local club are on TV, won't it kill attendances? Why would somebody march down to their local ground when they can watch their club from the comfort of their front room or, better yet, their local pub?

Well, here's the twist. For a game to be shown locally on TV it needs to be either an away match or, a home game that

sells out or, at the very least, reaches some prearranged attendance goal. Ideally, only sellouts would be on TV but, in practice, at some grounds, that's very difficult to do. Hillsborough has a capacity of 39,372, Sheffield Wednesday averaged 21,336 last season. Expecting them to sell out is a big ask. So you set an attendance goal of, say, 30,000. If they can hit that, they're on TV.

Doing it this way creates a virtuous cycle. Clubs would only get TV money if their home games are actually on TV. This would create an incentive for them to boost attendance which, in turn, would lead to better marketing of games and, above all, lower ticket prices. With extra TV revenue coming in, clubs could make games more affordable, especially for kids, without losing money. (Obviously it would take some tweaking to get the balance right, but it's a goal worth pursuing.) What's more, if a game hits its target and makes it on TV, it will be the only English game on TV at that time in that region.

There will be no competition except for foreign football (this isn't North Korea; you can't ban other broadcasters from showing overseas game). And if the game doesn't sell out, there will be no English football on TV in that time slot. So if you want to see it, you need to rock up to the box office.

Think for a minute what this would do. Increased attendance means more bums on seats, including young ones, who might not otherwise have gone. Packed stadiums also provide a better atmosphere which, in turn, provides more entertainment, both for those at the game and those watching at home. It also provides more and better sponsorship opportunities, which, in turn, means more revenue for the club.

Furthermore, you open up a whole new world of local commercial opportunities. A chain of curry houses in Sheffield won't want to advertise on Sky because most of those viewing won't ever set foot in Sheffield. But if they could advertise on a local broadcast of a Sheffield United or Rotherham game they'd be reaching a targeted audience of potential customers. Replicate this throughout the country and you could probably earn even more commercial income on aggregate than that raised from national advertising today.

What's more, a young Rotherham fan would know that every single one of his team's away matches would be on TV. And, when Rotherham are at home, he would always have the option of seeing them in person, or, if they sell out, on TV. What better way to build loyalty to a club?

But it's not just about maximising revenues, TV audience and bums on seats. There's a whole load of potential in having away games locally televised particularly for mid- to smaller-sized teams. You could gather fans together on match-days to watch together at churches, community halls or even the football ground itself on a big screen.

Obviously, different-sized clubs might do this in different ways. A Premier League or Championship side might host fans at the stadium and show the game on the big screen: charge a quid to get in, and make money by selling food, drinks and merchandise (ideally at non-matchday

prices)... after all, what else are you going to do with your stadium when the team are away from home? A League 2 side might rent a smaller venue, maybe different types of venues for different sets of fans: a kids' venue with face-painting and pizza, one for twentysomethings with lots of booze, a more laidback place for the older folks.

Imagine the excitement a young kid might feel every other week, when he goes with his friends — all kitted out — to the local community hall to watch his local club. If clubs were clever about it, they could maybe mix in retired stars or players recovering from injury or local celebs. Sure, it's another potential revenue stream, but it's not really about that as much as it is transforming following your team into a ritual. One week in person, the next with other fans on TV. Either way, it becomes an event of the kind that is not just entertaining but also captures the hearts and minds of young supporters. Sure, I can watch United on TV all the time, but can that match the excitement of following every minute of Rotherham's season with fellow Rotherham fans right here in Rotherham?

The whole purpose is to consolidate the link between a community and its local team and there are plenty ways to do it. When you stop and think about it, right now, clubs are wasting 50% of their output — their away matches — and getting nothing in return in terms of marketing their product. They're not on TV, except for a handful of travelling fans or a few minutes' worth of highlights, nobody gets to see any of it. Not to mention older fans, less well-off fans and those too young to go to home games: they too are denied their local club.

Right about this time I expect someone to pipe up and talk about local radio and the wonderful intimacy of the medium and how supporters can enjoy every match that way. I love radio myself, heck, I even work in radio sometimes. But let's not kid ourselves. You try persuading a 10 year old to sit and listen to radio commentary for two hours.

Especially when the alternative is actually watching the game. I'm told there's a whole generation of cricket fans who would rather listen to Test Match Special on long wave than actually see the game on TV. That's fine. That's cricket. This is football. And I simply don't see entire communities of people gathering around the wireless to cheer on their side away from home.

How about the counterarguments?

We'd lose the sanctity of the 3pm kick-offs. Fine. English football is, rightly, proud of its traditions. But the game has already grown and evolved. We've lost the "sanctity" of terracing in top flight football, we've lost the "sanctity" of shirts numbered 1 to 11. We've lost the "sanctity" of having just three subs on the bench (and, before that, two subs and one sub and no subs). The game grows and evolves — some of these "traditions" are worthwhile, others are just customs. We can grow accustomed to different ones. And if it means strengthening the bond of local football, with younger fans learning that, first and foremost, you support your local team, then it's worthwhile.

This could hurt travelling support. After all, if Rotherham are on TV, why should I make that six-hour round trip across the country to watch them play? Well, the harsh reality is that travelling supporters make up a tiny percentage of football fans. Sure, these are often the liveliest, most passionate fans. But they're also a privileged subset who can afford — both financially and in terms of time commitments — to go watch their team home and away. And, besides, TV is not a substitute for actually going to a game. If they're passionate fans, they'll still go. Just as supporters still go to away games in the Premier League, even when they're on TV.

Logistically and technologically it would be a nightmare, far too difficult to pull off. Actually, it wouldn't be. Every Premier League and Football League game is already filmed every week. Sure, not every game has 20 cameras like on Super Sunday. But you don't need 20 cameras at every match. Nor do you need stellar production values. If the option is either watching it filmed with just seven cameras or not watching it at all, it's not much of a choice is it? Besides, the costs of TV production shrink every year as technology advances. Sure, the fixture list would take some work. But that's what they have computers for. It's not the most complicated algorithm in the history of humanity. Put in the parameters and see what the machine spits out. Equally, regionalising the games is technologically rather straightforward. Ever notice how, if you're from, say, Sunderland and you move to London with your Sky receiver and smartcard you'll still get the local news from the North East until you tell Sky that you've actually moved and have a new address? That's because Sky sends you regional programming based on your post code. And, based on that, it would be a breeze for them to send you regional football matches as well. The same goes for geo-location and IP addresses.

The Premier League would never go for it. There would be fewer games on national television and, therefore, less TV revenue for everyone. Not necessarily. Sure, we'd go from four or five nationally televised games a week down to two. But so what? Every single game would be on TV somewhere. And the numbers would work out. Take Manchester United, the most extreme example since they are the biggest televised draw and they are on TV more than any other club. Last season, they were on 29 times. Under this plan, the number of national TV appearances might fall to, say, 14. Which, obviously, would be a blow in terms of audience. But that would be mitigated by the fact that all 38 of their games (assuming they always sell out, which they do) would be on live in the Manchester region. Plus, the fact that they sell out whenever they're on the road means they'd be on TV in every region they're visiting as well. United's total aggregate TV audience might fall slightly. But the vast majority of Premier League clubs and every single club in the Football League would see their aggregate TV audience skyrocket. And, overall, that translates to more viewers and a more valuable TV contract.

Sure, there are other issues that would need to be resolved. For example, you would need to figure out how to sell the TV rights packages and how to split them among the various broadcasters.

But that can be done. You also have the issue of several regions — London comes to mind — in which there are more than six league clubs. Doing it strictly by postcode and providing access to the six nearest teams by radius might penalise certain clubs. Geography doesn't always help.

And what of those clubs that are isolated? Bournemouth might be one of these six league clubs closest to Plymouth, but does it really make sense to screen their games there? Here, you could use some common sense. Maybe, when one of the six nearest clubs is more than 75 miles away, you don't fill all six slots. Maybe you just show another game that happens to be on at that time but which might draw some interest (a rival from the same division, perhaps). Common sense should prevail, sometimes fan bases don't always follow geography. But what you don't do is show Manchester United everywhere simply because they have more supporters.

It's easy to get bogged down in detail. But the key message remains: television is the ultimate marketing tool when it comes to football. And for most clubs, crazy as it sounds, it's actually underused. If done correctly and intelligently, a plan like this can ensure that one of England's greatest sporting treasures — the visceral attachment to local clubs that still exists away from the Premier League — is maintained through the next few generations even as the pressure to go the other way and simply back a "big club" becomes ever greater.

Location, Location, Location

Which is more important? How it looks or where a stadium is?

By Tom Dart

Strong chance he'd arch his eyebrows at the sight of folk in the parking lots grilling meat and sinking beers at the back of their pick-up trucks. But if LS Lowry were still alive, still painting, still a fan, he'd find going to the match a more familiar experience in Houston than Bolton.

It's the location of Houston Dynamo's new stadium. In the industrial East End, just a couple of blocks from the core of downtown, between an elevated freeway and railroad tracks, amid stiff grids of streets named for Texas heroes.

There is nascent gentrification. Mostly there is urban density and decay, warehouses and factories that don't let on whether they've been shut for years or are in business right now. Poor people. Pubs. A music venue. A scene that's a bit shabby, a bit shambolic, but organic and distinctive.

And from all directions, people walking to the match: noise, colour, anticipation, the kinship of a crowd of strangers. Buying beers from stalls, listening to bands and drinking in the street.

There are no cars in "Going to the Match", the Lancastrian artist's 1953 portrait of Bolton Wanderers' former home, Burnden Park. Everyone is walking. In the painting, as in Houston, people and buildings dominate the working-class landscape immediately surrounding the stadium.

Understand that this is not normal in Houston, this characterful and compact mass of pedestrians filling old city streets. Houston is a hymn to convenience and consumption, money and motor vehicles, the epic scale of Texas, the suburban American dream and the conviction that if plenty should sometimes tip over into excess, well, so what? That's our choice and our birthright.

We're not in 1950s England. It's sunny and sweaty-humid almost all season long. Most people drive to Dynamo games in big cars. The arena's naming rights were bought by a Spanish bank, its footprint and adjacent new apartments are as fresh, slick and precisely landscaped as the hair of a teen pop idol. The place has a giant video screen, an adidas store and lots of corporate seats.

At BBVA Compass Stadium it's the skyscraping headquarters of multinational energy companies you can see in the distance, not smoke stacks and chimneys. The colour scheme is so orange that doctors could prescribe visits to cure patients deficient in vitamin C.

Yet the experience feels old-European as well as modern-Texan. Thanks to its location this new-born stadium already has life and soul to add to its architectural elegance and flair. Even a short saunter from wherever you've parked will engage you visually, viscerally, with your surroundings. It will provoke reactions.

The site amply justifies the club's decision not to break ground in the suburbs amid one of the myriad outlet malls or generic housing estates, glossy and manicured as a model's fingernails. The Dynamo now feel like an immutable and storied thread of the city's fabric, yet they moved to Houston from San Jose in 2006.

"We were adamant about being downtown. We had opportunities to get [the stadium] built in the suburbs, probably via public money and it would probably have happened sooner, but we felt very strongly that we had to be a downtown location so we held out for that, and it's worked out perfectly," Chris Canetti, the Dynamo president of business operations, told me in May. "It's made us very relevant, it's made us very cool."

In time, the stadium will blend into its surroundings, encouraging attention, investment and regeneration, a rebirth of the East End. And whether that makes the rich richer or is truly a boon for everyone — well, that's up to the good people of Houston. But today, the team have brought hope and pride and publicity, and that seems like more than enough.

Houston's rivals, FC Dallas, do not play in Dallas. They are based in the nearby commuter city of Frisco. They are 28 miles north of downtown, just off a

highway, the stadium encircled by car parks, arterial roads and strip malls.

Bolton do not play in Bolton. In 1997 they moved from Burnden Park — a mile from the town centre, their home for more than a hundred years — to the Reebok Stadium in Horwich, five miles west. By a motorway, surrounded by car parks and shopping centres filled with the usual chain stores. It's the showpiece of a sports and leisure complex - misleading name, that, because life for the customer is simple.

The Reebok Stadium is really very good. It's just that it was built smack in the middle of a place called Anywhere. It is a homage to American car-friendly consumerism, Burnden Park to retail park. On any given Saturday you might be going to the match, or the mall, or the cinema, or the fast-food outlets. Or all of the above. Attending the football is one of a range of competing and comparable on-site entertainment options. Going to the match is like going shopping; what was once a ritualistic act of faith is now a conscious capitalist choice.

This way of life has some logic in the United States, where there is vast space and sports teams are bottom-line focused franchises that can be dismantled like flat-pack furniture and rebuilt thousands of miles away, leaving only hollow memories of their once-solid presence, like the impression of chair legs on a carpet.

It generally ensures high standards and competitiveness. It's discordant with the back-story of English football, where clubs sprang naturally from local communities long ago and were not just in their towns, but of them. These days, though, the English professional game is becoming a suburban pursuit, leagues of Reeboks.

Some 25 of the 92 clubs presently in England's top four divisions play in stadiums built since 1996, the first year of Major League Soccer. In all but five cases, the club has moved farther away from its town's centre.

There are good reasons for this, such as cost, logistics, the difficulty of finding suitable central land and the challenges of renovating existing grounds. Tottenham Hotspur were recently tempted to relocate to Enfield, near the M25, given the hassle of rebuilding White Hart Lane. Whatever the causes, it's a trend that changes a matchday's tone.

Coming in, you're not elbow-to-elbow with other fans, overhearing or engaging with them, smelling their food and the beer on their breath; you're isolated and sedate in a personal steel-and-glass bubble, sitting in traffic, listening to radio phone-ins in which supporters from across the nation bore you with the story of their day. You arrive and leave vacuum-packed.

The atmosphere is different, less intense, perhaps because opposing fans seem more like shoppers than invaders who've breached the city walls. And they've got their own car park, anyway. Might not even see them.

The club isn't your neighbour, as it would be if you lived around the corner. No matter how much it may matter to its fans, it's hard to see how a football team can be at the heart of its community if its

premises are on the outskirts. Or how it can reflect much beyond the neon glare of the adjacent Burger King.

Colchester United, Northampton Town, Stoke City, Swansea City: outsiders have to take a detour to visit the town. If you're looking for the stadium and come across something interesting, you've got lost.

It seems as if no club in England these days can build a stadium without the muscle of a major supermarket chain who use the emotional clout of football as a Trojan horse to win planning permission and part-fund the project. So it's not a shock that many new grounds are functional boxes that don't look much different from supermarkets.

With little incentive to be original they are often as bland as their surroundings. And what's chiefly being improved and regenerated: wasteland or the bank balances of landowners and property developers?

New, clean, standardised and sterilised, these arenas suit football's growing sense of itself as a family entertainment product. This seems to owe much to the high production values of the American major leagues, where sport is a spectacle, slickly marketed and brand aware, doing as much as it can to provide reliable fun around the inherently variable quality of the actual matches.

But England's present and future is already America's past. While England is copying the suburban American sporting model, city-centre venues are experiencing a renaissance in the US: attractive and highly-visible redevelopment catalysts that ensure downtowns remain a hub of activity after office hours.

In Major League Baseball, the opening of Oriole Park at Camden Yards in Baltimore in 1992 presaged the construction of many other charming, downtown, "retro" ballparks — there is one near the Dynamo's stadium — bringing to a close the "cookie-cutter" era of near-identical out-of-town, concrete, multi-purpose venues.

In MLS, which began by building or borrowing cheap out-of-town arenas, three downtown venues have opened since last year. Six of 18 stadiums are central. Despite the presence of the New York Red Bulls just across the water in New Jersey, MLS is obsessively pursuing the dream of a club in the most famous urban area on the planet, New York City. Imagine the attention, the energy, the credibility. All being enjoyed by the Nets basketball team, which has moved to hip Brooklyn from boring Newark.

England's new palaces primarily cater not to the traditions, history and geography of their clubs but to the affluence and mobility of the modern consumer. That physical location is now a matter of pragmatism not roots, choice not heritage, tallies with the philosophical shift prompted by the game's on-going globalisation.

Attending matches is no longer a prerequisite for serious fandom. Distant supporters identify with players, managers and victories, not buildings they will never visit.

What difference does a few miles make in a stadium's location in an era when

Manchester United might have more fans in Shanghai than Salford and a foreign supporter who logs on religiously to arsenal.com can consider himself as much a loyalist as a season-ticket holder? In which Fifa have polished and regulated their World Cup product so much and so well that the tournament is essentially portable and almost flavourless for spectators, as if each stadium was encased by a giant Truman Show-style dome and flown to the host country every four years?

In this context, a stadium's immediate surroundings are no longer significant. It's the inside that counts. Not because of ticket income, now dwarfed in the Barclays Premier League by television money. But it's still important that the stands are full and smart and orderly, so that the TV pictures look good. A stadium is no longer a traditional gathering place, a locus of civic pride and identity. It's a film set.

Fans are wallpaper, unlike in MLS, where broadcasting rights are paltry and wooing local people is critical to a team's prosperity. An urban venue such as Houston's is sound business sense and a symbolic act: football right in the middle of town, and for everyone, not only the SUV-driving suburban families of stereotype. The location and architecture engages where other arenas detach and prove that with effort and originality it's still possible to build an iconic football ground.

In Lowry's work, Burnden Park gives downtrodden factory workers a feeling of purpose, belonging and escape. What are most modern stadiums giving the community, other than excellent views of the action, clean toilets and a wide choice of food?

In England the smaller clubs trade quirks for functionality and lose part of what makes them distinctive. The top clubs increasingly see themselves as citizens of the world, their stadiums as the headquarters of global companies with multi-national workforces.

The balance between the local and international, the new and the old, the unique and the generic, is tense and strange. It's the recipe for an identity crisis, this strategy of dislocation, dislocation, dislocation.

156

Fiction

""Your father was a wizard at the dominoes," he had remarked gravely. "What are you good at, John?"

The Limping God

His football career ended by injury, John Brodie's life is going nowhere until he is sucked into the world of crime.

By David Ashton

I woke up with a mouth like a dead budgie. The skylight window let in a little pale light streaked with falling rain — this was Greenock after all. I could still taste the whisky from last night.

A cheap whisky. Fitted me to a T. Yessir, I was growing cheaper by the day and looking forward to my first signing on at the Buroo. Joining the long line of chancers to grace the windswept corner where they gathered in a shamefaced, barefaced clump.

My father pointed them out to me once. "See ye never end up there," he said, but he was dead now; soon after my mother, both of them martyrs — one to the Wild Woodbine, the other to Capstan Extra Strength.

I levered myself up, winced as I put inadvertent weight on a fragile ankle bone and then my eye was caught by a picture in a frame on the small rickety table that stood by my single bed.

A young boy in a football strip. Face alive, full of hope, black-and-white or you would have seen the blue-and-white hoops. Greenock Morton. Not that I ever played for them but a trial was on the cards; John Brodie, left-sided, cutting down the wing for the Juniors. I could run, oh I could run like the wind, but now I just broke it.

What was the name of that full-back? Tommy Boag, Bellahouston. He wasn't about to be diddled by some skinamalinkie kid. So he put the boot in. Hard. I don't suppose it was his intention to destroy my ankle but when the bone stuck through the sock like a graveyard relic, it was no longer a matter of intent.

Some of the other players spewed up at the sight but Boag looked down with a face like stone. "I warned ye," he said. I didn't remember the warning; it must have been during the kick-in. I was 17.

I still wore pyjamas, which I counted as a remnant of civilisation, not yet the scabby y-fronts, the Aertex vest in bed; they were in a heap on the floor. I still had class; I wore pyjamas.

On the peg of the bedroom door there was a yellow dressing-gown, a good colour for the boiled egg yolk should a shaking hand not make it to the dry lips with the bendy spoon. But from where I was to where it waited seemed a long way.

Everything seems a long way.

A pounding invaded these gladsome thoughts. At first I thought it was the blood celebrating it still had a few open conduits within which to operate, but then realised it was the front door. I lived at the top of the tenement, the attic rooms — a long way up. I looked at the clock. I had remembered to wind it last night, another mark of the valiant fight 'gainst disintegration. It said ten o'clock. Who would come a'knocking at this unearthly hour?

I put on the dressing-gown, fluffed out the imitation velvet collar and opened the door. It was Jimmy Lapsley, the barman from the Willow Bar that occupied the bottom left of the tenement. He was a good-hearted soul with an excitable nature and pop-eyes.

"There's a man wants tae see you," he spluttered, false teeth jerking askew.

"What's his moniker?"

Jimmy hesitated. "He didnae say."

"Can he not come up?"

"He's too fat."

That made sense. I nodded. It was decent of Jimmy to come all this way but he had been a great friend and partner to my father who was domino champion of the Willow till cancer played him a double six. Jimmy had not touched a tile since as a mark of respect and had a soft spot for me. It was painful to see the hope die a little in his eyes as the years went by.

"I'll be down directly. Tell him I just need to buff up my kidneys."

"Eh?"

"I'll be down directly, Jimmy. Thanks."

When I entered the pub it was empty

— as it should be at this time of the day — but Jimmy had set up a big mug of tea at a table in the snug where, indeed, he had not lied, a fat man sat at table sipping from another mug. He wore a Dublin Bookie's hat and had a friendly open face like a fresh scone. Frank Carlin. No wonder Jimmy hadn't mentioned the name. I'd have gone most definitely back to bed.

"You're looking grand, John,'" Frank averred in a soft Irish lilt. "Despite, ye know?"

"Despite?"

"Getting fired. Drunk. Shooting off at the mouth. Falling out with your employer, calling him I believe, a dirty capitalist bastard who was a shit-faced parasite on the dreams of the poor and other insults that were lost in the general clamour."

"A manky lickspittle," contributed Jimmy who was polishing the glasses with some vim. "I had tae look it up."

"It's Dickens. Part anyway. Uriah Heep," I muttered.

But they were both right. Two nights ago in this very bar, I had, under the influence of the aforesaid cheap whisky, lost connection to that part of myself which counsels not to unleash the rancid anger burning in the tender breast and told my runt of a boss Donny Dunlop that he could stick his job where the monkey stuck his nuts. It had of course been building up for a long time — the little bastard resented the splinters of intelligence still undefiled in the depths of his lowly cashier as he took in the betting slips at the grilled window.

He could sense I despised him almost as much as I did myself and hated the fact that I never tried to cheat him out of money. With the amount of coin and cash going mostly in and rarely out, I could have — but I didn't. Honesty is my one small triumph and it has got me absolutely nowhere in life. Nowhere. As it did two nights ago.

Donny had been boasting what mugs they all were, the working men who laid their intricate three cross doubles and accumulators that crumbled so often to dust, and how he pissed himself with laughter at the hope in their eyes. And how when they won that was fine because it hooked them in even deeper. That was when I lost contact with wisdom and said hello to the raging demon.

My father was a Clydeside Communist and I believe some of Karl Marx might even have been swirled in with the eruption.

A momentary elation, the Good Angel kicking the Bad Yin in the Luciferian knackers and then? As the man said. Fired. On the batter last night. Broke this morning. A sorry state.

Frank took out a surprisingly dainty handkerchief and wafted it under his nostrils like a priest with a holy wafer, before delicately blowing his nose. Jimmy took this as a signal and disappeared down to the other side of the long bar where the mirrors behind the various optics and bottles reflected his lanky, sallow frame.

Various pictures hung on the wall of some of the former Morton greats, Tommy Orr being my favourite, a lanky

decent horse-faced man with a pile-driving right boot, though he'd once missed a penalty for Scotland with that same trusty peg according to my father.

Other frames contained the motley collection of stiffs that sat with arms folded and a fixed grin on their face, sides without number or knowledge. The Willow was a dubious shrine to the broken dreams of Morton fans through the ages.

My arms were also folded. Frank Carlin was a menace and a Pape to boot. An old and chaste boyfriend of my then devoutly Catholic mother before she met my Protestant Communist father and reneged on the Holy Order — every time he came into my life I got into trouble.

But now I was already in it. Trouble. Frank smiled as if he sensed my predicament, leant forward and said, "I have a proposition for you, John. I need a guardian angel."

"Someone finally want to kill you?"

"Not for me. And I will pay the price."

He took a bulging wallet out of his immaculate inside pocket. Frank was a snappy dresser, his camelhair coat positively shone in the dingy surroundings of the Willow but I wasn't looking at the coat. I was looking at two five-pound notes, crisp and identical. To a T.

And so it happened that I found myself on a bitter cold Saturday afternoon watching a game at Broomhill Park near the top of our Greenockian uplands. It boasted two pitches and the balls, hoofed hopefully or thumped by a berserk wing back, sailed from the lower to higher field or vice versa. This often meant one game had no balls and the other had two, which might put the odd person in mind of a wartime song but did nothing to improve the quality of the gemme. The other possibility was the leather sphere being hammered out of the ground down the slope onto Drumfrochar Road where it might be flattened by a rare passing bus or stolen by the imps of that thoroughfare.

Brass-monkey weather, my ankle was aching from the long climb, and it was a terrible game.

Well, not completely terrible and here was the reason for my shivering presence. Billy Gourlay playing for a works team — Hastie's, to be precise, where my father had spent all his life from leaving school. A shipyard engineer, he biled his can of tea and did his job.

This boy was class, I could tell that in the first five minutes. He was ostensibly in the midfield but tiring of the ball being constantly fired over his head, collected it from a shy-in, ghosted past three Neanderthals down the wing then laid a cross precisely onto the centre-forward's head — from where it skittered off for a goal kick.

Billy had a fresh open face and blue choirboy eyes - not the usual Greenock physiognomy by a long shout - and hardly broke sweat for the rest of the game which Hastie's finally managed to win two-nil. One scored by the boy himself and the other a stonewall penalty where his legs were cawed from under him. A foul not even the baldy-heidit cross-eyed bastard of a referee (something both sets of supporters might agree on) could miss. Big Neil Forsyth who used to be my father's apprentice, thumped the ball home. Neil was lethal with a dead ball; it was just when it moved he had a problem.

Game over, I wandered up to Neilly who was wolfing into a gigantic doorstep sandwich, two more clutched in his meaty fist. His big red face split in a smile when he saw me, and he patted his ample belly in a friendly bear-like fashion. I had once seen Neil clear a pub in no time flat when someone had made a derogatory remark about his beloved Teddy Bears, the Glasgow Rangers, so I allowed him to slap me on the back and tried not to fall forwards onto my face.

"Ye want a tightener," he asked, waving the bread. "Spam fritters."

Spam was dead meat that lay in square tins like an unexploded mine and the only thing that might cause more harm to the recipient stomach was to deep fry it in batter.

"My mammy packed them," said Neil. "Good breid as well."

'I'll pass, Neilly," I replied. "But you may convey a wee message for me."

So it fell out that Billy Gourlay and I gazed across a plate of hot peas at each other in the nearest Tally café in Ann Street, Lugosi's. The name was really Rebecci's but the striking resemblance between the lugubrious owner and Bela Lugosi, the brooding Dracula who terrified virgins with his strange vowel sounds, had given rise to the nickname.

Billy was a puzzle. The note I had sent mentioned Frank Carlin and the boy had emerged from the changing rooms, hair plastered flat, nodded at me and said. "I'm starvin' hungry."

So far he had added nothing more but was on his second plate of peas.

I waited. He added a dollop more vinegar, cleaned his plate with a slice of bread and looked up at me with a total lack of curiosity.

"Uncle Frank worries too much," he stated flatly. "Ever since he got me that job in Hastie's."

"Job?"

"Office boy."

"How long since?"

"Three months but I'm no stayin' put. Jist till I'm 16."

"And then what?"

His lips quirked in a sly secret smile. "Whit do you think?"

Follow the dream. We all want to follow the dream. He had the talent no doubt, I could see it even in that clogging match. Balance, the most precious gift to a fitba' player. Billy rarely lost it. God grant he never came up against a full-back like Boag. But he had balance, ballast, back straight head always up. Looking for an opening.

It was up now. Eyes blue. Waiting. Yet there was something behind them. What was it? I have a strange intuitive side that does not help me avoid dangerous tackles but senses dark secrets. What was Billy's?

"Frank wants me to keep tabs on you for a wee while," I said. "He must have a reason but neglected to inform me."

Billy nodded. Unsurprised. "It'll be tae the final."

"Final?"

"The Works Cup Final." For a moment an expression of pride almost peeped through on his face. "Hastie's have never got there."

Undeniably true. My father forever lamented the fact that Hastie's, relatively small fry among the bigger factories like Scott's, Lithgow's and Kinkaid's, had not a net but a jam jar to cast into a minuscule pool of talent and the jar therefore came up with two or three shilpit minnows, easy prey for the sharp-toothed sticklebacks.

"Hey!" Lugosi shouted and brought me out of my piscine reverie, "Ye want mair tea?" Billy and I both nodded. A slight frown crossed the boy's hitherto untroubled countenance.

"Frank's no' my uncle. He's a Pape for starters. But he keeps pigeons."

I was lost now. The tea arrived. "Pigeons?"

"His doo hoose is jist beside my dad's. They're pally."

The idea of an immaculate Frank Carlin, keeping doos and getting covered with scabby pigeon excrement was a hard one to follow but, as the Irish say, every cripple has his own way of walkin'. Though something was beginning to percolate in the back of my head. "Do nothing for nothing," could well be inscribed on Frank's tombstone — behind that affable façade was a mind sharp as a Gillette Extra — what was unfolding cheek to cheek?

"Next Saturday," said Billy. "The final."

"Against?"

"Lithgow's. We'll gub them."

"It'll be the first time."

For a moment our eyes met and there was a flicker of unease in his gaze before Billy sniffed and stood up. I did the same. He was almost as tall as me, square in the shoulders and automatically shuffled left and right as if bamboozling an opponent before making for the door. He didn't offer to pay, talent never does.

I asked him in my guardian angel capacity where he was headed that evening and was told that it was an evening in with his Grandpa, listening to Perry Mason on the wireless.

The boy slid out of the door and I passed one of my crisp new fivers over to Lugosi then retired to the wooden booth where Billy and I had been ensconced, waited for the change and reflected on events so far.

Everybody was hiding something that's for sure; I could smell it in the air to go with the peas and vinegar. Frank definitely, Billy not a kick in the arse behind him — and why had Frank picked on me to nursemaid the boy?

Because he was once a sweetheart of my undoubtedly chaste mother?

Then I remembered a remark he had passed to me not all that long ago when he had breezed into the Willow Bar late night to find me reading a *Black Mask* magazine with some difficulty through the fag smoke and whisky fumes.

"Your father was a wizard at the dominoes," he had remarked gravely. "What are you good at, John?"

At the time that stuck in my craw. It was still lodged there. Now he had bought me for two fivers. Easy meat. Like the spam.

Lugosi banged down the change plus four single notes, then lurched off to hone up his fangs for the night as I poked at the bottom of my teacup. The leaves were supposed to predict coming attractions. Mine had huddled together in the form of a spindly arrow. It was pointed straight back at me.

Night fell. I did not leave Ann Street because Billie Gourlay lived not three blocks up from Lugosi's. I waited in a close opposite with a packet of spangles for company. No desire to light up a cigarette, not after watching both of your parents wither from the fell hand of cancer; my mother had vanished like a conjuring trick but my father lingered on, face swollen from the medication, intelligence still lurking in the dimmed eyes. He left me a note with a single sentence.

"Don't be a mug," it said.

Wise words but wasted. After the injury, then the year of the double coffins, I went to hell and couldn't hold down a job. Or a woman. The Limping God. Ha ha. I made my own bitter brew and swallowed it down. Then I ended up behind a grille. Story so far.

Now I waited. No one listens with their grandsire to Perry Mason on a Saturday because he and Della Street solve their cases on a Wednesday evening, so tell it to the birds.

Sure enough about nine o'clock Billy slipped out of his close and made his way down the street, keeping to the shadows. I stuck in another spangle and followed.

Then I hit a problem when my quarry slid into a snazzy dark blue Triumph Herald parked unobtrusively down a side street. I recognised the car and the woman inside who wrapped her arms round Billy like a hungry octopus and near devoured him in a long open-mouthed kiss. More anaconda than octopus.

Then she snapped back as if fearing disclosure and the car jolted into a rampant roar then sped off for parts unknown. Leaving me standing like a tumshie.

I had some excuse — who would have predicted that the internal combustion engine might take a hand? Plus the fact that I knew the car. And the driver.

As previously mentioned, a Triumph Herald. And the woman? Mamie Dunlop, wife of my ex-employer Donnie. When she walked in the bookies, pencil stubs quivered in the hand.

Blonde, red-lipped, hot as a pancake and better shaped.

Who had just disappeared with Billy Gourlay. Not to practise penalty kicks.

Things were getting interesting.

To be continued...

NATIONAL
FOOTBALL
MUSEUM

WE
ARE
A
SPECIAL
ONE
MANCHESTER

FREE
ADMISSION
OPEN DAILY

Cathedral Gardens
Urbis Building
Manchester

Follow us @footballmuseum
facebook.com/NationalFootballMuseum
www.nationalfootballmuseum.com

166

GREATEST GAMES

"I am aware now — as I was then —
of what an honour it was to play for
my country, but I felt I would not be
serving my country in any way by
going along with this racket."

Spain 1 Ireland 0

World Cup qualifying play-off, Parc des Princes, Paris, 10 November 1965

By Dermot Corrigan

This summer's Euro 2012 group game between Ireland and Spain was too one-sided to hold much lasting significance. Spain's stroll in Gdansk is unlikely to go down as much more than a footnote in their successful campaign to win a third successive major tournament, while most Irish fans will try to forget the 4-0 defeat as quickly as possible. More happily, the game acted as a reminder of a far more momentous meeting between the two countries, 47 years ago, in qualifying for the 1966 World Cup.

The draw in February 1964 grouped Ireland and Spain together with Syria in a three-team group. After a row over scheduling the Syrians pulled out, so a two legged play-off between the two European countries would decide who qualified for the tournament in England.

Qualification for the finals was even more important than usual for both teams. Real Madrid's success at club level during the 1950s hadn't translated into Spanish success on the international stage. Even with the naturalisation of the Argentina-born Alfredo di Stéfano and the Hungarians Ferenc Puskás and László Kubala, the Spanish did not qualify for Sweden 1958 and, unluckily but disappointingly, finished bottom of their group in Chile four years later with Helenio Herrera as coach.

That performance led to calls for the national side to be made more authentically Spanish. Herrera was replaced by the former nationalist soldier José Villalonga and, in 1963, foreign-born players were banned. Villalonga consciously implemented a more aggressive playing style for *la furia española* and Franco was delighted when the USSR were beaten in the following year's European Nations Cup final, held in Madrid and suffused with memories from the Spanish Civil War. That victory raised expectations of success at the World Cup, which remained the important tournament to win.

But many in Ireland also felt their time had come. The Irish had never reached a major finals, not even come close, but fans had jealously watched (or more likely listened to) Scotland, Wales and Northern Ireland all impress in Sweden in 1958 with teams they saw as being of a similar standard. Qualification was seen as part of a general trend opening up to the world, with Ireland almost joining the European Economic Community in 1963 and entering the Eurovision Song Contest in 1965. And the tournament was being played in England, where most of the team played and many Irish emigrants lived. The major handicap was the shambolic way the Football Association of Ireland

(FAI) was run. The team manager was the former player and Nottingham Forest boss Jackie Carey, but in reality a 'Big Five' selection committee decided everything, including the team line-up for each game. These decisions were often made for political or financial reasons. English clubs regularly refused to release players, teammates had little time to get to know each other, and line-ups varied wildly from game to game. At the simplest level, preparations were amateurish. Even training kit had to be provided by the players themselves. It was not an atmosphere conducive to success, no matter how proud the players were to represent their country.

Ireland 1-0 Spain, Dalymount Park, Dublin, 5 May 1965

Ireland v Spain was a familiar fixture in international football. Perhaps because of their religious and cultural similarities, the countries had already met 10 times, from a 1-1 draw in Barcelona in 1931 to the previous year's European Nations Cup quarter-finals, when Spain had eased through 7-1 over two legs.

Ireland had been below strength for both those matches, but Carey (or the Big Five) had access to almost their best side for the first leg in 1965. Seven changes were made to the team beaten 2-0 at home by Belgium earlier that year. The FAI took advantage of a recent change in Fifa's eligibility rules to call up the Manchester United defender Shay Brennan who became the first English-born Irishman to play for the national side. That 1964-65 championship-winning United team also provided

Brennan's fellow full-back Tony Dunne and goalkeeper Pat Dunne (making his debut as the first choice, Alan Kelly of Preston North End, was injured), while their reserve centre-forward Noel Cantwell was named up front.

Other well-known names in the side included the Leeds United midfielder Johnny Giles, the Sunderland centre-half Charlie Hurley and the Blackburn inside-forward Andy McEvoy, who had just finished level with Jimmy Greaves at the top of the English league goalscoring charts with 29 goals. Even the League of Ireland representatives Frank O'Neill and Jackie Hennessy were players of quality; in those days domestic Irish football was not the backwater it is today. This was about as strong an Irish team as had ever taken the field. Carey told reporters he was confident, as for the first time in four years the team had been together for three days before the game, giving them a chance to prepare properly.

Villalonga (referred to as the "sole selector" in the Irish papers) had fewer options. He was without the Italian exiles Luis Suárez (on European Cup duty with Internazionale against Liverpool) and Luis Del Sol, while injury ruled out the five-time European Cup winner Paco Gento of Madrid and Barcelona's 'Chus' Pereda. Six of the team that had beaten Ireland in the 1964 quarter-final remained, including the Athletic keeper José Ángel Iribar, the fearsome Real Madrid wing-half Ignacio Zoco and the Real Zaragoza centre-forward Marcelino, who had headed the winner in the European Nations Cup final against the Soviets. Luis Aragonés, then at Atlético Madrid, was an unused member of the travelling squad.

40,000 Irish fans packed into Dalyer for the afternoon kick-off. Both teams made bright starts. After eight minutes Hurley headed a Giles cross into the net but the Welsh referee Leo Callaghan whistled for a foul by Cantwell. At the other end the Ireland defence got in a tangle but the Atlético inside-forward Adelardo blazed over the bar from inside the area. McEvoy was soon running clear on goal but Iribar saved with his feet, Zoco getting to the rebound ahead of the Shamrock Rovers' outside-right O'Neill.

As the game settled down Carey's tactical preparations looked to have Ireland playing a more cautious defensive game than usual with Giles playing very deep. Spain gradually imposed themselves as Zoco and his fellow wing-half Jesús Glaría started to control the central areas, and they created a series of chances in the lead up to half-time.

The visitors began the second half again with more of the ball. Marcelino dithered over a shot having found space in the area. Pat Dunne beat the Valencia inside-forward Vicente Guillot to a deep cross. And then, on 63 minutes, against the run of play, Ireland went ahead.

Giles was fouled 40 yards from goal out on the right wing. O'Neill knocked the free-kick into the area and Cantwell jumped with Zoco. Neither got a touch but a distracted Iribar took his eye off the ball, letting it slip through his fingers into the net. Callaghan ignored Spanish complaints and the goal stood, as the legendary Irish commentator Philip Greene screamed, "Look at him, look at him in anguish!"

Their tails up, the Irish looked for a second. Iribar half-redeemed himself with a full-length stop from O'Neill and McEvoy hit the side netting from a narrow angle. The visitors rallied and spent the closing stages camped in the Irish half. Their best chance to equalise came with two minutes remaining as Zoco's cross found Guillot unmarked in front of goal. To Irish relief, his free header flew inches wide.

The Spanish players were unhappy with what they saw as hard tackling and weak refereeing and refused to swap jerseys on the final whistle. *Mundo Deportivo* placed the blame elsewhere, saying the team's defence had been fine (apart from Iribar who had been "bewitched" by the Celts) but its forward line had been very disappointing. The *Irish Times* took a different line: Hurley had been "once again a colossus" in an outstanding Irish defensive display which gave their side an advantage to take to Seville for the second game.

Spain 4-1 Ireland, Estadio Sánchez Pizjuán, Seville, 27 October 1965

Irish optimism was dimmed before they set off for Seville in late October, as Brennan and Hurley were both unable to travel because of injury. Theo Foley — then at Northampton Town, later to be George Graham's assistant manager at Arsenal — came in at full-back and Huddersfield's Mick Meagan replaced Hennessy at wing-half. Cantwell dropped back to centre-half with the Shelbourne centre-forward Eric Barber getting a first senior international call.

In an incident typical of the way the team was managed, Barber almost missed the flight to Spain. Suffering a toothache over the weekend, he decided to go to Dublin's dental hospital and have the tooth removed. Waking late on Monday morning due to the anaesthetic, he had to leap from his bed and take a taxi direct from the hospital to the airport. He just about made it in time and started the match despite "suffering from a badly swollen face" (and the fact that Carey had apparently never seen him play).

By contrast Spain were much closer to full-strength with the key *interiores* Pereda and Suárez both back. Iribar paid for his mistake in Dublin as the Real Madrid keeper Antonio Betancourt, making his debut, replaced him. The Spanish authorities brought the squad together for two weeks in advance to prepare, training on the pitch at the Sánchez Pizjuán. When the Irish tried to train there the evening before the match they were informed that heavy rain had made the surface unplayable, leading Carey to take the squad across town to Real Betis's Estadio Benito Villamarín.

A full house of about 50,000 Andalucian fans jammed in and, according to the Irish papers, the home team had further motivation in the form of a 50,000 pesetas (£300) a man win bonus. They began the game on top, with Foley clearing a Pereda shot off the line after only five minutes. As Ireland struggled to keep the ball, Marcelino crashed a header off the bar from a corner. It seemed only a matter of time before Spain took control.

But 19 minutes in the visitors forced a rare attack and Barber was obstructed inside the Spanish area. O'Neill touched the indirect free-kick to the Blackburn left-half Mick McGrath, whose 20-yard shot flew past Betancourt. After a moment's hesitation on all sides, the Spaniards rushed to the Portuguese referee Décio Freitas to complain. To Irish dismay, Freitas said the free-kick should be retaken, as he had not been ready. The momentum had nonetheless swung and, after 26 minutes, Giles's deep cross was volleyed in from close range by McEvoy to make it 1-0.

Both teams seemed to enter a state of shock. The crowd began to get on the home players' backs but the visitors lacked the belief to take advantage. Bit by bit the Spanish took control again and the game turned completely in four minutes just before half-time. First a cross from the Zaragoza winger Carlos Lapetra evaded both Marcelino and Cantwell and ran for Pereda to shoot powerfully home. With the Irish rocking, Zoco took a free-kick quickly. Dunne could only parry it as far as Pereda who knocked in the rebound to make it 2-1. This time Freitas saw nothing wrong.

Ireland's challenge faded further in the second half. Dunne saved from Pereda and Cantwell cleared a shot from Atlético's José Ufarte off the line before Pereda got his hat-trick from a tight angle. Lapetra's snapshot from the edge of the area removed any doubt. Giles had a late effort which flew too high but Ireland were well-beaten.

The Spanish press was in no doubt that the better side had won. *ABC*'s match report was headlined, "Spain achieve a fair and spectacular victory over Ireland," saying Freitas and his assistants were "impeccable" in their work and not mentioning the disallowed early goal. The Irish papers were less happy. "The

Portuguese referee was not at all helpful towards our efforts," protested the *Irish Times*. "He was too prone to hearken to the many appeals of the Spanish and in the long run spoiled what could have been a memorable game."

Under Fifa rules the teams had to settle the tie by meeting a third time in a neutral country, with goal difference only counting were this game to end level after extra-time. So the long-serving FAI general secretary Joe Wickham and Real Federación Española de Fútbol (RFEF) president Benito Pico sat down with Fifa officials to discuss their options. Wickham wanted Liverpool or London, Pico suggested Lisbon. Rotterdam was also floated as a possibility. After negotiations had dragged on until 3am all involved finally agreed on Paris. At the time this was reported as a fair compromise but even the FAI website now admits that the Spanish offered up both countries' share of the gate receipts to secure the agreement. The money involved was about £25,000, three times the FAI's annual income but much less than countries received for actually qualifying. Wickham and the rest of the Big Five showed what little faith they had in their own team's ability by taking the money on offer.

None of these details made the *Irish Times* story on the negotiations. The FAI claimed that there was "genuine relief" at the choice of Paris, as the other option, Lisbon, was to be feared given the "biased exhibition of refereeing by the Portuguese official" the night before. "Paris is within easy reach of both Dublin and Madrid," Wickham said. "And while

we cannot anticipate any great financial return, we should at least manage to keep our heads above water."

Ireland 0-1 Spain, Parc des Princes, Paris, 10 November 1965

Rumours of the back-room deal surfaced in the French and Spanish press, but the Irish players were reportedly none the wiser as they travelled to Paris the following month. Injuries were again the biggest concern, with McGrath, as well as Hurley and Kelly, not released by their clubs. There was puzzlement at the Big Five's eventual selection, with Foley first named at outside-right, then right-half when McGrath pulled out, despite never having played either position before. Moving Brennan forward to look after Suárez, who had been excellent in Seville, would have made more sense. The 20-year-old Eamon Dunphy, then at fourth-division York City, made his debut at inside-forward.

Any ideas the Irish players had about a neutral venue were quashed when they walked out onto the pitch at the Parc de Princes and saw a sea of red-and-yellow flags and banners. There was a full house of 36,000, most of whom were members of Paris's large ex-pat Spanish community, which included both political and economic refugees. It is not known if Samuel Beckett, who was living in Paris at the time, attended, but if he did he and his countrymen were outnumbered by about 200 to 1.

Villalonga was able to name the same side as in Seville and they again had two weeks together to prepare. They began

confidently but the Irish had the better early chances with Giles and McEvoy sending headers wide. Spain's first clear opening came on 17 minutes as Suárez's pass split the Irish defence and Pereda ran clear but shot wide.

Both teams played aggressively and just after the half hour Pereda danced past Tony Dunne inside the area, but the full-back got back to block the shot. Ireland's best chance of the game came after 34 minutes as Giles' right-wing cross picked out McEvoy inside the six-yard box. His first-time half-volley beat Betancourt only for Zoco to stick out a toe and divert the ball for a corner. Approaching the interval Irish keeper Pat Dunne saved well from Glaría and Zoco.

"In the second half the play grew in intensity, if not in class," the *Mundo Deportivo* match report read. Suárez

went down injured just after the break but Ireland carried on attacking, aggravating the crowd. Pereda and Ufarte both spurned chances while Giles almost caught out Betancourt with a dipping long-range effort.

The Spanish fans and players had perhaps been overconfident and had not expected the third game to be this close. Supporters began a slow handclap in the stands while the tension rose on the pitch. A running battle began between Glaría and Giles, with other players getting involved. With just a quarter of an hour remaining the game remained goalless. The Spanish had the aggregate lead, but everyone knew one piece of genius, a mistake, or bad luck could end their chances of playing in a World Cup.

Another strong challenge saw Foley leave the play for treatment and just as he returned, Spain struck. A pass from the liberated Suárez sent Pereda racing down the right-wing and the Barça man skipped past Tony Dunne before crossing towards the near post. Marcelino stopped Cantwell from clearing properly and the ball broke kindly for the unmarked Ufarte to shoot past Pat Dunne from close range.

McEvoy missed a chance to equalise but with gaps opening at the back Suárez was denied a Spanish second by another top-class save from Dunne. Tempers were now severely frayed and Ufarte needed treatment after a forceful tackle from O'Neill. At the final whistle Pat Dunne confronted some of the Spanish players, with Cantwell intervening to hold him back. According to the reports all involved quickly calmed down — Foley and Reija apologised to each other and the mood was soon friendly.

Cantwell told the Spanish papers afterwards that "Spain's win [was] fair. If we had managed to bring the game to extra-time, we could have imposed our greater fitness, but I want to congratulate Spanish football."

The *Irish Times* was also content with the performance, saying that "To a man the Irish team played magnificently, and with admirable skill as well as their usual fighting spirit... even though Ireland had failed, they gained greatly in prestige by this tremendous fight against one of the best teams in the world." This view was shared in the French media with *L'Equipe* headlining its report "Ireland would have been worthy winners" and saying "Spain did not steal their victory, but it is fair to say that Ireland, by their courage and the quality of their play during certain periods, would equally have deserved to qualify for the finals."

Giles remembers things differently. The episode features heavily in his excellent 2010 autobiography, in which he recalls how bitterly disappointing it was to miss out on a World Cup. Especially frustrating was the failure to press home their lead in Seville, when even a draw would have been enough to qualify. He "detested" the "inferiority complex" of some of his teammates and those around the team. This discontent resurfaced when Ireland and Spain were drawn together again in qualifying for the 1968 Euros. After a 0-0 draw at Dalymount, the breaking point came when an increasingly critical Giles was dropped in favour of Waterford United's Alfie Hale for the away game in Valencia, which the Spaniards easily won 2-0. Ireland's best player (maybe ever) soon decided that international football was just not worth the hassle.

"Weighing it all up, I didn't need much encouragement or excuse to miss a few matches," he recalls in his book. "I am aware now — as I was then — of what an honour it was to play for my country, but I felt I would not be serving my country in any way by going along with this racket."

Other players also grew fed up with the FAI's amateurism and decline set in. The team went six years without winning a match at home and crowds dwindled. This brought financial pressure on the Big Five to cede some power. Meagan was appointed national manager in 1970, but it was only when Giles himself was surprisingly offered a player-manager job in 1973 that things began to be organised professionally. Even so it wasn't until Euro 88 that Jack

Charlton's side finally reached a major international tournament.

Neither was joy unconfined in the winning camp after the third game in Paris. Villalonga admitted he was surprised how well Ireland had played, while apologising for his own side's lack of cutting edge. "I expected the Irish team to play so physically, and to use every means available to try and win, but I did not expect them to play their part in such a good game of football," he said. "Our objective is fulfilled, maybe we did not have too many shots at goal, but all the boys played with passion and a will to win as they had been instructed."

Unimpressed journalists argued the team would have to up their game considerably to achieve anything at the finals and — in phrases very familiar to 2012 ears — complained about players who were over-elaborate in possession and did not look to kill off games. "The national team always gave the impression of being superior technically, of being able to move the ball better than the Irish, adept at their typical triangular passing move, which they practice to exaggeration, including dangerous passes between defenders," wrote Carlos Pardo of the Barcelona-based *Mundo Deportivo*. "But technical superiority does not mark the difference between two teams on the scoreboard. That is the problem we will have to solve before London."

The Franco-friendly *ABC* even complained that the team was lacking a physical presence up front, and wanted Villalonga to drop Suárez, who was unpopular with the regime after moving to Italy. This was *la furía española*, which was supposed to steamroll opponents with its physical power and commitment to the cause. Villalonga chopped and changed from game to game at the following year's finals but Spain could not progress from a difficult group with West Germany, Argentina and Switzerland. Subsequent coaches up to and including Javier Clemente stuck to a physical and furious approach, with little success. Lacking a secure identity Spain failed to qualify for the 1970 or 1974 World Cups and then flopped as hosts in 1982. It was only in 2008 after Aragonés had put together a team packed with Suárez types such as Xavi, Iniesta and Silva that Spain began to win again.

With Ireland having at least qualified for this summer's tournament and Spain boasting perhaps the best international team in history, 1965 may seem like the distant past now — both countries eventually learned their lessons and made the changes in outlook required to bring success, at least relative to their population size and football tradition.

Or maybe not. Few who watched FAI president John Delaney's drunken antics in Poland will view today's organisation as professionally run. Giovanni Trapattoni's strange team selections at times echo those of the Big Five, while Roy Keane's comments about some fans and players being happy just to go along for the sing-song chime with Giles's thoughts in his book. Meanwhile many pundits in Madrid and elsewhere spent June debating whether Spain were too reliant on short passing and needed a more direct approach. Ⓑ

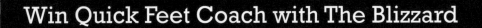

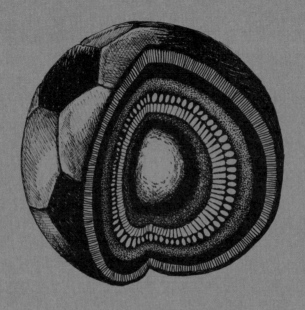

178

Eight Balls

"He looked less at ease flapping
a large golden sheet with three
gold-painted muscular men at the
Brandenburg Gate in 2006."

Classic Footballs

A selection of the best footballs through the ages

By Sheridan Bird

 Santiago (1963) & Telstar Elast (Euro 68 and subsequent models)

Ah, the 1962 World Cup. Vavá, Zito, Garrincha and Amarildo. The Brazilians threw off the loss of the injured Pelé and became the second team to defend the Jules Rimet trophy. Rejoice at the sunshine smiles and samba soccer of the glorious dancers in canary yellow. But it wasn't all happy faces and skipping. Aside from the street fight between hosts Chile and former champions Italy (intermittently disrupted by football) there was an equipment malfunction with historical ramifications.

The tournament ball looked fine on first inspection. Produced by the Señor Custodio Zamora company of San Miguel, Santiago, the Crack was an 18-panel, hand-stitched yellow leather affair with a valve and a prestigious 'Campeonato Mundial de Fútbol/ Copa Jules Rimet 1962' stamp. The previous World Cup ball, the Top Star, was selected after Fifa officials tested 100 contenders on a Stockholm playing field. Ominously, the process wasn't as rigorous for Chile '62. Zamora's yellow marvel didn't explode or break bones during the World Cup's early stages but it did occasionally lose colour and shape.

For some matches (including West Germany v Switzerland) the Crack was replaced with the tried and trusted Scandinavian Top Star. The rumour was Europeans didn't trust the local offering. Although unfortunate, this was not the PR disaster it would be if a ball were withdrawn (even temporarily) mid-tournament today. These disputes brought the ball into focus for the first time since the 1930 World Cup final. Then, Argentina used their favoured Tiento ball in the first half and Uruguay insisted on playing with their larger, harder T-Model after the break.

Harnessing the considerable power of a hunch we can assert that someone at adidas recognised the importance (and financial potential) of regulating match balls in the summer of 1962. The Crack's crack-up might have been the catalyst for the German company's venture into football manufacture.

A year later the fittingly-titled Santiago ball bounced out of adidas HQ. It was a lovely warm dark brown, the colour of Sir Roger Moore's voice [thanks to Alan Partridge for that line]. The structure was interlocking octagons, unmistakeably borrowed from the eye-catching yet flawed Crack and refined by the engineering skill of Adi Dassler & co. 'Hand-stitched nylon' and 'official' (in Fifa's preferred language, French) shone in luxurious gold capital letters on its plush cowhide. 'Santiago' and 'adidas' also took pride of place.

Adidas's transformation from early-sixties upstarts to official ball suppliers to Fifa and Uefa wasn't instant. In late 1965 the English FA invited manufacturers from all over the world to present their candidates to be match ball of the 1966 World Cup. The English company Slazenger, better known for its premium cricket equipment, won the contract. Their Challenge 4-Star ball, available in white, orange and lemon, consisted of 25 hand-stitched panels and crossed the line at least five times in the final. The top model cost 150 shillings — at the time about the same as three bottles of Moët & Chandon.

Beaten by England on the pitch and in the bidding process, the Germans didn't wallow in self-pity. They won the contract to supply the European Championship and World Cup, which they still hold. Brown, red and orange balls were booted into the museums. Design fuddy-duddies were shown the red card when the black-and-white Telstar Elast, official ball of Euro 68, rolled into town. It was the revolutionary, feather-ruffling 32-panel masterpiece of a mad football genius.

Created for better television visibility and retained (with technological updates) for the 1970 World Cup, Euro 72, 1974 World Cup and Euro 76, the Telstar featured 20 white hexagons and 12 shiny black pentagons. It became a classic, forever associated with Johan Cruyff's rubber-legged brilliance, the muscular goal hobbit Gerd Müller's unprecedented feats and Antonín Panenka's cheekily dinked penalty in the Euro 76 final.

Had the Crack been reliable, adidas might not have started their spherical odyssey. The Santiago was short lived and never used at a major tournament. But it was pivotal. A gateway ball. In football parlance, a through-ball to the strike-partnership of innovation and aesthetics.

② Emperor's Cup ball (various models 2009 onwards)

Japan, as the tourist brochures say, celebrates her past while embracing the future effortlessly. In one trip visitors experience a traditional tea ceremony in Kyoto. They see actors dressed as samurai and study authentic ninja artefacts from the Edo period at the Noboribetsu Date Jidaimura theme park in Sapporo. And of course they marvel at the latest technology in the exhilarating Shinjuku district of Tokyo.

Fittingly, the nation's club cup tournament ball combines state-of-the-art engineering with an exquisitely designed homage to heritage and the natural world. Until 2009 the Emperor's Cup balls were Fifa's flagship product with the Japanese FA's circular logo stamped on. No local flavour. But in 2009 the competition was awarded a bespoke match ball.

The central insignia on this sought-after item (selling for up to £210 on eBay) is one of Japan's national emblems, the sakura cherry blossom. The Japanese celebrate the intense, vibrant blossoming of the sakura with a sociable, relaxed ceremony called hanami dating back to the Nara Period of the eighth century. Marked today with long parties in the park with plenty of food and drink, it is a time of optimism and enthusiasm.

But the flower, which emerges between February and April depending on the region, has a short life and is a reminder of mortality. It appears frequently in Japanese art and poetry and is engrained in the country's psyche. During the Second World War kamikaze bombers painted sakura on their planes. It's an attractive, poignant and, above all, adored representation of Japan. The flower on the 2009 ball was a large, stylised, rich red rendering with blue outline on a pearlescent white background. Its simplicity introduced the concept but felt like a prototype. The more elaborate 2011 version displays a mainly red sakura motif with hints of yellow and more complex background pattern.

The technical specifications of the Emperor's Cup ball still follow Fifa's current highest-level adidas matchball. The 2009 edition featured the 14-panel construction and pimpled surface of the EuroPass, the ball of Euro 2008. The most recent model, used in 2011, was a Jabulani template of 8 panels and grooves of varying sizes.

Like the country it graces, the Emperor's Cup ball blends ground-breaking innovation with a respectful and charismatic tribute to history. This is one flower Japanese children can kick without their mother shouting at them.

③ Kopanya (2009 FIFA Confederations Cup)

Don't worry, this isn't the misunderstood 2010 World Cup ball. And that is the Kopanya's tragedy. Inspired by the indignous Ndebele tribe, this creation for the 2009 Confederations Cup in South

Africa looked better than the maligned Jabulani. The players loved it. But like the regrettable brown shorts Italy wore in the tournament, few remember it.

Any designer will verify that packing multiple colours onto one item while retaining aesthetic appeal is a headache. The unsettling Harlequins rugby shirt is an eyesore. Olympique Marseille's black 2010-11 Champions League shirt was an acceptable attempt, garnished with tasteful kaleidoscopic stitching and a large, vertical Bob Marley-esque red, gold and green stripe running through the badge and beyond. Keen to incorporate the host nation South Africa's six-coloured flag, and motivated by the Ndebele people, adidas immersed themselves in the Rainbow nation.

Ndebele women are famous for their colourful, symmetrical, geometric house painting. All the straight-edged designs feature a black outline and are created without rulers or other apparatus. Originally the colours were natural, muted reds, browns and pinks, but recent generations have added brighter colours. Everything springs from a white background for dramatic effect. The pattern on the Kopanya's propeller shaped panels was an Ndebele geometric mix of red, yellow, blue and green with silver partitions on a shiny white base. The ball looked perfect in photos, on television and in the flesh. The chassis and mechanics were the same as the pimpled 14-panel EuroPass and Champions League Finale 8. Most players at the Confederations Cup were used to the feel of this model from the 2008-09 Champions League; there were no complaints. Kaká, Giuseppe Rossi, Daniel Güiza and Katlego Mphela scored goals of the highest quality.

The Kopanya deserves to be remembered as a bold masterpiece. Meeting all criteria with flying colours, it would have been the ideal World Cup 2010 ball. Alas, after the 2009 Confederations Cup fans bade a sad farewell to the Kopanya and tried to forget Italy's unfortunate brown shorts.

④ +Teamgeist Berlin (2006 World Cup final)

As a libero, Franz Beckenbauer thrived against Johan Cruyff and Bobby Charlton. As coach he led West Germany to two World Cup finals without dislodging a hair in his thinning Kaiser Afro. But he looked less at ease flapping a large golden sheet with three gold-painted muscular men at the Brandenburg Gate in 2006. Underneath that shiny cover was a three-metre high football. Forget last-ditch tackle, this was vast, kitsch and tacky. Amid the gaudiness, Franz was unveiling something new in World Cup history.

The best, most simple advances sometimes take longest. After 76 years and 17 tournaments, someone found a way to recognise the prestige of the final: a one-off ball.

In reality this was the +Teamgeist, the match ball of the 2006 World Cup group stage to semi-finals, sprayed gold. In the postcard German village of Scheinfeld, adidas boffins called Hans, Klaus and Harald spent three years engineering the perfect ball so Ronaldinho, Zinedine Zidane and Philippe Senderos could light up the tournament. Breaking from the classic 32-panel pentagons and hexagons construction of the previous

nine world Cup balls, it had 14 panels. The new form removed the straight lines of older models for a smoother surface and truer flight. The central pieces were six propeller shapes.

To prevent unwanted water-retention, segments were thermally bonded instead of being stitched together. The ball was tested by robot feet and spun in a giant washing machine with a strategically uneven, roughened cylinder. You've probably seen matches which seemed to last years. This industrial washer replicated a year's wear and tear in four hours.

The +Teamgeist responded wonderfully to precision artistes such as Andrea Pirlo, Deco and Juan Román Riquelme. But what seals its place in legend were the visual tweaks for the France-Italy decider (the one-off ball was named the +Teamgeist Berlin). Sports equipment companies are often criticised for cash-ins and PR stunts. But this was a golden opportunity to enhance the World Cup final. And we got to see Herr Beckenbauer transported from his comfort zone into a camp vignette that would make Gianni Versace's eyes water.

⑤ Gamarada (Sydney Olympics) & Terrestra Silverstream (Euro 2000)

By 1999 ball watchers were blasé. They had seen the first fully synthetic World Cup effort (1986), the first major tournament ball with coloured logos (Euro 96) and France's high-speed trains and cockerels in the graphics of the 1998 World Cup's Tricolore. Some collectors splintered off, developing other pastimes like cookery or starting a family. Then one amazing sentence shattered the apathy: gas-filled micro balloons in a polyurethane matrix.

As Hunter Davies noted in his seminal book *Boots, Balls & Haircuts*, sports companies have long baffled consumers with jargon-heavy poncery to sell products. And succeeded. "Manufacturers' scientific claims and technological language are reminiscent of what they were saying a hundred years ago, amazing or astounding us with their latest astounding developments," said Davies.

After World Cup 98 adidas probably realised the world and its brother knew modern balls were souped-up with syntactic foam for rapid-rebound characteristics. When their competitors Nike and Puma entered the market, the German giants emphasised their experience and expertise. To retain the über-enthusiasts and remind rival brands who had the biggest balls, the Dassler Company released something contemporary and exotic for the Sydney Olympics and Euro 2000.

The Gamarada (Olympics) and Terrestra Silverstream (Euro 2000) had "ergonomically shaped syntactic foam panels coated in polyurethane". But the next layer was the showstopper. Underneath were compressed, gas-filled micro balloons distributing energy and providing a faster flight path.

The mind fixated on these micro balloons. What kind of gas was it? Did it expire? Who put it in? How big is micro? What if the ball rolled near flames? It was so magnificently outlandish every collector had to have one.

The pros had no problems with these millions of gas cells. Zidane conducted

the blue orchestra at Euro 2000 with the Terrestra Silverstream, Nuno Gomes made himself a world star. Jaap Stam gave his semi-final shootout penalty against Italy a bit too much gas.

At the Australian Olympics Samuel Eto'o, Xavi, Andrea Pirlo and the veteran Ivan Zamorano made merry with the Gamarada. Named after the Gadigal word for friendship, the Gamarada had dazzling red, thickened Tango trigons with dashes of cheerful yellow and orange evoking the relentless, outback sunshine.

The Terrestra Silverstream was dedicated to the trade waterways that gave the Netherlands and Belgium, the host nations, their livelihood. A pale grey base with chunky metallic blue and silver trigons, it looked like the Death Star from Star Wars ready for a spangly night out.

Today Nike, Puma, Penalty and Mitre all have magic balls designed using high-level physics and constructed from avant-garde materials. But nothing will ever sound as cool as tiny gas balloons. The Terrestra Silverstream was gone too quickly. After a short stay in the J. League, the Gamarada also vanished.

Beautiful to look at, concocted with frankly silly science and protagonists of two great competitions, we salute these non-identical twins. But we daren't dissect them in fear of gas leaks.

⑥ **Questra**
(1994 World Cup)

"They'll make the goals bigger"... "The games will be three thirds instead of

two halves" ... "The referees will dress like Buck Rogers!" During the build-up to the 1994 World Cup in the USA, sensible football fans spouted a lot of alarmist cack. Contrary to the fears of European football snobs, the only new development enriched the experience.

First we must travel back four years to Italia 90. Gazza's tears, Rijkaard's flob and Caniggia's homemade hairband. Emotion yes; penalties definitely; goals? Not really. There was an average of 2.21 goals per match at the 1990 World Cup — the lowest in the competition's history. Whether this was due to cautious tactics or rancid finishing didn't bother Fifa. What did interest the governing body was the success of the next contest in the glittering, unplundered land of Rocky Balboa, Dr Pepper and Elvis Presley.

This required excitement, action and goals. Industry consultants said a sport which can finish 0-0 would never catch the imagination of fans used to watching Michael Jordan score 50,000 points a week or Wayne Gretzky slamming the puck in the net every two seconds. This underestimated the passion many Americans had for football, but resonated with Fifa. Craving pizzazz, the organisers instructed their technical partners adidas to create a ball that would spice things up and wow apathetic viewers. Something responsive and light to fly unpredictably through the air.

After three years of hi-tech jiggery-pokery at their ball development centre in the tiny French town of La Walck and secret trials in youth matches across the globe, adidas unveiled the hallowed orb. Composed of five different materials, the outer shell was pliable but tough polyurethane over a thick layer of foam with high energy redistribution qualities. This meant if you kicked it cleanly and hard, it went like the clappers.

The name of the ground-breaking ball was Questra — a nod to the search for the stars. It paid tribute to the USA's rich history of space exploration. Like the host nation striving for perfection and knowledge of new frontiers through glitzy NASA projects, Fifa was hoping to conquer the States, a new 'planet', in the name of football. Visually the Questra featured the classic Tango trigon, filled with the interstellar imagery of black holes, planets and stars.

It was a huge success. Gheorghe Hagi floated in a long-distance wonder goal for Romania versus Colombia. Wim Jonk launched an unstoppable, swerving shot past Saudi Arabia keeper Mohammed Al Deayea with the outside of his boot. Roberto Baggio, Diego Maradona and Branco also scored with insanely accurate shots. Good players adapt to any ball. That will always be the case.

Combined with the host nation's ranging meteorological conditions, the Questra's flexibility produced unthinkable goals. It swung in the humid Florida air like a Wasim Akram delivery and whizzed ferociously through dry Californian conditions like a comet. The only complaints were from goalkeepers. But, to the joy of serial keeper-baiter Maradona, their gripes garnered scant sympathy.

With comically inaccurate misconceptions discredited, everyone enjoyed World Cup 1994. The all-singing all-dancing Questra played a starring role in the spectacular jamboree. The average went up to 2.71

goals per game, the highest since 1982 and superior to all subsequent tournaments. Even Spain, deploying coach Javier Clemente's heroically defensive 1-4-1-3-1, scored ten goals in five matches. The only party-pooper was the intriguing yet goalless final in Pasadena.

The Questra had a good life and illuminated games outside the States. It was the ball of Milan's net-busting 1994 Champions League final destruction of Johan Cruyff's Barcelona Dream Team in Athens. It graced the 1996 Olympics, Euro 96 and the Spanish league between 1994 and 1996 (with snazzy new graphics for each tournament).

Then the next innovation glided out of its shiny laboratory on to French turf for World Cup 98. Buck Rogers and referees were never linked again.

 Tango Durlast (1978 World Cup and subsequent models from Tango family)

Zambians in South Korea. The good folk of Székesfehérvár. Ray Wilkins. Anyone over 30 who likes football has a 'Tango moment'. Younger fans know of its legend from photos and YouTube. The explanation for this far reaching impact is simple. Between 1978 and 1989 the Tango and its derivatives were used for every big match, club and country. Every European Cup final between 1978 and 1989 (apart from 1987) featured the ball. The European Championships, the Olympics, Copa America, Intercontinental Cup... you get the idea.

Anyone watching football in that era saw the Tango. Zambia beat Italy

4-0 at the 1988 Olympics with one. Videoton, unfancied Hungarians from Székesfehérvár, tussled for a Tango with Emilio Butragueño's Real Madrid in the two-legged 1985 Uefa Cup final. They even won the second leg 1-0 at the Bernabéu (but went down 3-1 on aggregate).

After a tantalising cameo in the 1978 European Cup final, this design classic entered worldwide consciousness at the 1978 World Cup. Its full name was the Tango Durlast, the first part (by which it became known) a tribute to host country Argentina's famous, lusty dance, the latter the scuff-proof, robust treatment applied to its leather casing.

The logo was a black trigon with a thick outline on each of the 20 hexagons. The simple but enigmatic pattern had no beginning or end, creating the illusion of 12 large circles. An instant success, the motif survived for a decade. The carcass and materials were regularly improved but the trigons were only altered once (filled with Aztec mural-themed symbols by the designer Rebecca Martínez for the Azteca Mexico, ball of the 1986 World Cup).

The Tango River Plate (Euro 80), the wind-tunnel tested Tango España (World Cup 1982), the first non-leather model Tango Mundial (Euro 84) and the Tango Europa (Euro 88) improved weather resistance and durability but still looked as great as the original. Even after the Tango, World Cup balls retained the trigon emblem until 2002 when adidas revealed the Fevernova, the ultimate curate's egg of footballs.

Aston Villa fans link the Tango to their 1982 European Cup win. Italians loved the way it obeyed Bruno Conti at the

World Cup in the same year. Trevor Brooking shot with such accuracy he lodged one in the stanchion of the goal in England's 1981 win over Hungary. Marco van Basten secured Holland's first trophy with his outrageous volley in the Euro 88 final with it. Zico's mastery of the cult ball for Flamengo gave Liverpool a lesson in front of a mesmerised Tokyo crowd in the 1981 Intercontinental Cup. The list could go on forever. This piece of equipment will always summon beautiful memories in all four corners of the Earth.

If you're puzzled by Ray Wilkins's Tango moment, it was a delicious, deft, lobbed goal against eventual runners-up Belgium in Turin at Euro 80. Best not to mention when Raymond threw the ball at the referee during England's World Cup 1986 match against Morocco and was sent off.

 ### 8 Finale (2001 Champions League onwards)

"How do you brand a football match?" sounds like the question of a dusty old High Court judge among today's instantly recognisable, logo-sodden competitions. But in the early 1990s, Uefa were determined their new brainchild would change football consumption and perception forever. In the summer of 1992 the European Champion Clubs' Cup changed its name. Although there was a league stage after two rounds in 1991-92, the tournament was officially relaunched as the Uefa Champions League in 1992-93.

European football's governing body went to town with an anthem and a logo. The London-based company Design Bridge delivered a new identity to, in their words, "inspire supporters and attract global sponsors." Their enduring masterstroke was creating the black and white star-ball. "The eight leading teams (in the group stage) prompted the idea of the eight-star ball logo. The league has since expanded but this powerful emblem still holds strong," reads Design Bridge's statement. For the first eight years the device appeared on tickets, shirt sleeve patches and TV graphics. But it wasn't until the 2000-01 semi-final first leg between holders Real Madrid and Bayern Munich players actually kicked a star-ball.

That first generation ball debuted at the Bernabéu and was the same structure as the Terrestra Silverstream and Gamarada. The design was beautifully faithful and simple — a series of silver stars over the white background, shining in the floodlights. Titled the Finale, this silver star debutant was also used in Bayern's win in the 2001 final. It became an instant collector's item as shops sold out within weeks. Today the 'Silver' sells for £300.

A version of the Finale has been used in every final since, with evermore intricate designs. From 2006-07 onwards a non-final specific, generic model of the ball has also been used for every group and knock-out game en route to the decider (hitherto clubs used a ball of their choice). There have been disagreeable incarnations. The wretched 2007-08 group stage ball featured stars the colour of a depressed carrot in a sad grey and black rim.

Each city hosting the final is reflected in the ball's appearance. For the 2007 showpiece between Milan and Liverpool in Athens, the stars were blue and white (representing the Greek flag) and furnished with Hellenic patterns. Manchester United defeated Chelsea in Moscow in 2008 with a lavish ball brimming with ornate Russian imagery in gold on predominantly bright red stars.

As if that wasn't special enough, from 2006 until 2011 the winners of the previous year's final used the ball of that triumph exclusively for the next season. Next time you see Gareth Bale's glorious hat-trick for Spurs at Inter in 2010-11 look at the ball. It's the Finale Madrid from the Nerazzurri's José Mourinho-masterminded win six months earlier. Everyone else was playing with the standard version with electric blue stars.

As long as the final is played in cities of rich cultural interest, there will be something fresh about the Finale (we are yet to see a completely green star, for example). As a trademark it is perfection. Anyone viewing a game which includes a ball with stars knows they are watching the Champions League. And that is how to brand a football match, m'lud.

Contributors

The Blizzard, Issue Six

David Ashton is a playwright, TV and film screenwriter; creator of the BBC Radio 4 series, *McLevy*. He has written three novels, the latest being *A Trick of the Light*. Also an actor, he played Dr McDuff in *Brass*. His website is **www.david-ashton.co.uk**.

Philippe Auclair is the author of *The Enchanted Kingdom of Tony Blair* (in French) and *Cantona: the Rebel Who Would Be King*, which was named NSC Football Book of the Year. He writes for *France Football*, *Offside* and *Champions* and provides analysis and commentary for RMC Sport. He also pursues a parallel career in music under the name 'Louis Philippe'. **Twitter: @PhilippeAuclair**

Sheridan Bird writes for *Champions*, *World Soccer*, *Creative Review*, *Sporting iD*, *FourFourTwo* and the Manchester United and England match programmes. He has written for *Gazzetta dello Sport* online and appeared on Italian state radio RAI 1 during Euro 2012. **Twitter: @SheridanBird**

Andy Brassell is the European correspondent on BBC Five Live's World Football Phone-In and writes regularly for the likes of the *Independent* and ESPN Soccernet. He is also the author of *All Or Nothing: A Season In The Life Of The Champions League*. **Twitter: @andybrassell**

Luís Catarino is a Portuguese freelance journalist. He is the founder of the website Primeirotoque.pt and has written for several national magazines and newspapers. More recently, he was a commentator on the RTP television network. **Twitter: @LuisCatarino8**

Dermot Corrigan is an Irish sportswriter who lives in Madrid and covers Spanish football for publications including ESPN Soccernet, FOX Soccer, *When Saturday Comes* and Sport 360°. **Twitter: @dermotmcorrigan**

Tom Dart moved to Houston in 2011 from London, where he was a reporter, editor and columnist for *The Times*. He freelances for the *Guardian* and *The Times* and has made the occasional foray into si.com. **Twitter: @Tom_Dart**

Federico Farcomeni works as UK correspondent for the Italian radio station Manà Manà. He worked for *Calcio Italia* and now freelances for *FourFourTwo*. **Twitter: @fedefarco**

Anibal Greco has worked for Reuters, AP, Xinhua and WPN. He is currently a photographer for the newspaper *La Nación* of Buenos Aires.

Karel Häring has written for the Czech newspaper *Sport* since 2000 and is also contributor to *Champions* and the Japanese magazine *World Soccer Digest*. **Twitter: @KHaring75**

Iain Macintosh is the author of *Football Fables* and the *Everything You Ever Wanted To Know* series of sports guidebooks and a co-author of *Football Manager Ruined My Life*. He writes for *the New Paper* in Singapore, *the Irish Examiner*, si.com and anyone else who'll pay him. **Twitter: @iainmacintosh**

Gabriele Marcotti is the author of *The Italian Job, Fabio Capello: Portrait of a Winner* and *Paolo Di Canio: the Autobiography*. He writes for *The Times*, the *Wall Street Journal, Sports Illustrated, Corriere dello Sport* and *La Stampa* and is a regular contributor to ESPN and the BBC. **Twitter: @marcotti**

Antonis Oikonomidis is a Greek journalist who has worked for *France Football, FourFourTwo* and *World Soccer*.

Joel Richards works in print, TV and radio from Buenos Aires, and has written for *World Soccer*, the *Guardian, FourFourTwo, When Saturday Comes* and Fox Soccer. **Twitter: @JoelRichards**

Barney Ronay writes for the *Guardian* about sport. He is the author of several football books including *The Manager* and *Any Chance Of A Game?* and writes occasionally for film and television, most recently co-scripting the feature film *From The Ashes*. **Twitter: @BarneyRonay**

Ben Shave has followed and enjoyed Portuguese football since 2004, despite its best efforts. He is a co-editor of PortuGOAL.net. **Twitter: @benshave**

Vitor Sobral was born in Setúbal and works as a journalist for Australian television station SBS, primarily for the channel's flagship football programme *The World Game*. **Twitter: @Vitor_TWG**

Tim Vickery writes and broadcasts on South American football for the BBC, *World Soccer, Sports Illustrated*, SBS, Sambafoot and TalkSport.

Jonathan Wilson is the author of *Inverting the Pyramid*, a winner of the National Sporting Club's Football Book of the Year, *Behind the Curtain* and *The Anatomy of England*. His biography of Brian Clough, *Nobody Ever Says Thank You*, was published in November 2011. He writes for the *Guardian, World Soccer*, Foxsoccer, ESPN Star, *Sports Illustrated* and *the Irish Examiner*. **Twitter: @jonawils**

James Young writes about Brazilian football for the websites of *World Soccer* and the *Independent*, among others. He is the author of a novel and a collection of short stories, both of which remain stubbornly unpublished, and is currently at work on a third book, which might roughly be described as a 'favela *Fever Pitch*'. **Twitter: @seeadarkness**

Blizzard Subscriptions

Subscribe to the print version of The Blizzard, *be the first to receive new issues, get exclusive Blizzard offers and access digital versions of all back-issues FREE*

Subscription Options

Set Price for Four Issues

Get a four-issue subscription to *The Blizzard* — for you or as a gift — for a flat fee including postage and packing (P&P):

UK:	£35
Europe:	£45
Non-Euorpe:	£55

Recurring Pay-What-You-Like

Set up a quarterly recurring payment for each edition of *The Blizzard*. The recommended retail price (RRP) is £12, but pay what you like, subject to a minimum fee of £6 plus P&P

See www.theblizzard.co.uk for more

Digital Subscriptions

If the cost of postage is prohibitive, or you just want an excuse to use your new iPad or Kindle, you can set up a subscription to digital versions of *The Blizzard* for just £3 per issue.

See www.theblizzard.co.uk for more

Information for Existing Subscribers

Free Digital Downloads for *Blizzard* Subscribers

Whether you have taken advantage of our set price or pay-what-you-like offer, for the duration of your subscription to *The Blizzard* you are entitled to download every issue FREE.

See www.theblizzard.co.uk for more

We very much value the commitment of our print subscribers and have a policy to make available new issues, special offers and other limited access events and benefits to print subscribers first.

About *The Blizzard*

Distribution & Back Issues
Contact Information
About Issue Six

Buy *The Blizzard*

We want as many readers as possible for *The Blizzard*. We therefore operate as far as we are able on a pay-what-you-like basis for digital and print versions.

Digital Version
(Current & Back Issues)

All issues of *The Blizzard* are available to download for Kindle, Android, iOS and PC/Mac at: *www.theblizzard.co.uk*.

- *RRP: £3*
- *Pay-what-you-like minimum: £0.01*

Printed Version
(Current & Back Issues)

Purchase a physical copy of *The Blizzard* in all its luxurious, tactile, sensual glory at: *www.theblizzard.co.uk*. If you haven't felt our rough textured cover-varnish and smelled the inner genius, you haven't properly experienced its awesome true form. Read it, or leave it on your coffee table to wow visitors.

- *RRP: £12* (+P&P)
- *Pay-what-you-like min: £6* (+P&P)

Contact *The Blizzard*

All advertising, sales, press and business communication should be addressed to the Central Publishing Office:

The Blizzard
Ashmore Villa,
1, Ashmore Terrace,
Stockton Road,
Sunderland,
SR27DE

Email: info@theblizzard.co.uk
Telephone: +44 (0)7934 780 488
Website: www.theblizzard.co.uk
Facebook: www.facebook.com/blzzrd
Twitter: @blzzrd

About Issue Six

Editor	Jonathan Wilson
Publisher	The Blizzard Media Ltd
	www.theblizzard.co.uk
Design	Azure
	www.azure-design.com

Copyright

All content is ©Copyright The Blizzard Media Ltd and may not be reproduced without explicit consent. Thanks to Jeanette G Sturis at the Kingsley Motel, Manjimup, for kind use of Warren Walker's original sketches of Dog.

New T-Shirts

The latest additions to our range of top-quality fitted t-shirts have arrived – perfect for lazing on the beach this summer, or as a gift for the footy-geek in your life.

The Seconds of the Greats

From David Winner's interview with the Dutchman in Issue One, we've re-created his St James' Park masterpiece in tableau form.

Available in both black and white, much like Newcastle United.

Dolphins are Bastards

We've got nothing against Flipper and his chums, just don't question Platini for God's sake. Or wear this to a Greenpeace meeting.

Available in light blue.

Blizzard Tree

The seeds of the Blizzard were first planted a little over a year ago, and have now grown into our new cover illustration for our second year. The dog is gone, long live the tree.

Available in grey.

Order Online at
www.theblizzard.co.uk

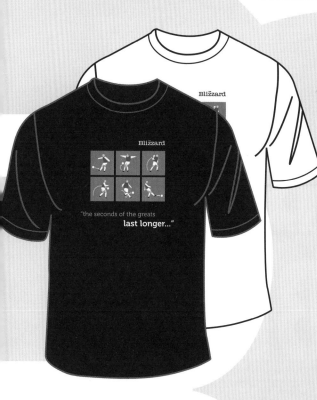

Product Details

All t-shirts are available for **£16 + (£1.45 P&P - UK)**. Shipping prices vary dependent on location — see **www.theblizzard.co.uk** for more details.

Subscribers get a £2 discount off all Blizzard clothing.

- 180 gsm 100% cotton t-shirts
- Fitted body shape
- Tubular constructed body for shape retention
- Extra-reinforced shoulder seams
- Available in S (36/38), M (38/40), L (40/42), XL (42/44), XXL (44/46)

THE FOOTBALL RAMBLE

Football's most entertaining
show—since 2007

Available every week on iTunes and
thefootballramble.com

@footballramble